# VW Super 1970 to 1972 Owners Workshop Manual

## by J H Haynes
Associate Member of the Guild of Motoring Writers

## and D H Stead

**Models covered**

UK : VW (1302S) Super Beetle, 1584 cc

USA : VW Super Beetle, 96.7 cu in

*Also covers VW 1302 Super Beetle, 1285 cc*
*(78.3 cu in) Does not cover VW 1303/1303S*

ISBN 978 0 85733 580 7

© J H Haynes and Company Limited 1974, 1987, 1989

ABCDE
FGHIJ
KLMN

2

Printed in the UK        (110 - 11P2)

**Haynes Publishing Group**
Sparkford  Nr Yeovil
Somerset  BA22 7JJ  England

**Haynes Publications, Inc**
861 Lawrence Drive
Newbury Park
California 91320  USA

# Acknowledgements

First, thanks are due to Volkswagen (UK) Limited for their co-operation and load of official manuals.

Secondly, thanks are due to Swallowdale Garage of Seaton, Devon, whose staff were always helpful with advice and information. Bill Kinchin, as usual, must get special mention for his patience and advice with layout and text matters.

Although all care has been tekan to ensure the correctness of the information given, it must be borne in mind that minor design changes occur continually during the production run of a model and they cannot all be detailed.

No liability is accepted for damage, loss or injury caused by errors or omissions in the information given.

# Introduction

In 1970 a further alternative became available in the range of 'Beetles'. The first alternatives to the basic 1200 had occurred in 1965 when larger engine sizes were introduced for the same body shell.

In 1970 the changes were much more significant in that the design of the suspension was radically altered. The rear suspension was changed from the simple swinging arm design to diagonal trailing arm combined with the double jointed axle shaft. This type of rear suspension was not entirely new as stick shift automatic models in 1300 and 1500 engine sizes had been fitted with it also. The past suspension, up till now exclusively based on twin transverse torsion bars for all Beetle models, changed to MacPherson struts - coil springs with integral damper/pivot units. This change permitted the front luggage compartment to be deepened giving a significant increase in capacity.

In the United Kingdom the new 'Beetle' model is called 1302S - a somewhat confusing identification in view of its 1600 engine (UK fitment) when the old Beetle with the original suspension systems is still sold under 1200 and 1300 designations. The 1302S has a 1584 cc engine. Further confusion can arise when versions not available in the UK are taken into account.

The 1302 is the same as the 1302S except that it has the 1285 cc engine fitted. There is also a 1302LS available. This is a 'super luxury' version.

This manual, based as it is on knowledge of the Beetle gained from experience on the 1302S model and the development of models leading up to it, gives a unique insight into the workings and repair of the latest model.

At the present time there is considerable development work going on with respect to exhaust emission control and this necessitates changes in carburettor and distributor specifications more frequently than any one manual can absorb. Some changes and modifications on later models may or may not be suitable for fitting on earlier types. The full details of these specification changes and the chassis and engine series to which they apply are held by the VW agencies.

We trust then that those owners who wish to embark on the maintenance and repairs of their cars will find this manual a helpful guide through the procedures needed. At the same time clear indications will be given of where it is considered necessary to call for professional experience and equipment. With the introduction of computer processed fault diagnosis, many owners will begin to wonder whether the manufacturers are actively trying to discourage those who take an interest in what makes their investment tick. We leave that to the reader to decide for himself.

As far as the computer diagnosis is concerned the reader is guided only so far as is possible to prevent him from disturbing the various connections. We have not devised a circuit (yet) which will send the computer into orbit when your car is plugged into it.

# Photographic captions and cross references

The book is divided into chapters and each chapter is divided into sections. The sections consist of serially numbered paragraphs.

All illustrations carry a caption. Where the illustration is designated as a figure the reference is merely a sequence number for the chapter. Where the illustration is not designated as a figure the reference number pinpoints the section and paragraph in that chapter to which the picture refers.

When the left or right of a car is referred to this is taken as if the viewer was looking in the forward direction of travel.

# Use of English

*As this book has been written in England, it uses the appropriate English component names, phrases, and spelling. Some of these differ from those used in America. Normally, these cause no difficulty, but to make sure, a glossary is printed below. In ordering spare parts remember the parts list may use some of these words:*

| English | American | English | American |
|---|---|---|---|
| Accelerator | Gas pedal | Locks | Latches |
| Aerial | Antenna | Methylated spirit | Denatured alcohol |
| Anti-roll bar | Stabiliser or sway bar | Motorway | Freeway, turnpike etc |
| Big-end bearing | Rod bearing | Number plate | License plate |
| Bonnet (engine cover) | Hood | Paraffin | Kerosene |
| Boot (luggage compartment) | Trunk | Petrol | Gasoline (gas) |
| Bulkhead | Firewall | Petrol tank | Gas tank |
| Bush | Bushing | 'Pinking' | 'Pinging' |
| Cam follower or tappet | Valve lifter or tappet | Prise (force apart) | Pry |
| Carburettor | Carburetor | Propeller shaft | Driveshaft |
| Catch | Latch | Quarterlight | Quarter window |
| Choke/venturi | Barrel | Retread | Recap |
| Circlip | Snap-ring | Reverse | Back-up |
| Clearance | Lash | Rocker cover | Valve cover |
| Crownwheel | Ring gear (of differential) | Saloon | Sedan |
| Damper | Shock absorber, shock | Seized | Frozen |
| Disc (brake) | Rotor/disk | Sidelight | Parking light |
| Distance piece | Spacer | Silencer | Muffler |
| Drop arm | Pitman arm | Sill panel (beneath doors) | Rocker panel |
| Drop head coupe | Convertible | Small end, little end | Piston pin or wrist pin |
| Dynamo | Generator (DC) | Spanner | Wrench |
| Earth (electrical) | Ground | Split cotter (for valve spring cap) | Lock (for valve spring retainer) |
| Engineer's blue | Prussian blue | Split pin | Cotter pin |
| Estate car | Station wagon | Steering arm | Spindle arm |
| Exhaust manifold | Header | Sump | Oil pan |
| Fault finding/diagnosis | Troubleshooting | Swarf | Metal chips or debris |
| Float chamber | Float bowl | Tab washer | Tang or lock |
| Free-play | Lash | Tappet | Valve lifter |
| Freewheel | Coast | Thrust bearing | Throw-out bearing |
| Gearbox | Transmission | Top gear | High |
| Gearchange | Shift | Torch | Flashlight |
| Grub screw | Setscrew, Allen screw | Trackrod (of steering) | Tie-rod (or connecting rod) |
| Gudgeon pin | Piston pin or wrist pin | Trailing shoe (of brake) | Secondary shoe |
| Halfshaft | Axleshaft | Transmission | Whole drive line |
| Handbrake | Parking brake | Tyre | Tire |
| Hood | Soft top | Van | Panel wagon/van |
| Hot spot | Heat riser | Vice | Vise |
| Indicator | Turn signal | Wheel nut | Lug nut |
| Interior light | Dome lamp | Windscreen | Windshield |
| Layshaft (of gearbox) | Countershaft | Wing/mudguard | Fender |
| Leading shoe (of brake) | Primary shoe | | |

# Contents

# Vehicle identification and spare parts

Although there are many parts common to all 'Beetles' it is unwise to assume that just because a part looks the same and fits it is automatically correct. This applies particularly to engine and transmission units where components are being developed continuously, even though the customer is not necessarily made aware of the fact.

You must know the chassis number and engine number before attempting to obtain a spare part. The chassis number is to be found on the frame fork under the rear seat, or in the front compartment on the lower edge just under the lid on a plate. The 'type' is indicated by an 11 for the beetle and there will be a third number under the 'type' heading which deals with certain options which may be fitted. The chassis serial number has 3 initial numbers, say, 111 which show that it is a Beetle made in model year 1971 - i.e. between August 1970 and July 1971.

The remaining numbers denote the serial number for that model year and they start again at 0 when the year changes.

The engine number is stamped on the crankcase below where the generator pedestal is bolted on. It has prefix letters and for the U.K. market these would normally be 'AD' denoting the 7.5 : 1 compression 1584 cc engine. 'AE' denotes that an exhaust emission control engine is fitted and 'AF' denotes a low compression engine (6.6 : 1. 'B' is used for a certain series of engines exported to the U.S.A. and Canada, and 'AH' is for those with exhaust recirculation systems in California. 'AB' is the prefix for 1285 cc engines.

As far as the UK is concerned the main source of spares is the VW dealer network. If they cannot supply you with what you want immediately then it is most probably due to the fact that they do not reckon on keeping large stocks for over the counter sales, and although they may have one or two of what you need, cannot afford to risk being out of stock for a customer who brings his car in for repair. VW agents are very helpful but one cannot blame them for this insistence on keeping a minimum stock level for their own use. It applies particularly to the less common items. So before tearing your vehicle to pieces check the spares position at your VW agency, you could save yourself a lot of trouble.

With gasket sets - for both engine and gearbox - do not be alarmed if there seem to be many items included in the set you buy, which do not fit your vehicle. To save a lot of variety of kits they include in one enough to cover a variety of types over a period of time so you are certain to have some left over. However it is a good idea to check the set before leaving the parts store. Some of the ones you may need could be omitted. Oil seals particularly are not all included - and this applies to some of the smaller ones (oil cooler).

# Routine maintenance

## Introduction

Because of their inherent. toughness and reputation for reliability and long life there is a tendency for owners to be a bit sketchy on VW maintenance - particularly with vehicles not in the first flush of youth.

The VW will put up with neglect for a much longer time than most cars but when the crunch eventually does come it is likely to be drastic.

Regular maintenance therefore, is just as important as on any other vehicle. If it is not neglected the Beetle is very much a long term investment with a low rate of depreciation in value.

The service procedures listed hereafter cover all the points of required regular service. The frequency of service tends to vary according to changes in design of various components, the conditions under which the vehicle is used, and the way in which it is driven. The frequencies given are based on a mileage of 12000 per year in a temperate climate which is mainly non dusty. Variations from this will be taken into account by VW service agencies in different conditions. Variations in driving style must be the responsibility of the driver where servicing requirements could be affected.

Where maintenance is solely a matter of inspection (rather than lubrication, cleaning or adjustment) the findings from such inspections will determine whether or not further action is required. Such further action is no longer within the scope of Routine Maintenance. It is a workshop procedure requiring repair or renewal. How to do the maintenance is detailed after the schedules. If the details are already in the main chapters then reference is made appropriately.

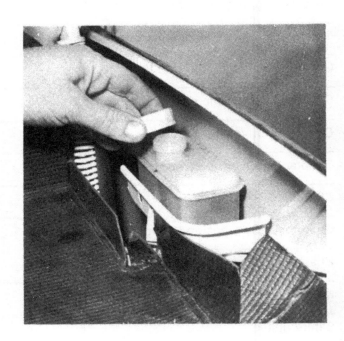

Topping up the brake fluid reservoir

## 1 SAFETY MAINTENANCE

a) Steering

| | |
|---|---|
| Steering tie rod ball joints - check for wear | 3 months |
| Steering gear - check worm to roller play and worm shaft bearings. Adjust if necessary. | 3 months |
| Front wheel bearings - check end play and adjust if necessary. | 3 months |
| Suspension strut upper and lower pivots - check for wear. | 3 months |

b) Brakes

| | |
|---|---|
| Hydraulic fluid reservoir level. | 1 month |
| Efficiency and foot pedal free play - check and adjust as required. | 3 months |
| Handbrake efficiency - check and adjust as required. | |
| Brake friction lining material - check thickness | 6 months |
| Hydraulic lines, hoses, master cylinder wheel cylinders and calipers - examine exteriors for leaks or corrosion. | 6 months |
| Renew all seals and fluid | 3 years |

Note: A significant drop in fluid reservoir level or any other indication of fluid leakage is a danger signal. A complete and thorough examination of the hydraulic system should be made.

c) Suspension

| | |
|---|---|
| Tyres - inflation pressure check | Weekly |
| Tyres - wear and damage check | As suspect |
| Dampers - check for leakage and malfunction | 3 months |

d) Vision

Lights functioning
Screen washer operative

## 2 SAFETY MAINTENANCE PROCEDURES

a) Steering

See Chapter 11.

b) Brakes

Hydraulic fluid reservoir level - Raise the front compartment lid. The fluid reservoir is mounted at the left hand side.
Clean round the filler cap before removing it and top up to the indicated level with approved fluid as required.
Remaining items - See Chapter 9.

c) Suspension

See Chapter 11.

d) Vision

Lights - See Chapter 10.
Screenwasher reservoir.

The screenwasher reservoir should be full of clean water - with an additive of anti-smear compound as wished. The tank should be pressurized from an ordinary type inflator to the maximum pressure of *42 lbs p.s.i.* which is marked on the tank.

If it is overinflated it will split and require renewal. If the jets do not direct water on to the screen as they should refer to Chapter 10 for details.

In the United Kingdom correctly functioning screenwashers are a legally obligatory fitment to all cars.

## 3 EFFICIENCY AND PERFORMANCE MAINTENANCE

a) Engine

| | |
|---|---|
| Lubricating oil - top up to level | Weekly |
|         - drain, clean filter and refill with fresh oil | 3 months |
| Fan belt - check tension and adjust if required | 1 month |
| Air cleaner - clean out bowl and refill with oil | 1 month |
|         - check correct operation of warm air control flaps | 1 month |
| Battery - check electrolyte level | Weekly |

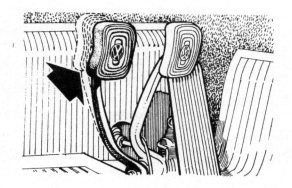

Check the clutch pedal free play

Underside of transmission showing drain and level plugs - the latter removed

Engine oil filler cap

Distributor - check contact points gap. Adjust
                     and/or renew                                    3 months
              - lubricate cam                                        3 months
Valve clearances - check and adjust as required
                     (renew rocker cover gaskets)                    6 months
Spark plugs - remove, clean and reset                                6 months
              - renew                                               12 months
Fuel pump - clean filter                                             6 months
Carburettor - check setting of throttle cable and
                     lubricate linkage                               6 months
Cover plates and fan housing - check security of
                     all screws and grommets                         3 months

b) Suspension
   Front wheel bearings - repack with grease                         2 years
   Rear wheel bearings - repack with grease                          2 years

c) Transmission and final drive
   Gearbox oil - check level and top up as needed                    3 months
              - drain and refill with fresh oil                      2 years
   Clutch pedal free play - check movement and
                     adjust                                       As necessary
   Axle shaft flexible gaiters - check for
              splits                                                 3 months

d) Automatic transmission
   Refer to Chapter 7.

**4 Efficiency and performance maintenance procedures**

a) Engine
   Lubricating oil
   To top up the oil, remove the filler cap from the filler pipe at
the right hand side of the engine. Remove the dipstick to prevent
possible blow back up the filler pipe when pouring oil in. A
funnel is necessary sometimes if spillage is to be avoided.
   When changing the engine oil the filter screen - which is simply
wire gauze - should also be flushed out with paraffin to clear the
gauze. This entails removing the circular retaining plate in the
centre of the bottom of the crankcase. Before starting, you must
obtain two new gaskets for it, and it is also desirable to get six
new copper washers for the stud nuts.
   First drain the oil by removing the centre plug and then
remove the cover plate. Take care when removing the strainer.
Do not distort it.
   The oil suction pipe which goes into the centre of the strainer
gauze must be quite firm. If it is loose then it is likely that
suction is being lost and the oil circulation is not 100% efficient.
(The engine needs completely stripping to put this right.)
   The strainer incorporates a relief valve in case the filter mesh
should get completely blocked up.
   Having thoroughly cleaned everything refit the strainer with a
gasket on each side of the flange. See that the suction pipe is
properly located in the strainer. Fit new copper washers followed
by the cap nuts. Do not overtighten the cap nuts - otherwise the
threads may strip.
   Replace the drain plug and refill with 4½ pints of approved
engine oil.
   Fan belt - see Chapter 2
   Air cleaner - see Chapter 3
   Battery - see Chapter 10
   Distributor - see Chapter 4
   Valve clearances - see Chapter 1
   Spark plugs - see Chapter 4
   Fuel pump - see Chapter 3
   Carburettor - see Chapter 3

b) Suspension
   Front wheel bearings - see Chapter 11
   Rear wheel bearings - see Chapter 8

c) Transmission and final drive
   Gearbox oil - To check the level stand the car on level ground

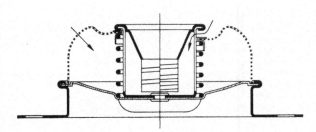

Cross section of engine oil filter screen showing normal oil flow
arrowed left and relief flow right, in the event of a blocked
filter screen

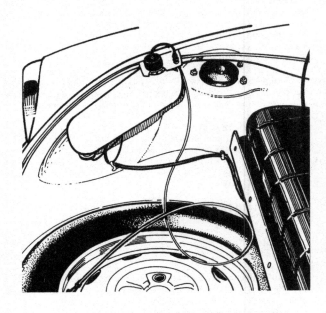

Filling and pressurising the windscreen washer reservoir

Checking for belt tension

and undo the level plug which is halfway up the side of the casing on the left - just ahead of the axle shafts. This plug is a recessed hexagon which could be very difficult to undo.

Use a tubular spanner or bolt head which fits snugly. If the plug is burred by makeshift methods it will get progressively difficult to remove. Add oil from a suitable oil gun or squeeze pack with flexible filler spout. Add oil slowly until it runs out from the filler/level hole. Clean the plug and replace it tightly.

When changing the transmission oil it is best to run it warm first. Then undo the magnetic drain plug in the bottom of the casing. Let the oil drain out for at least 15 minutes. Clean the magnetic drain plug and replace it. Before beginning to refill get the exact amount of oil needed ready, and then start to fill up through the filler/level plug. It is possible that oil will overflow before you have put it all in. Wait so that the air pockets have time to bubble out and then continue until all the oil is put in.

Clutch pedal free play - see Chapter 5.

Axle shaft gaiters - see Chapter 8.

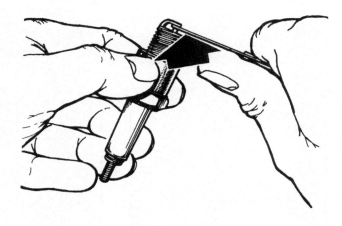

Checking spark plug gap

## VW COMPUTER DIAGNOSIS

As part of the VW service at 6000 miles (or 6 months) intervals a diagnosis check is carried out covering all aspects of maintenance. This system is described in more detail in Chapter 10. The diagnosis check list of 88 items is given below and covers all models of VW which are built.

1  Steering/ignition lock, warning lights*
2  Brake pedal push rod, clearance
3  Brake pedal, free travel
4  Clutch pedal, clearance
5  Play at steering wheel rim
6  Handbrake, free play
7  Windscreen washer operation
8  Windscreen wiper mechanism (mechanical)
9  Windscreen wiper blade rubber
10  Windscreen wiper blade assembly
11  Low beam
12  Fog lights*
13  High beam
14  Lights operating with ignition switched on
15  Reversing lights*
16  Instrument panel illumination
17  Fuel gauge*
18  Warning lamp, emergency warning system*
19  Control lamp, brake warning system*
20  Battery voltage, engine switched off
21  Condition of battery
22  Side, rear and number plate lights
23  Brake lights
24  Battery, electrolyte level
25  Indicator (left) - control light
26  Indicator (right) - control light
27  Heated rear window (operation)*
28  Tyre pressures, adjusted
29  Spare wheel tyre (pressure)
30  Spare tyre for damage
31  Level of brake fluid
32  Engine oil level
33  Front wheels, total toe                    + degrees/minutes
34  Front wheels, total toe                    — degrees/minutes
35  Front wheels left, camber                  + degrees/minutes
36  Front wheel left, camber                   — degrees/minutes
37  Front wheel right, camber                  + degrees/minutes
38  Front wheel right, camber                  — degrees/minutes
39  Upper torsion arm axial play*
40  Brake lines, inside vehicle
41  Engine oil temperature                     ($^{o}$C)
42  Starter motor current                      (amps)
43  Compression pressures: cylinder 1          (units)
44  Compression pressures: cylinder 2          (units)
45  Compression pressures: cylinder 3          (units)

46  Compression pressures: cylinder 4          (units)
47  Horn operation
48  Voltage control regulator, function at 2000 rpm
49  Distributor (dwell angle) degrees
50  Generator current (maximim output) amps
51  Kick down switch*
52  Kick down solenoid*
53  Coolant level, antifreeze content
54  Cooling and heating system
55  Engine, upper part
56  Pre-heating circuit and restrictor*
57  V-belt tension and condition
58  Ignition timing, adjust
59  Headlights
60  King pin and link pin, play*
61  Ball joint, axial play (upper left)*
62  Ball joint, axial play (lower left)*
63  Ball joint, axial play (upper right)*
64  Ball joint, axial play (lower right)*
65  Ball joint, dust covers and sealing plugs
66  Tie rod ends, play
67  Tie rods, mounting and dust covers
68  Steering rack bellows*
69  Steering gear
70  Brake lines and hoses (front)
71  Brake linings: thickness (front)
72  Suspension strut upper ball joints and dust covers*
73  Tyre (front left)
74  Tyre (front right)
75  Dust sleeve (CV joints)*
76  Final drive
77  Transmission
78  Engine lower part
79  Torque converter and lines (automatic, stick shift)*
80  Exhaust system
81  Brake lines and hoses (rear)
82  Brake regulator valve, linkage and dust seal*
83  Intake ducts, water drain flaps
84  Shift clutch (automatic, stick shift) play
85  Brake linings: thickness (rear)
86  Tyre (rear left)
87  Tyre (rear right)
88  Wheel bolts torque

* These test operations do not apply to all vehicles.

# Recommended lubricants and fluids

| Item | Type | Recommended |
|---|---|---|
| Engine lubricant ... ... ... ... ... ... ... | Multigrade engine oil * ... ... ... ... ... ... | CASTROL GTX |
| Transmission ... ... ... ... ... ... ... ... | SAE 90 gear oil ... ... ... ... ... ... | CASTROL HYPOY |
| Transmission with limited slip differential ... | SAE 90 gear oil ... ... ... ... ... ... | CASTROL HYPOY LS |
| Wheel bearings ... ... ... ... ... ... | Lithium based multipurpose grease ... ... | CASTROL LM |
| Contact breaker cam ... ... ... ... ... ... | Petroleum jelly ... ... ... ... ... ... | VASELINE |
| Battery terminals ... ... ... ... ... ... ... | Petroleum jelly ... ... ... ... ... ... | VASELINE |
| Brake hydraulic fluid ... ... ... ... ... ... | SAE 70 R3 ... ... ... ... ... ... ... | CASTROL GIRLING BRAKE FLUID |
| Torque converter (automatic transmission) | Dexron ... ... ... ... ... ... ... ... | CASTROL TQ, DEXRON® |

* In view of the small engine oil capacity and the heavy strains imposed on the oil none but the best quality should be used. Do not mix oils of different types.

# Lubrication Chart

**Frequencies are based on an average monthly mileage of 1000**

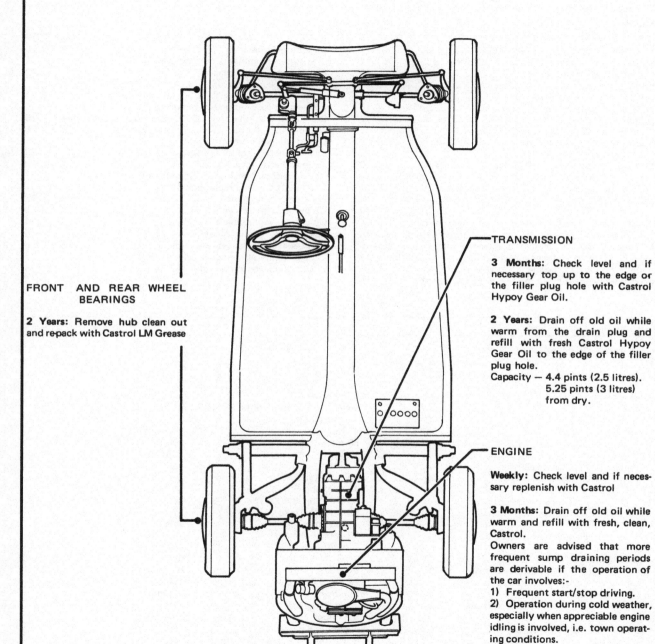

**FRONT AND REAR WHEEL BEARINGS**

**2 Years:** Remove hub clean out and re-pack with Castrol LM Grease

TRANSMISSION

**3 Months:** Check level and if necessary top up to the edge of the filler plug hole with Castrol Hypoy Gear Oil.

**2 Years:** Drain off old oil while warm from the drain plug and refill with fresh Castrol Hypoy Gear Oil to the edge of the filler plug hole.
Capacity — 4.4 pints (2.5 litres).
              5.25 pints (3 litres)
              from dry.

ENGINE

**Weekly:** Check level and if necessary replenish with Castrol

**3 Months:** Drain off old oil while warm and refill with fresh, clean, Castrol.
Owners are advised that more frequent sump draining periods are derivable if the operation of the car involves:-
1) Frequent start/stop driving.
2) Operation during cold weather, especially when appreciable engine idling is involved, i.e. town operating conditions.
Capacity — 4.4 pints (2.5 litres).

for **VEHICLES WITH AUTOMATIC TRANSMISSION** use Castrol TQ Dexron' R for torque converter — Capacity 7.8 pints (3.6 litres)

# Chapter 1 Engine

## Contents

## Specifications

### Engine specifications and data

| | |
|---|---|
| 1285 cc ... ... ... ... ... ... ... ... ... ... ... | 44 DIN bhp |
| 1584 cc ... ... ... ... ... ... ... ... ... ... ... | 50 DIN bhp |

### Engine general

| | 1300 Code AB | 1600 Code AD, AE |
|---|---|---|
| Type ... ... ... ... ... ... ... ... ... ... ... ... | 4 cylinders flat horizontally opposed. Pushrod ohv | |
| Weight (approx) ... ... ... ... ... ... ... ... ... ... | 115 kg/253 lbs | |
| Bore ... ... ... ... ... ... ... ... ... ... ... ... | 77 mm | 85.5 mm |
| Stroke ... ... ... ... ... ... ... ... ... ... ... ... | 69 mm | 69 mm |
| Cubic capacity ... ... ... ... ... ... ... ... ... ... | 1285 cc | 1584 cc |
| Compression ratio (normal) ... ... ... ... ... ... ... | 7.5 : 1 | 7.5 : 1 |
| - low | 6.6 : 1 (Code AC) | 6.6 : 1 (Code AF) |
| Power output (standard) ... ... ... ... ... ... ... ... | 44 DIN bhp @ 4100 rpm | 50 DIN bhp @ 4000 rpm |
| (low compression) ... ... ... ... ... ... ... | 40 DIN bhp @ 4000 rpm | 46 DIN bhp @ 4000 rpm |
| Max torque (standard) DIN ... ... ... ... ... ... ... | 63 ft lbs/8.7 mkg @ 3000 rpm | 77 ft lbs/10.7 mkg @ 2800 rpm |
| (low compression) DIN ... ... ... ... ... ... | 58 ft lbs/8.0 mkg @ 3000 rpm | 72 ft lbs/10 mkg @ 2600 rpm |
| Fuel octane required - standard ... ... ... ... ... ... | 91 RON | 91 RON |
| - low compression ... ... ... ... | 83 RON | 83 RON |
| Compression pressure - standard ... ... ... ... ... ... | 92 psi /6.5 kg/cm$^2$ minimum | 100 psi /7.0 kg/cm$^2$ minimum |
| - low compression ... ... ... ... | 71 psi/5 kg/cm$^2$ minimum | 71 psi/5 kg/cm$^2$ minimum |
| Location of No 1 cylinder ... ... ... ... ... ... ... ... | Right hand pair - front | |
| Firing order ... ... ... ... ... ... ... ... ... ... ... | 1 (r. front) 4 (l. rear) 3 (l front) 2 (r. rear) | |
| Engine mounting ... ... ... ... ... ... ... ... ... ... | Bolted direct to transmission casing | |

### Camshaft and camshaft bearings

| | |
|---|---|
| Camshaft drive ... ... ... ... ... ... ... ... ... ... | Lightweight alloy gear direct from crankshaft |
| Camshaft bearings ... ... ... ... ... ... ... ... ... | Steel backed white metal shells |
| Camshaft journal diameters ... ... ... ... ... ... ... | 24.99 - 25.00 mm (0.9837 - 0.9842 in) |
| Journal/bearing radial clearance ... ... ... ... ... ... | 0.02 - 0.12 mm (0.008 - 0.0047 in) |

End float ... ... ... ... ... ... ... ... ... ... ...          0.04 - 0.16 mm (0.0016 - 0.0063 in)
Gear backlash     ... ... ... ... ... ... ... ... ... ...      0.0 - 0.05 mm (0 - 0.002 in)

**Connecting rods and bearings**

Type   ... ... ... ... ... ... ... ... ... ... ... ...         Forged steel
Big end bearings ... ... ... ... ... ... ... ... ...           3 layer thin wall shells
Crankpin (big end) diameter  ... ... ... ... ...               54.98 - 55.00 mm (2.1644 - 2.1648 in)
Small end bush   ... ... ... ... ... ... ... ... ...           Lead/bronze coated steel - pressed in
Undersize big end shells available   ... ... ...               0.25 mm, 0.50 mm, 0.75 mm
Crankpin to bearing clearance limits ... ...                   0.02 - 0.15 mm (0.0008 - 0.006 in)
Crankpin end float ... ... ... ... ... ... ... ...             0.1 - 0.7 mm (0.004 - 0.028 in)
Gudgeon pin/bush radial clearance limit ... ...                0.01 - 0.04 mm (0.0004 - 0.0016 in)
Gudgeon pin diameter ... ... ... ... ... ... ...               21.996 - 22 mm (0.8658 - 0.8661 in)
Connecting rod weight - brown or white  ... ...                580 - 588 grams
                      - grey or black ... ... ... ... ...      592 - 600 grams
Maximum crankpin ovality  ... ... ... ... ... ...              0.03 mm (0.0011 in)

**Crankshaft and main bearings**

Number of bearings ... ... ... ... ... ... ... ...             4
Main bearing journal diameters Nos 1, 2 and 3   ... ...        54.97 - 54.99 mm (2.164 - 2.1648 in)
                               No 4   ... ...                  39.98 - 40.00 mm (1.5739 - 1.5748 in)
Regrind diameters undersize  ... ... ... ... ...               0.25 mm, 0.50 mm, 0.75 mm
Bearing shells - type Nos 1, 3 and 4 ... ... ... ...           Aluminium, lead coated 1 piece
                      No 2 ... ... ... ... ... ...             Split - 3 layer steel backed
Journal/bearing radial clearance limit
        Nos 1 and 3   ... ... ... ... ... ...                  0.04 - 0.18 mm (0.0016 - 0.007 in)
        No 2   ... ... ... ... ... ... ...                     0.03 - 0.17 mm (0.0011 - 0.0066 in)
        No 4   ... ... ... ... ... ... ...                     0.05 - 0.19 mm (0.0019 - 0.0074 in)
Crankshaft end float   ... ... ... ... ... ... ...             Taken by flange of No 1 main bearing and adjusted by shims
End float limits   ... ... ... ... ... ... ... ...             0.07 - 0.13 mm (0.0027 - 0.0051 in)
Main journal maximum ovality  ... ... ... ... ...              0.03 mm (0.0011 in)

**Crankcase**

Main bearing bore diameters Nos 1, 2 and 3   ... ...           65.00 - 65.03 mm (2.559 - 2.5601 in)
                            No 4   ... ...                     50.00 - 50.04 mm (1.9685 - 1.9700 in)
Oil seal bore diameter (flywheel end)  ... ... ...             90.00 - 90.05 mm (3.5433 - 3.5452 in)
Camshaft bearing bore diameter   ... ... ... ...               27.5 - 27.52 mm (1.0825 - 1.0852 in)
Oil pump housing bore diameter   ... ... ... ...               70.00 - 70.03 mm (2.756 - 2.758 in)
Tappet (cam follower) bore diameters ... ... ...               19.00 - 19.05 mm (0.748 - 0.750 in)

**Cylinders**

Type   ... ... ... ... ... ... ... ... ... ... ... ...         Single barrels - finned - cast iron
Distance between pair centres... ... ... ... ... ...           112 mm (4.41 in)

**Cylinder heads**

Type   ... ... ... ... ... ... ... ... ... ... ... ...         Aluminium - 1 per pair of cylinders
Port arrangement   ... ... ... ... ... ... ... ...             Each head has two inlet ports and two exhaust ports. The inlet
                                                               ports are side by side being fed from a twin branch induction
                                                               manifold to each head.

**Gudgeon pins**

Type   ... ... ... ... ... ... ... ... ... ... ... ...         Fully floating, steel tube retained by circlips
Diameter ... ... ... ... ... ... ... ... ... ... ...           21.996 - 22.00 mm (0.8658 - 0.8661 in)

**Lubrication system**

Type   ... ... ... ... ... ... ... ... ... ... ... ...         Wet sump - pressure and splash
Oil filter   ... ... ... ... ... ... ... ... ... ...           Wire gauze suction strainer in sump
Sump capacity   ... ... ... ... ... ... ... ... ...            2½ litres (4.4 Imp pints)
Oil pump type   ... ... ... ... ... ... ... ... ...            Twin gear
Oil pressure (SAE 30, 70ºC at 2500 rpm) ... ... ...            42 psi (min 28 psi)
Oil pressure warning light   ... ... ... ... ... ...           Comes on between 2 - 6 psi
Oil cooler ... ... ... ... ... ... ... ... ... ... ...         Pressure fed multitube type in cooling fan housing
Oil dipstick   ... ... ... ... ... ... ... ... ... ...         Upper mark indicates full capacity. Lower mark indicates half full

**Oil pump**

Gear/body end clearance (no gasket)   ... ... ...              0.1 mm (0.004 in) max
Gear backlash     ... ... ... ... ... ... ... ... ...          0 - 0.2 mm (0.008 in)

**Oil pressure relief valve**

Spring length loaded at 7.75 kg (17 lbs)  ... ... ...          23.6 mm (0.928 in)

Oil pressure regulating valve  ... ... ... ... ... ... ... ...        Maintains oil pressure at bearings at 28 psi

**Pistons**
Type  ... ... ... ... ... ... ... ... ... ... ... ... ...        Light alloy with steel inserts
Clearance in cylinder limits  ... ... ... ... ... ... ...        0.04 - 0.02 mm (0.0015 - 0.008 in)
Number of rings  ... ... ... ... ... ... ... ... ... ...        3 — Two compression, one oil control
Ring/groove side clearance - Top compression ... ... ... ...        0.07 - 0.12 mm (0.0027 - 0.0047 in)
                     - Lower compression ... ... ... ...        0.05 - 0.10 mm (0.0019 - 0.0039 in)
                     - Oil control  ... ... ... ...        0.03 - 0.10 mm (0.0012 - 0.0039 in)
Piston oversizes available  ... ... ... ... ... ... ... ...        0.5 mm and 1.0 mm (0.020 and 0.040 in)
Piston pin bore offset  ... ... ... ... ... ... ... ... ...        1.5 mm (0.060 in)

**Piston rings**
Top compression:
         Thickness  ... ... ... ... ... ... ...        2.5 mm (0.10 in)
         Gap limit  ... ... ... ... ... ... ...        0.3 - 0.9 mm (0.012 - 0.035 in)
         Bearing face ... ... ... ... ... ... ...        Bevelled, angle facing top of piston
Lower compression:
         Thickness  ... ... ... ... ... ... ...        2.5 mm (0.10 in)
         Gap limit  ... ... ... ... ... ... ...        0.3 - 0.9 mm (0.012 - 0.035 in)
         Bearing face ... ... ... ... ... ... ...        Parallel, lower edge cut back
Oil control:
         Gap  ... ... ... ... ... ... ... ... ...        0.25 - 0.95 mm (0.010 - 0.037 in)

**Tappets - (cam followers)**
Type  ... ... ... ... ... ... ... ... ... ... ...        Cylindrical flat based
Diameter ... ... ... ... ... ... ... ... ... ...        18.96 - 18.89 mm (0.7463 - 0.7471 in)

**Pushrods and rocker arms**
Pushrod type  ... ... ... ... ... ... ... ...        Tube with hemispherical ends
Pushrod length  ... ... ... ... ... ... ... ... ...        272.5 mm
Rocker arm bore size limits  ... ... ... ... ... ...        18.00 - 18.04 mm (0.7086 - 0.7093 in)
Rocker shaft diameter size limits ... ... ... ... ... ...        17.97 - 17.95 mm (0.7073 - 0.7066 in)

**Valves**
Inlet     - head diameter  ... ... ... ... ... ... ...        35.6 mm
        - stem diameter  ... ... ... ... ... ... ...        7.94 - 7.95 mm
        - seat width  ... ... ... ... ... ... ...        1.3 - 1.6 mm
        - seat angle  ... ... ... ... ... ...        44º
        - guide bore diameter  ... ... ... ...        8.00 - 8.06 mm
        - maximum rock in guide ... ... ... ...        0.8 mm
Exhaust - head diameter  ... ... ... ... ... ...        32.1 mm
        - stem diameter  ... ... ... ... ... ... ...        7.92 - 7.94 mm
        - seat width  ... ... ... ... ... ... ...        1.7 - 2.0 mm
        - seat angle  ... ... ... ... ... ...        45º
        - guide bore diameter  ... ... ... ...        8.00 - 8.06 mm
        - maximum rock in guide ... ... ... ...        0.8 mm
Seat width correction angle - inner  ... ... ... ...        75º
                              - outer  ... ... ... ...        15º
Rocker arm/valve clearance  ... ... ... ... ...        0.15 mm (0.006 in) all cold

**Timing**
Inlet opens  ... ... ... ... ... ... ... ... ... ...        7º 30' BTDC
Inlet closes  ... ... ... ... ... ... ... ... ...        37º ABDC
Exhaust opens  ... ... ... ... ... ... ... ...        44º 30' BBDC
Exhaust closes  ... ... ... ... ... ... ... ...        4º ATDC

**NOTE:** Rocker arm to valve clearances are set at 1 mm (0.040 in) for the purpose of valve timing only

**Valve springs**
Type  ... ... ... ... ... ... ... ... ... ... ... ... ... ...        Single coil spring
Loaded length  ... ... ... ... ... ... ... ... ... ... ...        31 mm at 53 - 61 kg (116 - 134 lbs)

**Torque wrench settings**
Crankshaft pulley nut  ... ... ... ... ... ... ...        33 lb ft (4.5 mkg)
Oil pump nuts  ... ... ... ... ... ... ... ... ...        14 lb ft (2.0 mkg)
Oil drain plug  ... ... ... ... ... ... ... ... ...        33 lb ft (4.5 mkg)
Oil strainer cover nuts ... ... ... ... ... ... ...        5 lb ft (0.7 mkg)
Cylinder head nuts  ... ... ... ... ... ... ... ...        23 lb ft (3.2 mkg)  See text
Flywheel screw  ... ... ... ... ... ... ... ... ...        253 lb ft (35 mkg)

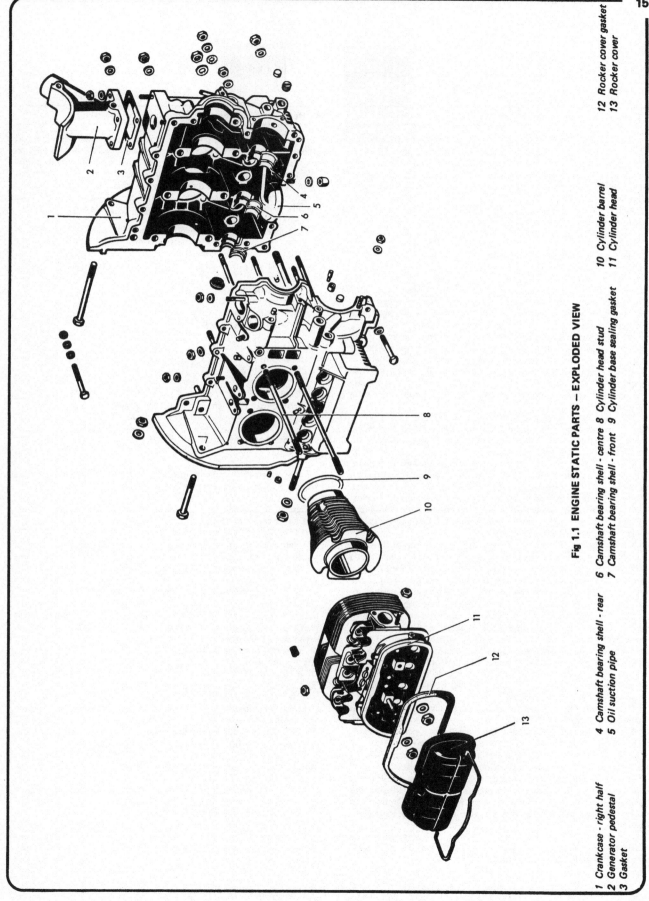

**Fig 1.1 ENGINE STATIC PARTS – EXPLODED VIEW**

1 Crankcase - right half
2 Generator pedestal
3 Gasket
4 Camshaft bearing shell - rear
5 Oil suction pipe
6 Camshaft bearing shell - centre
7 Camshaft bearing shell - front
8 Cylinder head stud
9 Cylinder base sealing gasket
10 Cylinder barrel
11 Cylinder head
12 Rocker cover gasket
13 Rocker cover

| | | |
|---|---|---|
| Crankcase nuts and screws M8 ... ... ... ... ... ... ... ... ... ... | | 14 lb ft (2.0 mkg) |
| M10 ... ... ... ... ... ... ... ... ... | | 25 lb ft (3.5 mkg) |
| Connecting rod cap nuts ... ... ... ... ... ... ... ... ... ... ... | | 24 lb ft (3.3 mkg) |
| Engine securing nuts ... ... ... ... ... ... ... ... ... ... ... | | 22 lb ft (3.0 mkg) |
| Rocker shaft nuts ... ... ... ... ... ... ... ... ... ... ... ... | | 18 lbs ft (2.5 mkg) |

## 1  General description and engine numbers

The 1302 series Beetle has two engine sizes fitted (only the larger is presently available in the U.K) the 1285 cc and 1584 cc. The larger engine is fitted in the 1302S. They are both direct descendents of the original flat four air cooled design, incorporating modification to improve cooling and bearing lubrication pressures.

As a guide to identification the engines have prefix letters in front of the 7 figure serial numbers, viz:

| | | | |
|---|---|---|---|
| 1285 cc | | | AB |
| 1584 cc | 7.5 : 1 CR | | AD |
| 1584 cc | exhaust emission control | | AE |
| 1584 cc | 6.6 : 1 CR | | AF |
| 1584 cc | US and Canada | | B |

The engine is an air-cooled horizontally opposed flat four cylinder design. The short crankshaft runs in aluminium alloy shell bearings located between the two halves of a magnesium alloy crankcase which join vertically. The camshaft runs centrally below the crankshaft and is gear driven from the rear end of the crankshaft. The camshaft is also located between the crankcase halves and runs in removable split shell bearings.

The distributor is driven by a removable shaft from a gear mounted on the rear end of the crankshaft. The same shaft incorporates a cam which operates the fuel pump operating plunger rod.

The gear type oil pump is mounted in the rear of the crankcase, held between the two halves and driven by a horizontal shaft. A tongue on the inner end of the shaft engages in a slot in the end of the camshaft.

The four, finned cylinder barrels are separately mounted and each pair has a common cylinder head containing the valves and rocker gear. The pushrods locate in cylindrical flat faced cam followers at the camshaft end and pass through sealed cylindrical tubes clamped between the head and crankcase outside the cylinder barrels. Each rocker cover is held to the head by spring hoops locating in a recess in the cover.

The flywheel is located on the front of the crankshaft by four dowel pegs and secured by a single central bolt which also incorporates needle roller bearings for the gearbox input shaft. The front crankcase oil seal bears on the centre hub land of the flywheel. The rear end of the crankshaft has an oil thrower plate and a helical groove machined in the pulley wheel hub to contain the oil. An oil filter screen is mounted in the bottom centre of the crankcase and the oil suction pipe for the pump comes from the centre of it. There is no other form of oil filter incorporated. The generator, which is mounted on a pedestal above the engine, is driven by a V-belt from the crankshaft pulley. On the forward end of the generator shaft the cooling fan is mounted. This runs in a sheet steel housing which ducts air down to the cylinder barrels.

There is no separate oil sump - the crankcase acting as an oil reservoir of just under 4½ pints.

Engine cooling is regulated by a bellows type thermostat which is mounted in the air flow under the right hand pair of cylinders. The thermostat operates two linked control flaps in the fan housing lower ducting section at left and right.

The car heating system is integral with the engine cooling and is achieved by directing air through ducts which shroud the exhaust pipes. Two flexible ducts lead from the fan housing to the heat exchangers - and then via two more ducts to the car interior.

The cooling system also incorporates an oil cooler which is a multitube heat exchanger mounted vertically on the crankcase. Air from the cooling fan is ducted past it.

## 2  Repair and maintenance procedures - dismantling

The VW beetle engine has always been easier to work on when removed from the car. It has been possible in the past to do a certain amount of work, however, with the engine in place. With the various design developments there are now fewer opportunities, in the Super Beetle for this. Apart from routine maintenance tasks the parts or sub-assemblies which can be repaired and/or removed with the engine in place are:

| | |
|---|---|
| Fan housing          ) | |
| Oil pressure relief valve  ) | |
| Oil cooler          ) | |
| Oil pressure control valve  ) | |
| Crankshaft pulley wheel   ) | Details in Chapter 2 |
| Oil pump          ) | |
| Thermostat         ) | |
| Exhaust manifold       ) | |
| Heat exchangers       ) | |
| Fan (with generator)    ) | |
| | |
| Carburettor        ) | |
| Fuel pump         ) | Details in Chapter 3 |
| Inlet manifold       ) | |
| | |
| Distributor         ) | |
| Distributor drive shaft    ) | Details in Chapter 4 |
| Coil           ) | |
| | |
| Generator (with fan)    ) | Details in Chapter 10 |
| Starter          ) | |

For any other work on the engine to be carried out it must be removed from the car.

## 3  Engine removal - preparation

Removal of the Beetle engine is quite straightforward and speedy provided that the correct tools and lifting tackle are assembled beforehand. The engine is held to the transmission unit by two studs and two bolts - nothing more. It has to be drawn back from these and lowered out of the car. If you have a pit or raised ramp, a firm stand or platform will be needed to support the engine as soon as it is detached. It weighs 240 lbs and attempts to draw it off without providing support under the ramp or in the pit will result in disaster.

Without a pit or ramp a method must be devised to support the engine as soon as it is detached so that the supports may then be removed and the engine readily lowered to ground level. The car body is then lifted up at the rear and the engine drawn out from under - or the car rolled forward over the engine. Four strong men can lift the car the required three feet to clear the engine. Alternatively a conventional hoist can be used to lift the car with the sling fastened between the rear bumper support brackets. If no hoist is available then at least two conventional scissor jacks or hydraulic jacks will be needed together with suitable wooden or concrete blocks, to raise and support the car at each side near the jacking points.

A 17 mm ring spanner - of the non-cranked sort you get on a combination - is essential for undoing the mounting nuts and bolts as there is no space to get a socket on.

If the car is very dirty underneath it would be worthwhile getting it thoroughly cleaned off away from the removal area first. The lower mounting stud nuts are exposed to the elements and the top bolts and nuts call for a certain amount of

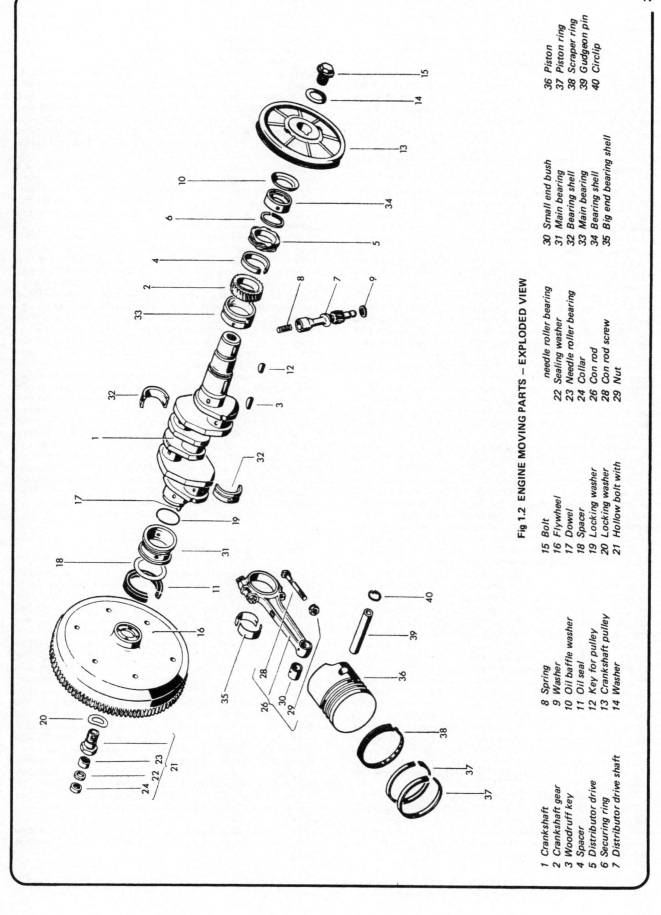

**Fig 1.2 ENGINE MOVING PARTS – EXPLODED VIEW**

1 Crankshaft
2 Crankshaft gear
3 Woodruff key
4 Spacer
5 Distributor drive
6 Securing ring
7 Distributor drive shaft

8 Spring
9 Washer
10 Oil baffle washer
11 Oil seal
12 Key for pulley
13 Crankshaft pulley
14 Washer

15 Bolt
16 Flywheel
17 Dowel
18 Spacer
19 Locking washer
20 Locking washer
21 Hollow bolt with

    needle roller bearing
22 Sealing washer
23 Needle roller bearing
24 Collar
26 Con rod
28 Con rod screw
29 Nut

30 Small end bush
31 Main bearing
32 Bearing shell
33 Main bearing
34 Bearing shell
35 Big end bearing shell

36 Piston
37 Piston ring
38 Scraper ring
39 Gudgeon pin
40 Circlip

reaching around. If you are working on your back at floor level, dirt falling in the eyes can be a major irritation.

It is possible to get the engine out and clear single-handed if all the foregoing equipment is available but the trickiest part is lowering the engine to floor level. Assistance is insurance against dropping it. Even a few inches fall could crack the aluminium crankcase - there being no conventional sump. Note that the engine is back-to-front as compared with a conventional layout so that the flywheel is at the front. All references to front and rear of the engine will, therefore, be in relation to its position in the car.

### 4 Engine - removal

1  Stand the car on a level hard surface with sufficient room to roll it forward about six feet if you wish to lift the car over the engine rather than drag the engine back from under the car. Disconnect the battery (photo). Now is the time to drain the engine oil into a container - whilst you are disconnecting the ancillaries described next.

2  Open the engine compartment cover and then remove the carburettor air cleaner by slackening the clamp, removing also the pre-heater hose and the oil breather pipe. The air cleaner, complete with hoses, is then lifted off.

3  Remove the heat insulating plates from round the intake manifold pre-heater pipe at each side (photo). Undo the screws securing the small cover plate over the crankshaft pulley (photo). Then remove the remaining screws and the large rear cover plate (photo).

4  Disconnect the three leads from the dynamo noting their colours and the terminals they came from (photo).

5  Undo the connectors to the auto choke and solenoid cut-off valve (one each side of the carburettor), from the oil pressure sender switch and coil (photos). The loom containing all these wires may then be taken from the clips and tucked to one side of the engine compartment.

6  Remove the distributor cap and then slacken the clamping screw which holds the distributor in position. Lift the distributor out (photo).

7  The accelerator cable connected to the carburettor is the next item to be detached. This is somewhat unusual arrangement as the cable has to pass through the fan housing en route to the carburettor. First undo the locking screw which clamps the end of the cable to the link pin on the operating lever (photo). Pull the cable out and do not lose the link. The cable itself need not be pulled through from the back of the fan housing until the engine has been disengaged from the transmission.

8  Now jack up the car, using the vehicle jack to enable you to get underneath the rear end comfortably but keep the tyres touching the ground. Replace the oil drain plug. From underneath, first disconnect the control wires that run to the heater flaps, one on each side. They are held to the flap control arms by cable clamps as used on the carburettor but are quite likely to be dirty and rusted up so be prepared with penetrating oil and suitable self-grip wrenches as necessary. If you have difficulty in identifying them get someone to operate the heater control while you are underneath. You will see them move. The fuel pipe runs along on the left side of the engine and if you feel around you will be able to locate the point where the flexible hose connection occurs (photo). This should be pulled off at the end of the hose nearest the engine so that the end of the flexible pipe can be clamped, or plugged with a pencil stub, to prevent the fuel leaking out. If the fuel level in the tank is fairly low it may not be necessary to do this. Next unclip and pull off the flexible hoses which fit onto the heat exchangers on each side of the engine.

9  The two lower mounting nuts can now be removed and this is where the 17 mm ring spanner mentioned earlier is needed. The nuts are positioned about four inches from each side of the engine centre line and about two inches up from the bottom of the flange where the engine joins the transmission unit. Remove the two nuts and washers (if any), (photo).

10  Then remove the left hand top mounting bolt, also from underneath. This is best done with a socket and extension with a universal joint (photo).

11  Lower the vehicle to the ground once more.

12  The fourth mounting bolt is in front of the fan housing to the right. The nut can be felt so put an arm around and undo it. Strictly speaking, it is safer to support the engine underneath now before the last mounting bolt is removed although the likelihood of the engine moving 3 to 4 inches rearward and falling down of its own accord is fairly remote. The bolt head has a flat on it which should lock into the transmission. This enables the nut to be taken off without any difficulty provided the bolt is not pushed out.

13  Support the engine, preferably on a trolley jack with the jack head under the central circular plate in the crankcase. If another method is used bear in mind that the engine has to be drawn back about 3 inches to disengage it from the transmission. When this is done draw the accelerator cable out of the tube in the fan housing and tape it up on the bulkhead.

14  As said earlier the engine is a tight fit in the compartment. When drawn back it should not be tilted otherwise the anti-rattle springs on the clutch release levers may get damaged by the gearbox input shaft when it is lowered. Grip the fan housing and silencer to pull the engine back. It may need a bit of jiggling to get it clear. Lower carefully until it rests on the ground (photo). All that remains is to raise the rear of the car sufficiently to enable it to be rolled forward over the engine or for the engine to be drawn out from underneath. This can be achieved by four strong men or by hoisting the rear of the car with a sling stretched between the two rear bumper support brackets (photo). Alternatively the car can be raised on two jacks, one on each side and supported progressively on blocks near the body jacking points. Great care must be taken to chock the front wheels securely when using this latter method and the blocks used must be perfectly square and large enough to provide a stable 'pillar' when stacked up. Each support under the body at each side will have to be at least 2 ft 6 ins high so collect sufficient blocks beforehand. Do not use odd bits and pieces. The base blocks should be at least 9 inch x 12 inch square. When the car is raised sufficiently the engine can be pulled out from the rear. It is a little more work to lower the car to the ground at this stage but if you are going to leave it then the extra effort is worthwhile. It is better to be sure than sorry, particularly if there are children about.

### 5 Engine dismantling - general

1  Unlike the majority of conventional engines the Volkswagen is one which does not make it easy to carry out most tasks with the engine still in the car. In view of the relative ease with which it can be taken out and lifted on to a bench this manual does not, in general, recommend that engine repair work of any significance is carried out with the engine still in the car. If you have a pit or ramp that enables you to work conveniently under the car there are instances when it is justifiable. Otherwise the inconvenient 'flat on your back' method is far too risky in view of the likelihood of dirt getting into the wrong places and mistakes occurring.

2  For an engine which is obviously in need of a complete overhaul the economies against a replacement engine must also be carefully considered. The dismantling and reassembly of a Volkswagen engine is more complex than for a conventional four cylinder block. Each cylinder is separate and the crankshaft and camshaft run in bearings mounted between the two halves of a precision faced, split crankcase. The number of individual parts is far greater. It is not our intention to put you off - far from it - but we must, in fairness to the owner, point out that it is much easier to make an assembly mistake than on a conventional engine.

3  The dismantling, inspection, repair and reassembly as described in this Chapter follows the procedure as for a complete overhaul.

Disconnect the battery (Sec 4.1)

Remove sealer plates round the inlet manifold pre-heater pipe (Sec 4.3a

Take out the small plate over the crank-shaft pulley (Sec 4.3b)

Take out the large cover plate (Sec 4.3c)

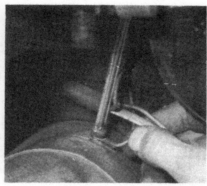
Disconnect the dynamo leads (Sec 4.4)

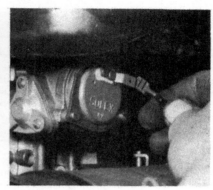
Disconnect the automatic choke lead (Sec 4.5a)

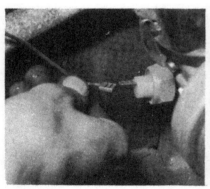
Disconnect the oil pressure switch lead (Sec 4.5b)

Disconnect the solenoid valve and coil leads (Sec 4.5c)

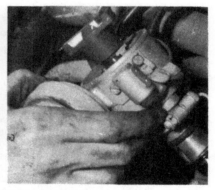
Remove the distributor (Sec 4.6)

Disconnect the throttle cable (Sec 4.7)

Disconnect the fuel pipe (and block it) (Sec 4.8)

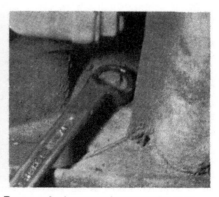
Remove the lower engine mounting nuts (Sec 4.9)

4  Before starting work on any part it is strongly recommended that time is spent in first reading the whole Chapter. It would be too cumbersome and confusing to cross reference the implications of each and every activity. So if you think that the big end bearings are your problem, for example, do not think that by turning to the heading 'Big end bearings' all the implications of repairing them will be contained in that single section above. Mention will be made in brief of the operations necessary which may lead up to it and the details of these should be read first.

5  Whatever degree of dismantling is carried out, components can only be examined properly after they have been thoroughly cleaned. This is best carried out using paraffin and a stiff bristled brush. Some engines can be particularly bad, with a stubborn coating of hard sludgy deposits - generally denoting neglect of regular oil changing - and it can take some time and effort to get this off. Afterwards, the paraffin can be hosed off with a water jet. Cleaning may sometimes seem to take a disproportionate amount of time but there is no doubt that it is time well spent.

## 6  Engine ancillaries - removal

Having removed the engine from the car it may be assumed that all the tinware will have to come off before any major overhauls are carried out. Once the fan housing assembly is removed together with the manifolds and heat exchangers, the dismantling of the other components is dealt with in this chapter.

## 7  Fan housing - removal

Although the removal of the fan housing forms an integral part of the total dismantling procedures of the engine, it is possible to remove it with the engine still in position in the car. As it is part of the cooling system it is therefore dealt with in detail in Chapter 2.

## 8  Oil cooler - removal and renovation

1  It is possible to remove the oil cooler with the engine installed provided the fan housing is first completely removed as described in Chapter 2.

2  Undo the three nuts holding the oil cooler mounting adaptor to the crankcase.

3  Undo the nuts holding the cooler to the adaptor.

4  It will be fairly obvious if the cooler leaks severely but if there is no apparent damage it may be difficult to decide whether it functions correctly. If suspect it should be subjected to a pressure test by a Volkswagen agent equipped with the proper equipment. If there is any doubt about it the only sure remedy is a new one. If the cooler is found to be leaking the oil pressure relief valve should also be checked as it could have caused the failure of the cooler.

5  It is rare for the fins of the cooler to get clogged up but if they have, soak them in a solvent such as 'Gunk' and then flush and blow them through with a high pressure air line. Do not try and poke dirt out with sharp pointed instruments.

## 9  Oil pressure relief and control valves - removal and renovation

1  These may be removed from underneath with the engine in the car. They are spring loaded pistons held into the left hand half of the crankcase at front and rear by large screw plugs (photo).

2  It is not necessary to drain the engine oil but be prepared to catch a small quantity when either of the valves is removed.

3  When the plugs are removed the springs and plungers should drop out. If a plunger sticks in the bore in the crankcase it may need a little assistance and poking with a screwdriver.

4  If a piston seems seized and will not move it may be

necessary to start the engine. Oil pressure should blow it out. Such drastic action being necessary would indicate serious neglect in the matter of regular oil changes. Note that the plungers and springs are not interchangeable so do not mix them up (photo).

5  Both pistons should be a sliding fit in the crankcase bores. Minor signs of seizure may be cleaned up. If there is severe scoring in the piston it may be renewed but if the crankcase bore is damaged the consequences could be serious and expensive, calling for a new one also.

6  The larger of the two springs is for the oil pressure relief valve and goes into the rear bore near the oil pump (photo). The shorter spring is for the pressure regulating valve and goes into the front bore near the transmission mounting (photo).

7  When refitting ensure that the springs locate in their recesses in both piston and plug and that a new plug seal is used. The relief valve serves to relieve excessive oil pressure from the oil cooler when the oil is cold and thick. The regulating valve serves to maintain oil pressure at the crankshaft bearings when the oil is hot and thin.

## 10  Crankshaft pulley wheel - removal and replacement

1  Take off the cover plate held by three screws.

2  The pulley wheel is a straight keyed fit on the end of the crankshaft. It is secured by a single, central bolt. To lock the pulley when undoing or tightening the bolt push a suitable article through one of the holes in the pulley and jam it against the crankcase flange.

2  If, when the nut has been removed, the pulley is a very tight fit, do not apply force at the edges or you are likely to distort it. Soak the boss with penetrating oil and hook something through the two holes if any leverage is necessary.

3  If the pulley has been removed during the course of an overhaul remember that the lower rear engine plate has to be re-fixed before the pulley (photo). There is no access to the two securing screws after the pulley is in position.

4  The nut should be tightened to a torque of 33 ft/lbs when the pulley has been replaced (photos).

## 11  Oil pump - removal and renovation

1  Remove the crankshaft pulley wheel and the lower rear cover plate.

2  The oil pump gears may be removed relatively easily because once the oil pump cover plate has been released by removing the four retaining nuts, the gears may be drawn out of the pump body.

3  The pump body itself is mounted over the same four studs as the cover plate and is clamped between the two halves of the crankcase. To remove the pump body from the engine without splitting the crankcase is best done with a special tool which fits over the studs, locks to the inside of the body and draws it out. If you do not have such a tool then the best way is first to slacken the crankcase clamping stud nuts above and below the pump. This relieves the pressure on the body. A suitable tool can then be tapped against the edge of the pump body and, in easy stages, it can be eased out over the studs. Do not force a tool into the gap between the pump body and the crankcase as this could damage the mating faces and upset the correct alignment of the pump on replacement.

4  If the crankcase is to be split anyway leave the pump body to be taken out then.

5  It is possible to check the pump fairly comprehensively without removing the body from the crankcase but it is, of course, far less convenient and liable to cause measurement inaccuracies.

6  First check the cover plate. If it is very badly scored it should be renewed anyway. Light scoring can be ground out using carborundum paste on a piece of plate glass.

7  Check that the driving spindle is a good fit in the body. Any apparent rocking indicates that the inside of the pump body

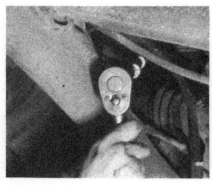
Remove the left upper engine mounting bolt (Sec 4.10)

Engine lowered to the ground (Sec 4.14a)

Car raised with a sling to clear the engine (Sec 4.14b)

Undo stubborn oil pressure regulator plugs with an improvised screwdriver (Sec 9.1)

The relief valve spring is longer than the regulator valve spring (Sec 9.4)

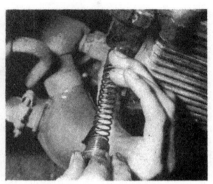
Replacing the relief valve piston, spring and plug (Sec 9.6a)

Replacing the regulator valve piston, spring and plug (Sec 9.6b)

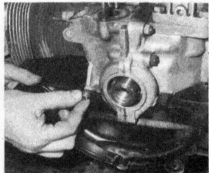
Fitting the lower cover before the crankshaft pulley (Sec 10.3)

Replace the pulley nut (Sec 10.4a)

Tightening the pulley nut (Sec 10.4b)

must also be worn. The driven gear spindle should be tight in the body. The gear should be a good fit on it with no play.

8  Provided both gear spindles are in good shape refit the gears and measure the end clearance between them and the end of the pump body. This is done by putting a straight edge across the body and using a feeler gauge to measure the gap between the straight edge and the gears. Make sure no traces of gasket remain on the flange of the body when doing this. The gap should not .exceed 0.1 mm (0.004 inch) or inadequate oil pressure will result. The wear is most likely to be in the pump body in this case and this will need renewal.

## 12 Cylinder heads - removal

1  Take the engine out of the car.
2  Remove the exhaust system, heat exchangers and upper cylinder cover plates as described in the Fuel and Cooling Chapters. The inlet manifold together with carburettor should also be taken off. See the Fuel System Chapter for details.
3  Prise off the spring clip, downwards, which clamps the rocker cover to the head. Take off the cover.
4  Undo the two nuts, evenly, which secure the rocker shaft standards and then pull off the standards, shaft and rockers as a complete assembly. Pull out the four pushrods and push them through a piece of cardboard so that the location of each one is known and which is the top and bottom end.
5  Before starting to undo the eight nuts which hold the cylinder head down onto the cylinder barrels it must be appreciated that when the head is released the four pushrod tubes will be freed and the cylinder barrels also. If the cylinder barrels are not being taken off the pistons they will rest in position but the engine must not be turned. If the engine is to be turned the barrels should be temporarily tied down to the crankcase with string or wire.
6  Using a socket spanner, the cylinder head stud nuts should be slackened ¼ to ½ turn each only, in the reverse order of the final tightening sequence as given in Fig 1.12. Continue releasing each nut a little at a time until they are all slack. When all are removed the head may be drawn back a little way.
7  Remove the pushrod tubes from between the head and crankcase and make sure the cylinders are disengaged from the head before pulling the head right off.

## 13 Cylinder heads - dismantling and renovation of rocker gear, valves and springs

1  To remove the rocker arms from the shaft the spring clips at each end should be removed and the thrust washers and wave washers taken off. The end rockers may then be removed. The rocker shaft support standards may need tapping off if they are tight in order to remove the two inner rocker arms, clips and washers. If possible lay out the parts in the order in which they were dismantled in a place where they need not be disturbed.
2  To remove the valves it is necessary to use a proper tool to compress the valve springs. The tops of the springs are almost level with the edge of the head casting. If you are unable to obtain a G clamp with extended ends (to clear the edge of the head when the spring is compressed) it will be necessary to use a short piece of tube, with an aperture cut in the side, in conjunction with a conventional spring compressor. The aperture is to enable one to get at the split collars on the valve stem.
3  Compress the spring using the clamp and if the tubular spacer is being used make sure that the pressure is applied squarely and that the tube cannot slip. As soon as the two split conical collars round the valve stem are revealed, use a small screwdriver through the aperture to hook them off the valve stem. It is advisable to maintain one's hold on the spring clamp while doing this to prevent anything from slipping. When the collars are clear release the spring clamp.
4  The spring retainer collar and spring may then be lifted off. There will be small sealing rings round the valve stems and these

too should be taken off. The valve can now be pushed through the guide and taken out. If it tends to stick then it will be because of carbon or sludge deposits on the end of the valve stems and these should be cleaned off as necessary. The end of the valve stem could also be burred due to the 'hammering' action of the rocker arm; in which case the burrs should be carefully stoned off. Do not force a tight valve through the guide or you will score the guide. Keep valves in order so that they may be replaced in the same port. Push them through a piece of cardboard to avoid getting them mixed up.
5  After the cylinder head has been removed and the valves taken out, the head itself should be thoroughly cleaned of carbon in the combustion chambers and examined for cracks. If there are any visible cracks the head should be scrapped. Cracks are most likely to occur round the valve seats or spark plug holes. Bearing in mind that one head will cost (new) nearly 20% of the cost of a complete replacement engine economies should be considered as well as the likelihood of obtaining a used head from a breaker's yard. If the latter, make sure that the head you get is the same type as the old one - and in better condition!
6  The valve seats should be examined for signs of burning away or pitting and ridging. If there is slight pitting the refacing of the seats by grinding in the valve with carborundum paste will probably cure the problem. If the seat needs re-cutting, due to severe pitting, then the seat width should not exceed specification. Fitting new valve seat inserts is a specialist task as they are chilled and shrunk in order to fit them. Check with the nearest Volkswagen dealer because you could have difficulty in getting this problem solved cheaply.
7  The rocker gear should be dismantled and thoroughly cleaned of the sludge deposits which normally tend to accumulate on it. The rocker arms should be a smooth fit on the shaft with no play. If there is any play it is up to the owner to decide whether it is worth the cost of renewal. The effects on engine performance and noise may not be serious although wear tends to accelerate once it is started. The valve clearance adjusting screws should also be examined. The domed ends that bear on the valve stems tend to get hammered out of shape. If bad, replacement is relatively cheap and easy.
8  The valves themselves must be thoroughly cleaned of carbon. The head should be completely free of cracks or pitting and must be perfectly circular. The edge which seats into the cylinder head should also be unpitted and unridged although very minor blemishes may be ground out when re-seating the valve face.
9  Replace the valve into its guide in the head and note if there is any sideways movement which denotes wear between the stem and guide. Here again the degree of wear can vary, if excessive, the performance of the engine can be noticeably affected and oil consumption increased. The maximum tolerable sideways rock, measured at the valve head with the end of the valve stem flush with the end of the guide, is 0.8 mm (0.031 inch). Wear is normally in the guide rather than on the valve stem but check a new valve in the guide if possible first. Valve guide renewal is a tricky operation in these cylinder heads and you may find it difficult to get it done. Check with the nearest Volkswagen dealer first. Do not attempt it yourself. One final part of the examination involves the end of the valve stem where the rocker arm bears. It should be flat but often gets 'hammered' into a concave shape or ridged. Special caps are available to put over the ends. Alternatively the ends can be ground off flat with a fine oil stone. Remember that it is difficult to set the valve clearances accurately with the adjusting screw and valve stem in a battered condition.

## 14 Cylinders, pistons and rings - removal and renovation

1  The cylinders may be removed, after the cylinder heads are off, simply by drawing them from over the pistons. Make sure that the piston and rings are not damaged after the cylinder has been removed. It must also be remembered that if the crankshaft is turned after removing the cylinder the piston skirts can foul

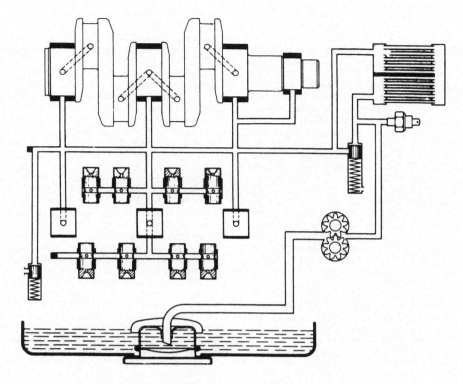

**Fig 1.3 LUBRICATION SYSTEM — DIAGRAMMATIC**

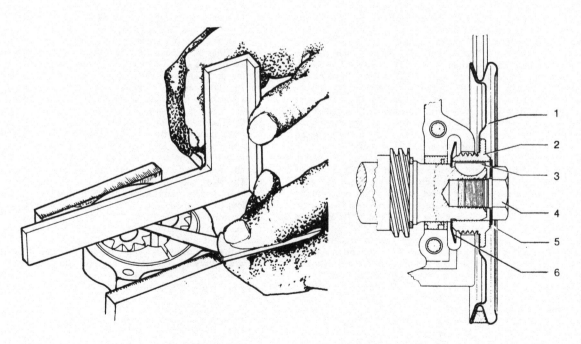

**Fig 1.4  MEASURING OIL PUMP GEAR END CLEARANCE**
(Sec 11)

**Fig 1.5 CRANKSHAFT PULLEY
WHEEL — CROSS SECTION**
(Sec 10)

1 Pulley
2 Oil return scroll
3 Woodruff key
4 Securing bolt
5 Lockwasher
6 Oil thrower disc

the crankcase unless they are guided at the bottom of the stroke.

2   The piston rings may be removed from the pistons by carefully spreading the ends of each ring so that it comes out of its groove and then drawing it off over the top of the piston.

3   To remove the piston it is necessary to separate it from the connecting rod as it is not possible to get at the connecting rod bolts with the piston fitted.

4   Remove the circlip from one side of the piston boss where the gudgeon pin is retained and it will be possible to push out the gudgeon pin. If it resists then warm up the piston with an electric light bulb held next to it for a while. Do not try and drive out the gudgeon pin from a cold piston. You will possibly bend a connecting rod. It is only necessary to push out the pin far enough to enable the connecting rod to be released from the piston. If the pistons are to be put back make sure that each one is marked suitably so that you know (a) which number cylinder it came from and (b) which way faces forward. A good way is to scratch the number and an arrow, pointing forward, on the crown before removal. If you do make a nonsense and forget how it came off then carefully clean the top of the crown and look for identifying marks which indicate the front or flywheel side. Volkswagen pistons are stamped with an arrow at the edge of the crown pointing towards the flywheel. British made pistons have the word 'flywheel' stamped on in that position.

5   Piston and cylinder bore wear are contributory factors to excessive oil consumption (over 1 pint to 300 miles) and general engine noise. They also affect engine power output due to loss of compression. If you have been able to check the individual cylinder pressures before dismantling so much the better. They will indicate whether one or more is losing compression which may be due to cylinders and pistons if the valves are satisfactory.

6   The piston rings should be removed from the pistons first by carefully spreading the open ends and easing them from their grooves over the crown of the piston. Each one should then be pushed into the cylinder bore from the bottom using the head of the piston to make sure they rest square in position about 5 mm from the bottom edge. The gap between the ends of the ring can then be measured with a feeler gauge. For the two compression rings it should not exceed 0.90 mm (0.035 inch) and for the oil scraper ring 0.95 mm (0.037 inch). If the gaps are greater you know that new rings at least are required.

7   Determining the degree of wear on pistons and cylinders is complementary. In some circumstances the pistons alone may need renewal - the cylinders not needing reboring. If the cylinders need reboring then new pistons must be fitted. First check the cylinders. A preliminary check can be done simply by feeling the inside walls about ½ inch down from the top edge. If a ridge can be felt at any point then the bores should be measured with an inside micrometer or calipers to see how far they vary from standard. The measurement should be taken across the bore of the cylinder about 15 mm (0.6 inch) down from the top edge at right angles to the axis of the gudgeon pin. Then measure the piston, also at right angles to the gudgeon pin across the skirt at the bottom. The two measurements should not differ by more than 0.20 mm (0.008 inch).

8   Further measurement of the cylinder across the bore will indicate whether or not the wear is mostly on the piston. If the cylinder bore is uniform in size fitting new pistons alone is possible. However, it is a very short sighted policy. If new pistons are needed anyway the cost of reboring will add 20—25% to the cost of the pistons so it would be as well to get it done whilst the cylinders are off.

9   Another feature of the pistons to check is the piston ring side clearance in the grooves. This should not exceed 0.12 mm (0.0047 inch) for the top ring and 0.10 mm (0.004 inch) for the other two. Usually however, this wear is proportionate to the rest of the piston wear and will not occur in a piston which is otherwise apparently little worn. If you think that only a new set of rings is required it would be a good idea to take your pistons to the supplier of the new rings and check the new rings in the gaps. You may change your mind about how worn

the pistons really are! Once a cylinder has been rebored twice it must not be rebored again. New cylinders must be obtained.

## 15  Connecting rods and bearings - removal and renovation

1   Connecting rods may be removed only after the pistons have been taken off. It is not necessary to split the crankcase although if you are going to do so anyway it will be simpler to take the connecting rods off the crankshaft afterwards. Start with No 1 and, using a socket with an extension, slacken the two connecting rod cap nuts by inserting the extension into the crankcase. It is important to have the crankshaft positioned so that the socket spanner fits squarely and completely onto the head of each nut.

2   Once both are loose, carefully undo each one and keep them captive in the socket when undoing them so as not to drop them in the crankcase. The cap will be left behind and may be awkward to retrieve. Tip the engine to shake it out if necessary. Retrieve both halves of the bearing shells also. Loosely refit the cap to the connecting rod noting the two matching numbers on the shoulders of the rod and cap which must line up on replacement. It is a good idea to note on a piece of paper which serial number applies to which cylinder number. This avoids the need to mark the connecting rods further. If the same rods and pistons are being put back it is very desirable that they should go back in the same position as they came out.

3   It is unlikely that a connecting rod will be bent except in cases of severe piston damage and seizure. It is not normally within the scope of the owner to check the alignment of a connecting rod with the necessary accuracy so if in doubt have it checked by someone with the proper facilities. It is in order to have slightly bent connecting rods straightened - the manufacturers provide special jigs for the purpose. If a rod needs replacement, care should be taken to ensure that it is within 10 grams in weight of the others. If too heavy, connecting rods may be lightened by removing metal from the shoulders near the big end of the wider parts where the bearing cap mates up to it.

4   The small end bushes are also subject to wear. At a temperature of 70°F the piston (gudgeon) pin should be a push fit. No axial or rocking movement should be apparent. The fitting of new bushes is a specialist task and although the bushes themselves may be easily pressed in it is necessary to ream them to fit the gudgeon pins. Unless you have reamers readily available and the knowledge of how to use them this should be done by a firm (or individual) specialising in engine reconditioning. Remember that if you are fitting new pistons it may be necessary to fit new connecting rod bushes. If you are lucky the new gudgeon pins may fit the old bushes properly however make sure that the new bushes have been drilled to match the oil holes in the connecting rod. This should be done before reaming so that there are no burrs on the bush bore.

5   The shell bearings from the big end are matt grey in colour when in good condition. If the engine has done a considerable mileage it is good policy to renew them anyway when the opportunity presents itself. To make sure you get the correct replacement size make a note of the numbers on the back of the bearing shell or take it along to the supplier.

6   If the crankshaft is being reground new bearing shells will be required anyway and these are normally available from the firm which does the regrinding and will be matched to the degree of regrinding carried out.

## 16  Camshaft and tappets - removal and renovation

1   The camshaft and tappets can be removed only after splitting the crankcase and this procedure is described in the section on crankshaft removal.

2   Having split the crankcase the tappets should be checked in their respective bores in the crankcase and no excessive side-play should be apparent. The faces of the tappets which bear against the camshaft lobes should also have a clear,

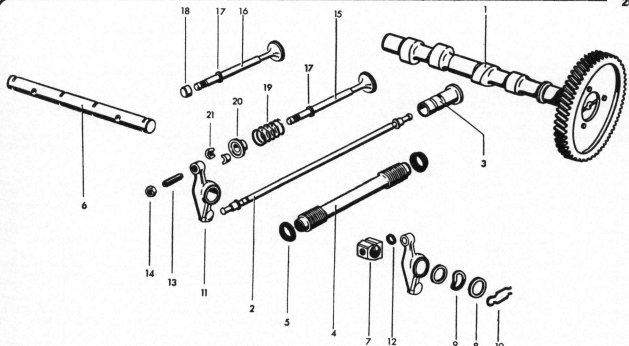

**Fig 1.6 CAMSHAFT AND VALVES – EXPLODED VIEW (Sec 13)**

| | | |
|---|---|---|
| 1 Camshaft and gear assembly | 6 Rocker shaft | 12 Sealing ring |
| 2 Pushrod | 7 Shaft support bracket | 13 Tappet adjusting screw |
| 3 Tappet | 8 Thrust washer | 14 Locknut |
| 4 Pushrod tube | 9 Corrugated washer | 15 Inlet valve |
| 5 Pushrod tube seal | 10 Securing clip | 16 Exhaust valve |
| | 11 Rocker arm | 17 Oil wiper |
| | | 18 Valve cap |
| | | 19 Valve spring |
| | | 20 Valve spring seat |
| | | 21 Valve cotter halves |

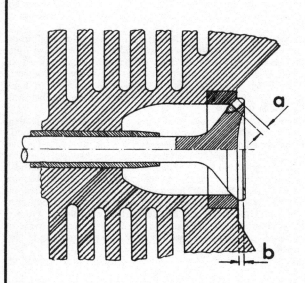

**Fig 1.7  VALVES – CROSS SECTION OF SEAT (Sec 13)**

a = seat width 1.7 - 2 mm exhaust and 1.25 - 1.65 mm inlet

b = 1 mm minimum, all valves

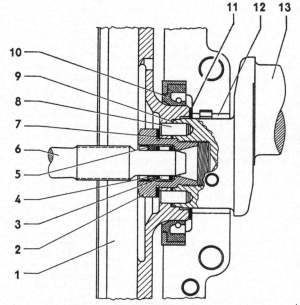

**Fig 1.8  CROSS SECTION VIEW OF THE FLYWHEEL END OF THE CRANKSHAFT (Sec 17)**

| | |
|---|---|
| 1 Flywheel | 8 Dowel peg |
| 2 Gland nut | 9 O ring |
| 3 Needle bearing | 10 Crankshaft oil seal |
| 4 Felt ring | 11 Shims |
| 5 Retaining ring | 12 Rear main bearing |
| 6 Gearbox input shaft | 13 Crankshaft |
| 7 Lock washer | |

smooth, shiny surface. If they show signs of pitting or serious wear they should be renewed. Refacing is possible with proper grinding facilities but the economics of this need investigating first. The lobes of the camshaft should be examined for any indications of flat spots, pitting or extreme wear on the bearing surfaces. If in doubt get the profiles checked against specification dimensions with a micrometer. Minor blemishes may be smoothed down with a 120 grain oil stone and polished with one of 300 grain. The bearing journals also should be checked in the same way as those on the crankshaft. The camshaft bearings are renewable.

3   The gear wheel which is riveted to the end of the camshaft must be perfectly tight and the teeth should be examined for any signs of breakage or excessive wear. It may be possible to have a new gear wheel fitted to the existing camshaft - much depends on the facilities available in your area. It is not a job to be attempted by the owner.

## 17 Flywheel - removal and renovation

1   With the engine removed from the car the flywheel may be removed after the clutch cover has been taken off (as described in Chapter 5).

2   The flywheel is held by a single centre bolt which is tightened up to 253 ft/lbs so do not think you can get it undone just like that. It was necessary to obtain a piece of angle iron to lock the flywheel by putting the angle iron across two of the clutch bolts which were put back into the flywheel. If by yourself the other end of the angle iron (or flat bar will do) can then be held in the vice with the engine on the bench.

3   A 36 mm socket is then put on the bolt with the longest handle from the socket set (do not under any circumstances try to use anything other than a correct sized socket - you could easily cause serious damage or even hurt yourself). A piece of steel pipe is then put over the socket handle and leaned on with considerable weight. The bolt slackens with no fuss at all. It may cost you a little money to get the stuff to do this job properly but we cannot recommend any other way.

4   Remove the bolt and large washer and before going any further make an identifiable mark on the flywheel hub so that you can re-locate the flywheel in the same place. The matching mark on the crankshaft cannot be made until the flywheel is off, so remember not to move the flywheel when it has come off until you can make a corresponding line up mark on the crank-shaft flange. This is important as there may be no other way of knowing the correct position of balance.

5   The flywheel is now located only by four dowel pegs which fit into holes in the crankshaft flange and flywheel boss. Put a piece of wood under the edge of the flywheel starter teeth to support the weight and then use a soft mallet or block of wood to tap the edges of the flywheel and draw it off. Do not try and lever it off with anything against the crankcase or you are likely to crack the casting and that will be very expensive.

5   When the flywheel is free, hold it steady, and remove the metal or paper gasket fitted over the four dowel pegs in the flange. Then make the second line-up mark on the crankshaft referred to in paragraph 4.

6   The dowel pegs are a precision fit into both the flange and flywheel. If any of these should be a slack fit there is considerable risk of the flywheel working loose, despite the tightness of the securing bolt. Where a flywheel has worked loose and caused the holes to become oval a new flywheel will be needed. (The precision work of boring and fitting oversize dowel pegs would cost more).

7   Another area of wear is in the starter teeth. These are machined into the flywheel itself so there is no question of fitting a new ring gear. If the teeth have become seriously chewed up it is in order to have up to 2 mm (0.08 inch) machined off on the clutch side of the teeth. The teeth should then be chamfered and de-burred. Any good machine shop should be able to carry out this work.

8   Examine also the land on the flywheel boss where the oil

seal runs. If this is severely ridged it may need cleaning up on a lathe also. Any such ridging is very exceptional.

## 18 Crankshaft oil seal - removal

1   The crankshaft oil seal may be removed after taking the engine from the car and removing the flywheel.

2   The oil seal may be levered out of the crankcase with a screwdriver or similar but great care must be taken to avoid damaging the crankcase where the seal seats. This means that the point of the tool used must not be allowed to dig into the crankcase.

3   When the oil seal is removed a number of shims which fit between the flywheel hub and the flange on the front main bearing will be observed. There should be three of them normally. These govern the amount of crankshaft endfloat. Make sure they are kept safely and not damaged.

4   If the crankcase is being split anyway it is simpler to wait until this is done when the oil seal may be easily lifted out.

## 19 Crankshaft and main bearings - removal and renovation

1   In order to remove the crankshaft, camshaft and cam followers (tappets) the two halves of the crankcase will need to be separated. Unless you are quite sure that this is essential do not do it. It is not worth opening the crankcase up just to 'have a look'. Remember also that the main bearing shells are much more expensive than on conventional cars (three of the four are not split) and before you can remove one of them two gears must be removed from the crankshaft. These gears are on very tight and are difficult to draw off.

2   Having decided to split the crankcase, remove the generator pedestal and prop the crankcase on its left side. All pistons and cylinders should already have been removed as should the flywheel. If the flywheel is left on it will add to the difficulty of controlling the weight of the crankshaft when the two halves release it. It will also be much more difficult to remove from the crankshaft afterwards. The connecting rods may be left on as these will be easier to remove after the crankcase is split.

3   The two halves are held together by large and small studs and nuts and two bolts and nuts. Slacken all the smaller nuts followed by the large nuts. Before starting to separate the two halves remember that the crankshaft and camshaft are held between them and you do not want either to fall out haphazardly. So if you keep the crankcase tilted to the left they will both rest in that half.

4   Separate the two halves by tapping lightly at the projecting lugs on the left half with a soft faced mallet or piece of wood. Do not hit anything hard. This progressive gentle tapping at the four corners will gradually increase the gap between the two until the right hand half will be free enough to lift off the studs. If you have a second pair of hands to help so much the better. When the right hand half has moved out a little way there will probably be a light clatter as one or more of the four cam followers in the right hand half fall out. If possible try and get hold of these and arrange them somewhere (in an egg box or numbered row on a shelf) so that they may be put back in the same bores.

5   Put the crankcase half in a safe place where it cannot fall or be damaged.

6   Lift out the camshaft from the other half of the crankcase. The bearing shells may be left in position. If they fall out note where they came from. If being renewed anyway take them out. One half of one shell is flanged to take the camshaft end thrust and the crankcase is suitably machined to accept it.

7   The tappets from the left hand half of the crankcase may now be taken out. Keep them in order like the others so they may be replaced in the same bores.

8   The crankshaft can now be lifted out and should be carefully put somewhere safe. The bearing shell halves for No 2 main

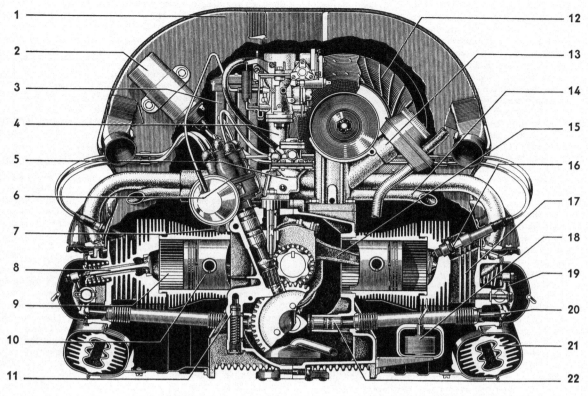

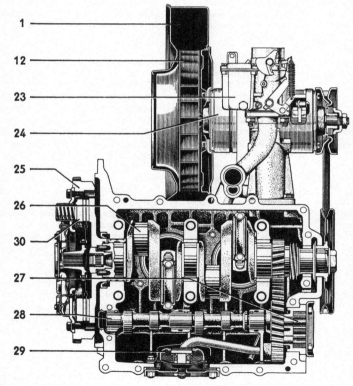

**Fig 1.9 ENGINE — CROSS SECTION VIEWS**

1 Fan housing
2 Coil
3 Oil cooler
4 Inlet manifold
5 Fuel pump
6 Distributor
7 Oil pressure switch
8 Valve
9 Cylinder
10 Piston
11 Oil pressure relief valve
12 Fan
13 Oil filler
14 Intake manifold preheater pipe
15 Connecting rod
16 Spark plug
17 Cylinder head
18 Thermostat
19 Rocker arm
20 Pushrod
21 Heat exchanger
22 Cam follower (tappet)
23 Carburettor
24 Dynamo
25 Flywheel
26 Crankshaft
27 Oil pump
28 Camshaft
29 Oil strainer
30 Clutch

*Note: This drawing does not show all the later modifications (eg: 3 section inlet manifold, one-piece fuel pump) but the basic format is the same.*

bearing should be removed from their locations in each half of the crankcase. Note that the location of each main bearing is by a dowel peg which locates each bearing shell. These normally remain in the crankcase but if any have come out with the bearings retrieve them now before they get lost.

9 It is possible to examine the connecting rod big end journals after removing the pistons and connecting rods without splitting the crankcase, but only visually. They cannot be measured satisfactorily. Provided there is no good reason to suspect that the big end bearings were seriously worn and that the surfaces of the journal are bright and smooth with no signs of pitting or scoring then there should be no need to proceed further.

10 The main crankshaft bearing journals may be examined only when the crankcase has been split and the crankshaft taken out. An indication of serious wear in these bearings can be obtained by checking the crankshaft for signs of slackness in the bearings before the crankcase is split. A wooden lever put through one of the cylinder apertures can be used to test for any indications of rocking in the bearings. If there is any then the bearing shells will almost certainly need renewal, even though the crankshaft journals themselves may be serviceable. The journals should be perfectly smooth with a bright mirror finish. They should be measured with a micrometer across the diameter for signs of ovality. If any measurement should differ by more than 0.03 mm (0.0011 inch) from any other the crankshaft should be reground. This means taking it to a specialist engineering firm who can grind it to the undersizes permissible and supply the matching new bearing shells. In view of the need to remove the two gears in order to examine No 3 main bearing journal the condition of the gears should also be checked, in conjunction with their respective mating gears on the camshaft and distributor drive spindle. The bronze worm gear which drives the distributor drive spindle is the most likely to show signs of wear. Any noticeable ridging of 'feathering' and variations in thickness of each spiral tooth indicate wear and renewal is probably justifiable.

11 Three of the four main bearings may be removed as soon as the crankshaft is taken from the crankcase. No 1 is a circular flanged shell which is drawn off the flywheel end, No 2 is the split bearing and No 4 is a narrow circular bearing which can be drawn off the crankshaft pulley end. No 3 however, is trapped by the helical gear which drives the camshaft. In front of this gear is a spacer and the distributor drive shaft worm gear, an oil thrower disc and woodruff key.

12 To remove No 3 main bearing first tap the woodruff key out of the shaft and keep it safe. Take off the oil thrower disc. The two gears are a tight keyed fit onto the shaft and the only way to get them off is by using a proper sprocket puller which has grips which will fit snugly and completely behind the helical gear so that both the gears and the spacer can be drawn off together. If you have difficulty in fitting the puller in the small gap between the bearing and gear do not try and pull off the gear gripping only against the gear teeth. You will either chip them or break them off. If you are committed to new bearings anyhow, cut the old bearing off to enable you to get the puller properly seated behind the gear.

13 If, when you start putting the pressure on it is obvious that considerable force is going to be needed it is best to clamp the legs of the puller to prevent them spreading and possibly flying off and causing damage to the gear. Some pullers have a clamp incorporated for such a purpose. If you have press facilities available so much the better but on no account should you try to hammer the gears off. It is virtually impossible to do this without damaging the gears.

14 With the two gears removed the bearing can be taken off the shaft.

15 Having taken off the No 3 bearing it would be unwise not to renew the complete set as a matter of course. If the crankshaft needs re-grinding then the new bearings will need to be of the correct undersize to suit the amount removed during re-grinding. Such bearings will normally be supplied by the firm doing the re-grinding work. If the crankshaft is not being re-ground make sure that the bearings obtained are exactly the same dimensions as those removed. This can be verified by checking the numbers

on the bearings which normally include an indication of whether they are standard or undersize. Do not forget that it is always possible that the crankshaft may have been re-ground already.

## 20 Distributor drive shaft - removal

1 The procedure for removing and replacing the distributor drive shaft from an assembled engine is given in Chapter 4. It is mentioned here because it is in order to leave it in position right up until the time when the crankcase is divided. It should, however, be removed before the crankcase is reassembled.

## 21 Crankcase - examination and renovation

The crankcase should be free from cracks or any other form of damage and the two mating edges must be quite free from dents, scratches and burrs which could in any way affect their precise alignment when both are clamped together. The crankshaft bearing locations should also be examined for any signs of damage or distortion. In an engine which has been permitted to run on with worn out main bearings it is possible that the bearing shells themselves will have been 'hammered' by the vibration of the crankshaft into the crankcase. This will mean that new bearings will not be a tight fit in their crankcase locations. In such instances the crankcase must be scrapped. In these circumstances the best action would be to abandon ideas of renovating the engine and obtain a complete replacement. Make sure that the camshaft bearing surfaces are in good condition.

The studs in the crankcase, both for attaching the cylinder heads and for the two halves, must be tight in their threads. Any sign of looseness which may be due to worn threads in the alloy crankcase is reparable. It will mean drilling and fitting a 'Helicoil' insert - which is a new thread in effect. This can be done at the Volkswagen agents for certain and at many other places where aluminium engines and castings are often being repaired. In any case check the economics before buying a lot of other parts.

## 22 Engine reassembly - general

1 As mentioned earlier, the Volkswagen engine is more complex in assembly than a conventional engine with a single cylinder block. It is therefore essential to get everything right first time and this means DO NOT RUSH IT. More than likely you will not have assembled an engine like this before so the order of assembly on other types cannot be relied upon for experience.

2 Before starting work clear the bench and arrange all the components nearby. The assembly surface must be particularly clean and it is a good idea to cover the working surface with sheets of strong paper. Have all the necessary gaskets and seals available together with clean oil in a can or convenient dispenser pack. If you are replacing bearing shells, cam followers and various other parts make sure the old parts are kept away from the assembly area in a carton or something. It is very easy to pick up an old cam follower for instance by mistake. At each stage, get the relevant batch of nuts and bolts ready - having cleaned the grit from them in a paraffin bath. A plentiful supply of clean cloths is the final requirement. Do not forget to clean the tools you will use as well. It is easy to transfer grit from a spanner to the engine with your hands and any small pieces of grit can ruin many hours and pounds worth of work. Again finally, take your time!

## 23 Crankshaft - assembly of gears and nos 3 and 4 main bearings

1 With the crankshaft thoroughly clean and the oilways blown out lubricate No 3 journal with clean engine oil (photo) No 3 main bearing is one of the two largest one-piece circular shells. It does not have a flange on it. This bearing goes on to the journal

Clean the crankshaft oilways and lubricate the journal surface (Sec 23.1a)

No 3 main bearing shell showing the dowel peg hole towards the flywheel (Sec 23.1b)

Replace the camshaft gear with the chamfered edge inwards (Sec 23.2a)

Line up the gear keyway (Sec 23.2b)

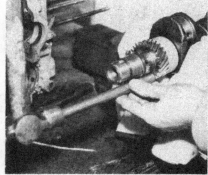
Drift the gear fully home (Sec 23.2c)

Replace the spacer collar (Sec 23.3a)

Replace the distributor drive worm gear (Sec 23.3b)

Line up the keyway before driving it home (Sec 23.3c)

Fit the circlip (Sec 23.3d)

The end bearing shell locating peg hole must be towards the flywheel end of the crankshaft (Sec 23.4)

Fit the oil thrower disc (Sec 23.5a)

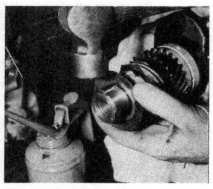
Tap the Woodruff key into the keyway (Sec 23.5b)

one way only - that is with the small dowel peg hole (which is not central) towards the flywheel end of the crankshaft (photo). Do not get this wrong or assembly will grind to a halt when you try to locate the bearing in the crankcase halves.

2  Next replace the camshaft drive gear. Before putting it on examine the surfaces of the crankshaft and key and the bore of the gear. If there are signs of slight scoring as a result of seizure when the gear was drawn off, clean them up with a very fine file. This will avoid a tendency to bind on replacement. The gear keyway should be lined up with the key in the shaft and the chamfered edge of the gear bore must face the flywheel end - i.e. it goes on first (photo). The gear may be difficult to start on the shaft so keep it square and make sure that the keyway is precisely lined up (photo). This is most important because if wrong you will have to draw the gear off and start again. It can then be drifted on with firm evenly spaced strikes around the gear (away from the teeth). Keep it square, particularly at the start, and drive it fully home. The crankshaft should be clamped between padded vice jaws for this operation.

3  Next the spacer ring followed by the spiral distributor drive gear are fitted. They can go on either way round and the gear should be carefully drifted up to the spacer without damaging the spiral teeth (photos). Finally, fit the retaining circlip and make sure it fits snugly in its groove (photo). If it will not go in the groove then one of the gears has not been fully driven onto the crankshaft and this must be rectified.

4  Next fit the small circular bearing over the end journal, once again making sure that the offset dowel peg hole is towards the flywheel end of the crankshaft (photo). Do not confuse the dowel peg hole with the circular groove machined in the outside of this bearing. Lubricate the journal.

5  Next fit the oil thrower disc with the concave face outwards (photo). Fit the woodruff key (for the crankshaft pulley wheel) into the keyway now as this will prevent the disc from falling off inadvertently (photo).

## 24  Connecting rods - assembly to crankshaft

1  If the crankcase has been split the connecting rods (without the pistons) should first be fitted to the crankshaft. Check that the gudgeon pins fit correctly in their respective small end bushes, otherwise difficulty will be encountered in fitting the pistons later. If you are refitting the connecting rods to the crankshaft in the assembled crankcase, note the additional information at the end of this section.

2  Lay the crankshaft down on the bench with the flywheel flange end away from you.

3  Arrange the connecting rods, two on each side of the crankshaft with Nos.1 and 2 on the right, No.1 nearest the flywheel end and No.3 and 4 on the left with No.3 nearest the flywheel end. The numbers on each connecting rod and cap must face downward for each cylinder (photo). There is a forging mark on each rod on the opposite side which obviously faces upwards (photo). If you are fitting new connecting rods check with the supplier first about any changes which may possibly have occurred in this principle of marking. The first crank on the crankshaft, from the flywheel end, is No.3, left. Pick up the connecting rod and after wiping the bearing surface perfectly clean, fit the bearing shell with the notch engaging in the corresponding notch in the rod. Fit the other half of the shell bearing to the cap in the same fashion (photo). Next, liberally oil the bearing journal with clean oil and assemble the rod to the crankshaft (photo). Match the two numbers on the shoulders and with the rod pointing to the left face them downwards. Replace the cap and nuts, finger tight so that the assembly is not loose on the crankshaft (photo).

4  Repeat this for No.1, right, which is the second crank from the flywheel end followed by No.4, left, and No.2, right. It is easy to get confused while doing this. If your crankshaft assembly does not look like the one in Fig 1.10 rotate the crankshaft 180° but keep the connecting rods pointing the same way. Then it should look familiar! Above all, think and do not rush.

5  Once the rods are correctly fitted to the crankshaft the bolts will need tightening to the correct torque of 3.3 mkg (24 ft lbs). The best way to do this is to mount the crankshaft vertically in the vice, clamping the No.4 bearing journal firmly between two pieces of wood (photo). All the connecting rod bolts can then be tightened. It is advisable to tap the shoulders of each rod with a hammer to relieve any pre-tension which can be set up between the mating surfaces of the cap and the rod. When the cap bolts are fully tightened the connecting rods should be able to rotate around the journals under their own weight. There should be no tight or 'free' spots anywhere although if you are fitting new shells to an un-reground crankshaft this is possible. If very noticeable however, it indicates that the journal is out of round. If rods on a reground crankshaft are slightly tight the engine will need running-in. If very tight then the regrinding tolerances are wrong and it should be returned to the machinists for correction.

6  Place the assembled crankshaft on the bench once more, as before, with each connecting rod facing its proper cylinder position.

7  If you are fitting the connecting rods to an assembled crankcase/crankshaft lay out the rods alongside their respective cylinder positions as already explained and fit the shells into the rods and caps. Turn the crankshaft so that the journal for the rod to be fitted is nearest its crankcase opening. The cap must then be placed on the journal and the rod fitted to it. This is easy if you have four hands and fingers ten inches long! It is helpful to have a piece of bent metal rod which can be put through from the opposite side of the crankcase to hold the cap on the journal whilst the rod and nuts are being fitted. A certain amount of patience is essential as it is more than likely that you will drop a bolt or bearing cap into the crankcase at some stage and have to shake it out. Do not use grease to hold parts together for this assembly. It will probably affect lubrication seriously. The most important thing to ensure is that a bearing shell does not drop out unnoticed and get trapped and damaged while you are fiddling about. So if a shell drops in the crankcase go easy on rotating the crankshaft until you get it out. As soon as the first connecting rod is fitted tighten the bolts to the correct torque and check that it moves freely but without any clearance. You will be refitting new shells to the original journal sizes so if something seems amiss - bearing too tight or too loose - make sure you have bought the correct shells by comparing the numbers and oversizes (if any) with the old ones removed.

## 25  Crankcase, crankshaft, camshaft and cam followers - reassembly

1  The items in the section heading are grouped together for the very good reason that they all have to be assembled together. None may be omitted (see Fig 1.10).

2  Both crankcase halves must be perfectly clean, inside and out. All traces of jointing compound must be removed from the mating faces, the roots of the studs, and the chamfers in the stud hole mating faces. Use a solvent such as carbon tetrachloride to remove sealing compound and not a scraper which could damage the aluminium surfaces. The distributor drive gear should have been removed. The oil pump suction pipe must be tightly fitted. If loose it must be peened in position as necessary.

3  Place the left hand half of the crankcase on the bench with the flywheel end away from you and leaning over so that it rests on the cylinder head studs.

4  Oil the four cam followers for the left half and place them in their bores. If new followers are being fitted it is possible that their heads may be slightly thicker than the originals, so compare them (photo). If they are thicker then it is essential to check the clearance between them and the crankcase with the cam lift at its highest point. So having placed the cam followers in position replace the camshaft temporarily, with its shell bearings and revolve it (photos). If any of the cam lobes should jam the followers against the crankcase then clearance will have to be provided by relieving the crankcase by about 1—2 mm behind

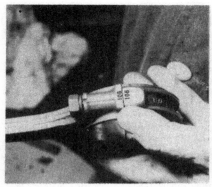

The connecting rod and cap have matching numbers (Sec 24.3a)

... and a forge mark on the opposite side (Sec 24.3b)

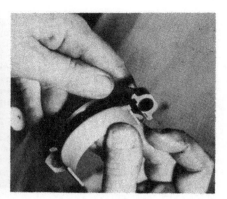

Fit the bearing shell into the cap (Sec 24.3c)

Put the rod into position on the journal (Sec 24.3d)

... and mate up the cap (Sec 24.3e)

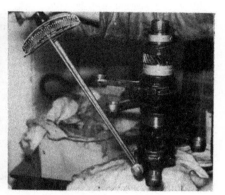

Tighten all the cap nuts (Sec 24.5)

Fig 1.10 CRANKCASE, CRANKSHAFT AND CAMSHAFT READY FOR REASSEMBLY (SEE SECTION 35)

each cam follower head. This can be done by a small, end face grindstone in a power drill by a competent handyman. Great precision is not important provided that there is no damage to the actual cam follower bore and the resulting clearance is adequate to permit full unobstructed movement of the cam and follower. Be sure to remove all traces of metal after such work. Repeat this check for the four cam followers in the right hand half of the crankcase.

5 Fit the flanged No.1 bearing shell at the flywheel end of the crankshaft. Once again make sure that the off-centre locating dowel peg hole goes towards the flywheel end (photo). Look to see that the corresponding dowel pegs in the crankcase will mate up. The bearing surfaces of the journal should be well lubricated with clean oil but keep the outside surfaces of the bearing shell clean and dry.

6 Place one half of the split shell in position at No.2 bearing in the crankcase, engaging the dowel pin in the hole (photo). Lubricate the bearing with clean oil.

7 The crankshaft assembly should now be placed into position in the left hand crankcase half (photo). The three dowel holes in the circular bearings will need lining up so that they will locate snugly and Nos.3 and 4 connecting rods must pass through their respective apertures. It is a good idea to lift the assembly up by Nos.1 and 2 connecting rods for this operation. Do not force anything into place. The circular bearings may need rotating a little until you can feel the pegs engage. Ensure the thrower disc locates within the oil thrower recess in the casting. Once all the bearing pegs are located a little pressure will ensure that the assembly and bearings are completely seated. If it is stubborn for any reason lift it out, pause, look, think and have another go.

8 Next fit the camshaft bearing shells into clean locations, engaging the notches in the crankcase (photo). Then oil the bearings in readiness for the camshaft.

9 Turn the crankshaft carefully until two teeth, each marked with a centre punch, are visible and well clear of the edge of the crankcase. There is a single tooth on the camshaft gear similarly marked which must mesh between them (photo). Engage the teeth and roll the camshaft round, in mesh still, into its bearing location. Then turn the gears again to check that the timing marks are still correctly aligned.

10 Now fit the four tappets (cam followers) into the right hand half of the crankcase and if it seems as though they might fall out when it is lifted and tilted then put a dab of grease behind the lip of each one to help stick it in position.

11 Fit the other half of No.2 bearing shell into the right half of the crankcase locating it over its dowel peg correctly.

12 Now thinly coat the two clean, smooth mating surfaces of the crankcase halves with aluminium alloy jointing compound (photo). Use a good quality product such as Volkswagen themselves recommend or 'Hylomar'. Neither is cheap but then you do not want your crankcase to leak oil when it gets hot. Make sure the two surfaces are coated completely but thinly and evenly. Take care to cover round the base of the studs. Do not let any compound get into oilways or other places where it is not wanted and may cause obstruction or binding.

13 The six larger studs have rubber sealing rings at the roots and these should all be renewed.

14 Place the right hand half of the crankcase over the studs of the left and carefully slide it down until it just touches the crankshaft bearings (photo).

15 Coat the circular camshaft sealing plug with jointing compound and place it in position in its groove in the left hand half at the flywheel end of the camshaft, with the recess facing inwards (photo).

16 Move the two halves together, tapping lightly with a block of wood if necessary. Use no force - none should be necessary.

17 Now stop and check:

1 Are all the connecting rods protruding from their proper holes? Cap nuts tight?
2 Are all four bearings, two gears and oil thrower disc fitted to the crankshaft?

3 Are all eight cam followers in position?
4 You did not forget the camshaft? (It has been known!). Did you mesh the timing properly.
5 Camshaft sealer plug?
All in order, replace all the nuts on the studs finger tight. Revolve the crankshaft just to make sure that everything moves freely at this stage at least.

18 It is important to tighten down the stud nuts evenly and in the correct order. Tighten first the six large nuts to a torque of 1.5 mkg (11 ft lbs) only, followed by all the smaller nuts to the same torques. Then tighten the small nut near the lower large stud clamping round No.1 main bearing to its full torque of 2 mkg (14 ft lbs).

19 Tighten the large nuts progressively to a torque of 20 ft lbs and then to 25 ft lbs. Finally tighten the smaller nuts to 14 ft lbs (photo).

20 Now rotate the crankshaft - it should revolve smoothly without any stiffness. If there is stiffness however, slacken all the crankcase nuts. If it then turns freely something is wrong and you should separate the crankcase again. Then check that all the bearings have been properly located on their dowel pegs and that the split bearings of the camshaft are seated properly. Any pressure spots on bearings will be visible. The cause is normally due to dirt or burrs behind them, particularly on the corners of the bearing bore corners and mating face edges. These can be chamfered lightly if necessary. Whatever happens do not press on until you have found the reason for any tightness. Start again from the beginning if necessary.

## 26 Pistons, rings and connecting rods - reassembly

1 If you are only fitting new rings to existing pistons make sure you have examined the pistons properly as detailed in Section 14 and checked the new ring gaps in the cylinder bores.

2 The new rings should be fitted over the piston crown replacing the bottom ring first. If you do not have a proper ring expander tool spread the ends of the ring so that it goes over the top of the piston. Then carefully ease it down over the other grooves a little at a time. The blade of a feeler gauge or some shim steel will be of great assistance in sliding it over the grooves. Do not bend the ring in any way more than necessary to move it. It breaks easily. The top two rings are different. The lower of the two has a cut-away lower edge and the top ring is chamfered on its outer face. Both rings will be marked 'open' or 'top' which denotes which way up they go. The lower of the two is fitted first. (See Fig 1.14).

3 When new pistons are supplied for rebored cylinders the rings are already fitted and the gaps should automatically be correct. It does no harm however, to take the top ring off each piston and check it in the bore to make sure.

4 Assuming the small end bushes have been correctly sized for the gudgeon pins remove one circlip from each piston - if not already done - and push out the gudgeon pin until the piston boss is clear to permit the end of the connecting rod to be positioned (photo). If the pins are too tight to push out do not force them. Warm up the pistons in front of the fire or on a radiator or next to an electric light bulb. Do not play over them with a blow lamp or gas torch. They only need warming - not heating.

5 If new pistons are being fitted they can go to any connecting rod and all that matters is that the side of the piston marked on the crown 'flywheel' or with a pointing arrow goes towards the flywheel end of the engine (photo). Push the gudgeon pin back into place and replace the circlip. Make sure that you use only the circlips supplied with the pistons. Do not use the old circlips just because they are easier to contract. (Volkswagen pistons have wire circlips with long legs (photo). English pistons have spring steel clips with small eyes needing proper circlip pliers to release them).

6 As soon as one piston has been fitted take care because when the crankshaft is rotated the skirt of the piston can foul

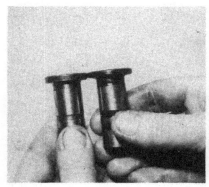
Compare new tappet flange thicknesses with the old (Sec 25.4a)

Put the tappets into the crankcase (Sec 25.4b)

Check the cam lobe clearances (Sec 25.4c)

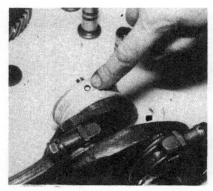
No 1 main bearing is flanged. The dowel peg hole goes towards the flywheel (Sec 25.5)

The only split main bearing is No 2. Fit each half into the crankcase halves (Sec 25.6)

Place the crankshaft and connecting rod assembly into the left half of the crankcase (Sec 25.7)

Fit the 3 camshaft bearing shells. The rear one is flanged (Sec 25.8)

Mesh the dot on the camshaft gear tooth between the two dots on the crankshaft gear teeth (Sec 25.9)

Coat the crankcase mating surfaces with jointing compound (Sec 25.12)

Fit the two crankcase halves together (Sec 25.14)

Don't forget the camshaft sealing plug (Sec 25.15)

Tighten the stud nuts in the correct sequence (Sec 25.19)

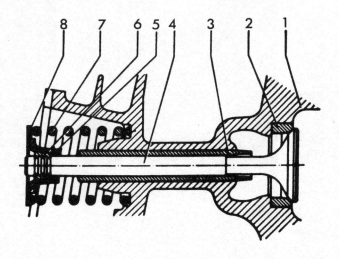

**Fig 1.11 VALVE ASSEMBLY – CROSS SECTION (SEC 28)**

| | | | |
|---|---|---|---|
| 1 Cylinder head | 3 Guide | 5 Oil seal ring | 7 Valve spring |
| 2 Seat insert | 4 Valve | 6 Split collar | 8 Spring retainer |

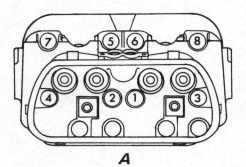

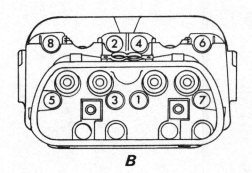

**Fig 1.12 CYLINDER HEAD NUTS. TIGHTENING SEQUENCE (SEC 29)**

A  up to 7 lb ft (1 mkg)
B  up to 23 lb ft (3.2 mkg)

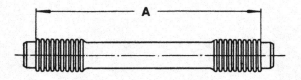

**Fig 1.13 PUSHROD TUBE – OVERALL LENGTH (SEC 29)**

A = 191 mm (7.5 ins) minimum before  installation

osition the piston over the connecting
d small end (Sec 26.4)

The makers put an arrow on the piston
crown pointing towards the flywheel.
Note the arrow pointing upwards and the
piston No 1 scratched on the crown as
well (Sec 26.5a)

Fitting a circlip for a VW piston (Sec
26.5b)

rinding the cylinders into the head
Sec 27.2a)

Fitting the cylinder base gasket (Sec
27.2b)

Piston rings clamped (Sec 27.6)

itting the cylinder over the piston
Sec 27.9)

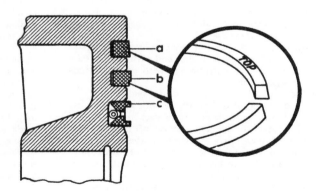

Fig 1.14 PISTON RINGS (SEC 26)

(a) Top compression ring
(b) Lower compression ring with stepped
lower edge
(c) Oil control ring

the crankcase at bottom dead centre unless it is guided into the cylinder aperture. This could break it. Watch too that the piston rings do not get snagged up on anything which could break them.

## 27 Cylinders - replacement

1  Cylinders should normally go back in their original locations unless new pistons are being fitted or they have been rebored, in which case it does not matter.
2  Before fitting the cylinders you may wish to lightly grind them into the seats in the cylinder head. This can be done using fine carborundum paste. Make sure that all traces of paste are flushed away afterwards. Light grinding in this way helps to ensure a gastight seal but do not over do it (photo). Make sure that the mating faces at top and bottom of the cylinders are perfectly clean and clear of old gaskets. Select the new thin, cylinder base gaskets from the set and separate them. It is easy for two to stick together. Hang one over each connecting rod now so you do not forget to put them on. Alternatively they may be put in position on the cylinder base - held by a proprietary jointing compound (photo).
3  Cylinders will only go on one way, that is with the narrow fins at the base and the flat fin edges of a pair of cylinders facing each other. This should be remembered for the first cylinder of each pair. You could get it wrong and have to take it off again when the second one is ready to go on!
4  The piston ring gaps should be spaced round the upper 180° of each piston with the gap in the oil control ring facing the top of the engine.
5  The rings must be compressed into the piston grooves in order to get the cylinder over them. The type of compressor used must be such that it will split and come off round the piston because once the cylinder is on it will not be possible to lift it off over the top of the piston. A Jubilee hose clip may be used quite satisfactorily. The cylinder bore is chamfered at the bottom which also facilitates assembly.
6  Fit the clip round the rings and tighten it so that all three are compressed (photo). Take care to see that no ring slips out from under the clip. This can easily happen, particularly when first tightening up the clip screw when a screw type hose clip is used.
7  Tighten the clip until the rings are flush with the piston but do not tighten it so much that the clip grips the piston tightly. Otherwise it will be difficult to slide the clip down the piston when the cylinder barrel takes over.
8  Not forgetting the lower cylinder gasket, place the cylinder over the piston crown narrow end first and with the fin flats facing the adjacent cylinder position and with the four studs aligned in the passages in the fins.
9  Press the base of the cylinder against the piston ring compressor or clip and tap it down with a wooden block or soft hammer (photo). If the clip does not move slacken it a fraction and try again. Do not let the cylinder 'bounce' off the clip when tapping it otherwise you are likely to release an otherwise captive ring. If a ring does escape it will be necessary to start again. If you break a ring you will probably have to buy a set of three for that piston - rarely can you buy a single ring unless you are lucky and a supplier has a part set or is prepared to split a set.
10  Once all rings are inside the cylinder remove the compressor. With the 'Jubilee' clip this means unscrewing it until the end can be drawn out to release it.
11  Next, carefully position the base gasket onto the bottom of the cylinder barrel. Then move the barrel down and locate it into the crankcase. It will not be a tight fit. It is important to make sure that the gasket is not dislodged and trapped incorrectly. If it is, the joint may leak and, worse the cylinder tilt fractionally out of line.
12  It will be necessary to rotate the crankshaft as each cylinder is fitted. When this is done, precautions must be taken to keep the other cylinders in position, otherwise you will have to keep checking the gasket seating. Also guard against the pistons jamming the crankcase at bottom dead centre. The cylinders

may be tied down with string to prevent them moving.

## 28 Cylinder heads, valve and springs - reassembly

1  The valves removed should be refitted in their original positions unless, of course, new ones are being fitted.
2  If possible treat the valve stem with molybdenum disulphide or some other form of anti-scuffing paste to prevent excessive initial wear in the guide.
3  Place the valve in the guide (photo). Fit the oil ring round the valve stem and then the spring and spring collar. Note that the close coils of the spring go against the head (photo).
4  Next arrange the valve spring compressor with the spacer tube fitted if required and carefully compress the spring (photos). Watch that there is no likelihood of the spring flying out. Often the spring tends to tilt on compression and this can impede the fitting of the split collars. If you can straighten the spring up without risk of releasing it all is well.
5  Compress the spring far enough to expose the grooves into which the split collars locate.
6  It will be necessary to fit the split collars through the slot in the tube if you have used this method. Fingers will be found too be too fat so put a blob of grease on the end of a screwdriver and use this to pick up the collet and put it in position with the narrow end downwards (photos). You may have difficulty with the second half because of the spring not being centrally spaced round the valve stem. This can be overcome by carefully tipping the spring with the compressor or by a little extra compression.
7  When both split collars are properly located in the grooves in the valve stems slowly release the compressor tool making sure that neither of the split collars is pushed out of position. When the spring compressor is fully released the two halves of the split collar should be flush. If not, one is not properly bedded in the grooves of the valve stem.
8  Repeat the procedure for each valve in turn.

## 29 Cylinder heads - replacement

1  First check the pushrod tubes. They have compressible concertina ends and these should be stretched out a little by pulling them so that the distance between the outer ends of the concertina sections is no less than 191 mm (photo). A new sealing ring should be fitted over each end so that the radiused face will go into the head or crankcase as appropriate (photo). When stretching the tubes pull straight so as to avoid any possibility of cracking them. If they are fractured a positive oil leak will result so check their condition carefully (Fig 1.13).
2  Next fit the sheet steel air deflector plate, of which there is one to each pair of cylinders (photo). It is a spring fit to the two centre studs and to make sure it is tight, the clip flange may be bent out a little. Note that these deflectors (which guide air into the cooling fins) are on the lower side, i.e. the same side as the pushrod tubes. They follow the contour of the cooling fins when installed so make sure they are the right way round. They cannot be fitted after putting the cylinder head and tubes in position.
3  One head should now be put on to the eight head studs just far enough to be secure (photo). Then place the four pushrod tubes into position and hold them loosely in position by putting the pushrods back through them (photo).
4  Move the head further into position so that the tube ends locate in their respective seats at both ends. Make sure that the pushrod seals seat firm and square and that the recesses are clean. The seams in the tube should face the cylinders.
5  The cylinder head studs should not be touching any of the cylinder barrel fins so if necessary turn the barrels a little to achieve this. A piece of postcard placed behind each stud will establish the presence of a gap.
6  Replace the stud washers and nuts and tighten them lightly and evenly as far as is possible with a socket and extension using no lever bar.

Inserting an exhaust valve into the head (Sec 28.3a)

Fitting the spring and retainer (Sec 28.3b)

The spring compressor needs elongated ends ... (Sec 28.4a)

... or use a piece of tube with a hole in it (Sec 28.4b)

Use grease to hold the collets on replacement (Sec 28.6a)

Collets in position (Sec 28.6b)

Stretching the pushrod tubes (Sec 29.1a)

Fitting the pushrod tube seals (Sec 29.1b)

Fitting the lower air deflector plates (Sec 29.2)

Offer up the cylinder head (Sec 29.3a)

Hold the pushrod tubes with the pushrods to start with (Sec 29.3b)

Tighten the head nuts in the proper sequence (Sec 29.7)

7 The tightening progression of the nuts is important and is in two stages (photo). First tighten the nuts to 1 mkg (7 ft lbs) in the order shown in Fig 1.12. Then tighten them to 3.2 mkg (23 ft lbs) in the final diagonal pattern sequence as shown in Fig 1.12. There is a temptation to overtighten these head nuts. Resist it! Otherwise you will distort the head.

8 Repeat the operation for the second head.

## 30 Rocker gear and pushrods - replacement

1 See that the lower ends of the pushrods are properly located in the recesses in the tappets (cam followers).

2 Place a new seal over each rocker assembly mounting stud (photo). Place the rocker shaft support blocks over the studs so that the socketed ends of the rocker arms will line up with the pushrods and the adjusters over the valve stems. The rocker shaft support blocks are chamfered and slotted. They are fitted with the chamfers outwards and slots upwards (photo).

3 Replace the washers and nuts and tighten the two nuts down evenly ensuring that the pushrods are properly engaged in the rocker arms. Tightening torque is 2.5 mkg (18 ft lbs). Slacken all the rocker adjuster screws for later adjustment (photo).

## 31 Crankshaft oil seal - replacement

1 The seal must be replaced (if it has been removed) before the flywheel is fitted. Do not fit it however, until the crankshaft endfloat has been checked as this involves temporary replacement of the flywheel and the movement of shims.

2 Before fitting the seal, place the necessary circular shims over the crankshaft flange and make sure they are perfectly clean and lightly oiled (photo).

3 Coat the outer metal edge of the new oil seal with jointing compound and place it squarely in position into the crankcase with the inner lip of the seal facing inwards (photo). It may then be tapped squarely home using a suitable mallet or piece of wood.

## 32 Flywheel - replacement

1 If you have taken the flywheel off you will presumably have the same equipment still available for replacing it. You will need it.

2 If you have overhauled the complete engine it will be advisable to check the crankshaft endfloat. This is governed by the gap between the inner face of the flywheel boss and the flange of the rear main bearing shell. Shims are introduced to reduce the gap and these shims need to be fitted before the oil seal. Although it is possible for them to be pushed in past the oil seal it is very difficult to get them out again without buckling or kinking them. If the main bearing shell has been renewed it is most likely that the shims originally fitted will be correct as the main wear takes place on the bearing shell flange. Three shims are always used to make up the required total thickness and they come in six thicknesses (0.24 mm, 0.30 mm, 0.32 mm, 0.34 mm, 0.36 mm, 0.38 mm). Fit two shims to start with, when the thickness of the third may then be calculated.

3 The four dowel pegs should all be placed in the crankshaft flange after having been checked for fitting in both the flange and the flywheel (photo). If any of these should be slack there is considerable risk of the flywheel working loose, despite the tightness of the nut, and this could be disastrous.

4 In the flywheel flange recess there will be the fine 'O' ring seal. Renew this before placing the flywheel in position and before measuring any crankshaft end float.

5 Grip the flywheel firmly and, with the marks lined up, locate it over the dowel pegs (photo). It is most important for the flywheel to be kept square. If it proves a bit of a strain and a fiddle to get in position find a piece of wood of a thickness suitable to support it at the right height. Once the flywheel is

positively located on the pegs replace the centre bolt and washer and take it up as far as it will go finger tight. Then very carefully tighten the bolt to draw the flywheel on, at the same time keeping it perfectly square by tapping the rim as necessary with a soft faced mallet. If the bolt is tightened with the flywheel out of square the dowel pegs and holes will be damaged.

6 It will be necessary to tighten the centre bolt to at least 75 ft lbs in order that the crankshaft endfloat may be accurately read. To do this a clock gauge micrometer is used against the face of the flywheel. The crankshaft is then moved in and out and the float measured. The thickness of the third shim is the measured float less 0.10 mm. Any three shims will do of course provided they add up in total thickness to the sum of the two in position and the calculated third.

7 Once the correct shims have been selected the flywheel should be removed and the three shims put in position and the oil seal fitted as described in Section 31. The flywheel is then replaced in the same fashion.

8 Final tightening of the centre bolt involves a torque of 253 ft lbs (35 mkg) and the locking of the flywheel for this purpose should be arranged in the same way as for removal (photo). It is important to get this torque as accurate as possible because the flywheel may vibrate loose if it is insufficient. Too much, on the other hand, could cause unwanted stresses.

9 It should also be remembered that the flywheel bolt has a built-in roller bearing which supports the transmission input shaft. This bearing should be in good condition and not over-greased.

## 33 Oil pump - replacement

1 Make sure that the mating faces of the crankcase and pump body are perfectly clean and unmarked.

2 Using a new gasket fit the pump body over the studs so that the fixed spindle is towards the bottom of the crankcase (photos).

3 Carefully tap the body fully home over the studs, taking care that the gasket does not get trapped incorrectly.

4 When the body is fully home tighten the two crankcase stud nuts, above and below, to the correct torque.

5 Next fit the two gears, turning the driving spindle so that the tongue engages in the slot in the end of the camshaft (photos). With both gears fully home the engine should now be turned through at least two complete revolutions. This ensures that the pump body is correctly centred by the revolving gears. The body should not be disturbed again after this has been done. Fit a new cover plate gasket followed by the cover plate (photo). Replace the four nuts. Whilst tightening up the nuts to the recommended torque of 14 ft lbs it is worthwhile rotating the engine once or twice more in case the pump body should inadvertently have moved during tightening.

## 34 Oil cooler - replacement

1 Using new special seals for the oil ways fit the cooler over the studs on the mounting adaptor. Fit the small sealer plate with the foam rubber strip over the same studs before fitting and tightening the nuts (photos).

2 Put two new special seals for the oilways between the adaptor and the crankcase and fit the whole assembly to the crankcase. Tighten the nuts firmly but take care not to shear the studs (photos).

## 35 Fan housing - replacement

The same remarks as made in Section 7 about removing the fan housing apply. For details refer to Chapter 2.

Fit new rocker shaft mounting stud seals (Sec 30.2a)

Replace the rocker shaft assembly ... (Sec 30.2b)

... making sure the pushrods are seated correctly (Sec 30.3)

Crankshaft end float shims being assembled (Sec 31.2)

Replacing the oil seal (Sec 31.3)

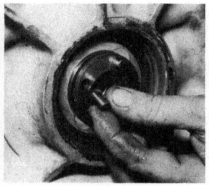
Flywheel/crankshaft dowel pegs in position (Sec 32.3)

Offer up the flywheel (Sec 32.5)

A piece of flat bar or angle on 2 clutch securing screws will hold the flywheel firm whilst the nut is tightened (Sec 32.8)

Fit a new oil pump body gasket ... (Sec 32.2a)

... and replace the body in the crankcase (Sec 33.2b)

Replace the driving gear ... (Sec 33.5a)

... and driven gear (Sec 33.5b)

## 36 Valve to rocker clearances - adjustment

1 Valve clearances are important. If they should be too great the valves will not open as fully as they should. They will also open late and close early. This will affect engine performance. Similarly, if the clearances are too small the valves may not close completely, which will result in lack of compression and power. It will cause damage to valves and seatings.

2 The valve clearances should be set for each cylinder when the piston is at the top of its firing stroke. With the engine in the car this may be first found on No.1 cylinder (right, front) by removing the distributor cap and turning the engine so that the notch on the crankshaft pulley lines up with the centre of the crankcase and the rotor arm points to the notch in the edge of the distributor body.

3 With the engine out of the car and distributor not yet installed the easiest method is to turn the crankshaft pulley wheel clockwise up to the mark and at the same time keep a finger over No.1 cylinder plug hole to check that there is compression. This indicates that you are on the firing stroke.

4 Both valves on No.1 cylinder may then be adjusted. First slacken the locknut on each rocker arm adjusting screw. Then put a feeler blade of the appropriate thickness between the adjuster and the end of the valve stem and turn the adjusting screw until a light drag can be felt when the blade is moved (photo). Tighten the locknut, holding the adjuster simultaneously with a screwdriver (photo). Check the gap once again.

5 Continue with the subsequent cylinders; the order is 2, 3, 4 and the crankshaft pulley wheel should be rotated ½ turn (180°) anti-clockwise. The distributor rotor arm will turn ¼ turn (90°). The valve clearances for No.2 cylinder may then be set. Continue the same way for cylinders 3 and 4 in that order.

6 Do not forget that the valve clearance settings have recently been increased. If there is a sticker on the fan housing saying the clearance is .004 inches ignore it. Put your own sticker on instead (photo).

## 37 Engine - reassembly of ancillaries

1 In Section 2 of this Chapter details were given of items which could be removed with the engine in the car. With the exception of the distributor all these items can and should be refitted, however, before replacement of the engine. Some things have to be fitted before others and the following points should be noted:

a) As mentioned in Section 35 the inlet manifold centre section must be replaced before the fan housing assembly, or before the generator/fan assembly if the two have been separated. The two outer sections of the manifold should be assembled loosely after that. Do not tighten the inlet manifold securing nuts at this stage.

b) Assemble the heat exchangers and exhaust system to the engine, to each other and to the inlet manifold with all clips, gaskets screws and sleeves loosely put together. Do not fit any one unit and tighten up the screws or nuts before assembling the other parts which join it. Then tighten up in the following sequence:

    Inlet manifold flange to cylinder head nuts
    Heat exchanger flange to cylinder head nuts
    Exhaust manifold flange to cylinder head nuts
    Exhaust manifold to heat exchanger pipe clamp bolts and nuts
    Inlet manifold pre-heater pipe flange to exhaust manifold flange screws
    Inlet manifold centre section to crankcase clamp nut
    Heat exchanger connecting sleeve screws
    Inlet manifold flexible connector clips

c) Fit the fuel pump before the carburettor.

d) Attach the thermostat bellows to the pull rod and adjust the setting before fitting the lower right hand duct plate.

## 38 Engine - replacement and starting up

1 If the starter motor has been removed refit it to the transmission and connect the leads before replacing the engine. It is much easier. Put the right hand top mounting bolt in position into the casing also and check that the nut runs easily on it.

2 Make sure the clutch assembly is fitted and the friction disc has been properly centralised.

3 Put the accelerator guide tube in position through the fan housing. Also ensure that the accelerator cable is in a position where it will not get trapped or kinked (photo).

4 With the rear of the car raised move the engine into position underneath so that it can be lifted. Ideally it will be raised on a trolley jack. Otherwise it will be necessary to raise it by some other means so that the car can be lowered to line up with it.

5 There is very little fore and aft clearance inside the engine compartment. For this reason the engine must not be tilted otherwise the gearbox input shaft will get snagged up with the clutch cover.

6 As soon as the input shaft is lined up with the clutch centre, feed the accelerator cable through the guide tube in the fan housing (photo).

7 Push the engine forward so that the lower mounting studs engage in the holes and the crankcase moves right up to the transmission casing. It may be necessary to waggle the engine about a little to achieve this. It is important to note that any attempt to draw the engine into position with the mounting bolts when there is a considerable gap may crack the crankcase or transmission casing.

8 The upper right hand mounting bolt should engage its head into the transmission casing and the nut can be fitted from inside the engine compartment. The two lower nuts and the upper left hand bolt are fitted from underneath the car. The bolt goes into a captive nut in the crankcase.

9 When the engine is in position reconnect or adjust the following from underneath:

1 Fuel line
2 Heater hoses
3 Heater flap control wires
4 Starter cables
5 Adjust the clutch pedal free play

    The following items must be connected from above:

1 Accelerator cable (see adjustment details in Chapter 3)
2 Generator leads (3) brown at the fan end, red on the left D+ terminal near the pulley, and green on the D— terminal
3 Automatic choke lead (black)
4 Solenoid cut off valve on carburettor (black)
5 Coil — black to 15 — green from distributor to terminal 13
6 HT leads (see Chapter 4).
7 Oil pressure switch (blue/green)
8 Fuel line at carburettor
9 All hoses
10 Replace distributor and set ignition timing (see Chapter 4)
11 Replace the rear cover plate, ensuring that all screws are correctly fitted and the small insulator plates secured round the inlet manifold pre-heater pipes. The edge of the plate should fit neatly in the rubber beading round the edge of the engine compartment.
12 Remove the dipstick (to prevent blow back up the filler pipe) and fill the engine to the top mark on the dipstick. Take care not to spill oil.
13 Reconnect the battery

10 If the engine does not fire and run fairly quickly it is likely to get flooded due to the operation of the automatic choke. In such cases press the accelerator to the floor and hold it there until the engine fires. If it still fails to start go through the ignition and fuel system fault diagnosis as outlined in the respective chapters.

11 Once the engine starts see that the oil warning light goes out

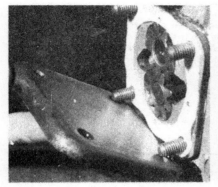
The oil pump cover plate gasket goes on last (Sec 33.5c)

Oil cooler seals on the mounting bracket (Sec 34.1a)

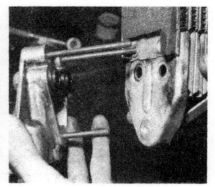
Fitting the oil cooler to the bracket (Sec 34.1b)

The small sealer plate goes on the bracket studs (Sec 34.1c)

Oil cooler seals on the crankcase (Sec 34.2a)

Fitting the cooler assembly to the crankcase (Sec 34.2b)

Tighten the oil cooler mounting nuts (Sec 34.2c)

Adjust valve clearance with the screw ... (Sec 36.4a)

... and tighten the locknut (Sec 36.4b)

Get the valve clearance correct (Sec 36.6)

Get the accelerator cable out of the way before the engine goes back ... (Sec 38.3)

... then feed it into the tube through the fan housing before the engine is fully home (Sec 38.6)

and then go immediately to the engine compartment to see if there is anything going on which should not. Let the engine run until normal working temperature is reached and then adjust the carburettor as necessary. Then stop the engine, let it stand for

a minute or so and recheck the oil level.
12 Road test the car and if the performance is not satisfactory make small alterations to the distributor timing setting, testing on the road after each adjustment.

## 39 Fault finding

| Symptom | Reason/s | Remedy |
| --- | --- | --- |
| Engine will not turn over when starter switch is operated | Flat battery<br>Bad battery connections<br>Bad connections at solenoid switch and/or starter motor | Check that battery is fully charged and that all connections are clean and tight. |
| | Starter motor jammed | Rock car back and forth with a gear engaged. If ineffective remove starter. |
| | Defective solenoid | Remove starter and check solenoid. |
| | Starter motor defective | Remove starter and overhaul. |
| Engine turns over normally but fails to fire and run | No spark at plugs | Check ignition system according to procedures given in Chapter 4. |
| | No fuel reaching engine | Check fuel system according to procedures given in Chapter 3. |
| | Too much fuel reaching engine (flooding) | Slowly depress accelerator pedal to floor and keep it there while operating starter motor until engine fires. Check fuel system if necessary as described in Chapter 3. |
| Engine starts but runs unevenly and misfires | Ignition and/or fuel system faults | Check ignition and fuel systems as though the engine had failed to start |
| | Incorrect valve clearances | Check and reset clearances. |
| | Burnt out valves | Remove cylinder heads and examine and overhaul as necessary. |
| Lack of power | Ignition and/or fuel system faults | Check ignition and fuel systems for correct ignition timing and carburettor settings. |
| | Incorrect valve clearances | Check and reset the clearances. |
| | Burnt out valves | Remove cylinder heads and examine and overhaul as necessary. |
| | Worn out piston or cylinder bores | Remove cylinder heads and examine pistons and cylinder bores. Overhaul as necessary. |
| Excessive oil consumption | Oil leaks from crankshaft oil seal, rocker cover gasket, oil pump, drain plug gasket, sump plug washer, oil cooler | Identify source of leak and repair as appropriate. |
| | Worn piston rings or cylinder bores resulting in oil being burnt by engine (smoky exhaust is an indication) | Fit new rings or rebore cylinders and fit new pistons, depending on degree of wear. |
| | Worn valve guides and/or defective valve stem seals | Remove cylinder heads and recondition valve stem bores and valves and seals as necessary. |
| Excessive mechanical noise from engine | Wrong valve to rocker clearances | Adjust valve clearances. |
| | Worn crankshaft bearings<br>Worn cylinders (piston slap) | Inspect and overhaul where necessary. |
| Unusual vibration | Misfiring on one or more cylinders | Check ignition system. |
| | Loose mounting bolts | Check tightness of bolts and condition of flexible mountings. |

NOTE: When investigating starting and uneven running faults do not be tempted into snap diagnosis. Start from the beginning of the check procedure and follow it through. It will take less time in the long run. Poor performance from an engine in terms of power and economy is not normally diagnosed quickly. In any event the ignition and fuel systems must be checked first before assuming any further investigation needs to be made.

# Chapter 2 Cooling, heating and exhaust systems

## Contents

## Specifications

| | |
|---|---|
| Fan capacity at 4000 rpm ... ... ... ... ... ... ... ... ... ... | 600 litres (22 cu ft) per second approximately |
| Thermostat opens at   ... ... ... ... ... ... ... ... ... | 65 – 70°C (149 – 158°F) |

### Torque wrench settings

| | |
|---|---|
| Fan securing nut   ... ... ... ... ... ... ... ... ... | 43 lb/ft (6.0 mkg) |
| Fan/generator drive pulley nut   ... ... ... ... ... ... ... | 43 lb/ft (6.0 mkg) |

## 1 General description

One of the most famous and well known features of the Volkswagen engine throughout its life has been the fact that it is air cooled. The advantages are obvious - none of the problems and cost of maintaining a water cooling system with the attendant problems of extreme temperatures. There are certain disadvantages of an air cooled system however - there is greater engine noise, more engine power used to drive the cooling fan and a less precise control of engine temperatures. Air cooled engines are not at their best in dense traffic in hot weather. Great care must also be taken to ensure that the lubrication system is not neglected as the engine oil plays a more significant part in engine cooling.

The Volkswagen system is neat and simple. A multi-bladed turbo fan is mounted on the shaft which drives the generator. It rotates in a sheet steel, semi-circular housing, drawing in air through the fan centre and directing it down to each pair of finned cylinders. The cylinders are shrouded above with carefully designed sheet steel covers. Below each pair of cylinders a contoured deflection plate is mounted centrally. Thus the air is directed over the full surface area of the cylinder cooling fins.

In order to shorten the warming up time a thermostat is mounted below the right hand pair of cylinders. This is a conventional bellows type and it operates a restriction on the through flow of air when the engine is cold. Flaps in the fan housing are opened by the thermostat when the engine warms up, so allowing the full air flow to pass round the cylinders.

The car heating system is linked with the cooling system. In addition to the cooling air circuit there are two heat exchangers mounted one below each pair of cylinders. In effect these heat exchangers consist of a finned section of exhaust pipe from the front cylinder at each side which is encased in a sheet steel 'tank'. A smaller 'tank' also encases the short piece of exhaust from the rear cylinders. The two tanks are connected together.

Air from the fan housing passes through a flexible hose to the top of the small heat exchanger and then through the larger one. Hot air then passes from the heat exchanger to the ducts in the car body. A control flap at the front of each large heat exchanger can shut off the air flow.

The heat exchangers are made from special corrosion and rust resistant metals so that under normal circumstances their life is indefinite. The exhaust silencer box also is of above average durability.

Models which are exported to arctic climates cannot generate enough heat from this system to be effective so petrol burning heater units are fitted to supplement the interior heating system. These devices are not dealt with in this manual.

The condition and fit of all the covers is important. Sealing strips and grommets must all be properly positioned. If air leaks out the cooling capacity is reduced.

## 2 Removal of cooling and heating system components - general remarks

1 It is more difficult to dismantle the cooling and heating systems with the engine in the car than after the engine has been removed. There may be occasions when it will be necessary to remove components from the system without disturbing the engine, for example:
a) The fan and fan housing may be removed to service a damaged fan, for generator overhaul, or to give access to the oil cooler.
b) The heat exchangers may be leaking and need renewal.
2 As the cooling system is so much an integral part of the engine assembly this chapter deals primarily with those items which are easily accessible with the engine in the car.

## 3 Fan belt - adjustment, removal and replacement

1 The Volkswagen fan belt needs more regular inspection than a water cooled engine fan belt usually gets because if it slips or breaks the consequences are more serious more quickly.
2 Adjustment takes a little more time than usual. There is no tension pulley. The pulley on the generator is split into two and the gap between the two halves governs the effective diameter. The gap is regulated by spacer rings (photo). If the belt is too slack the gap between the two halves is decreased by removing

44

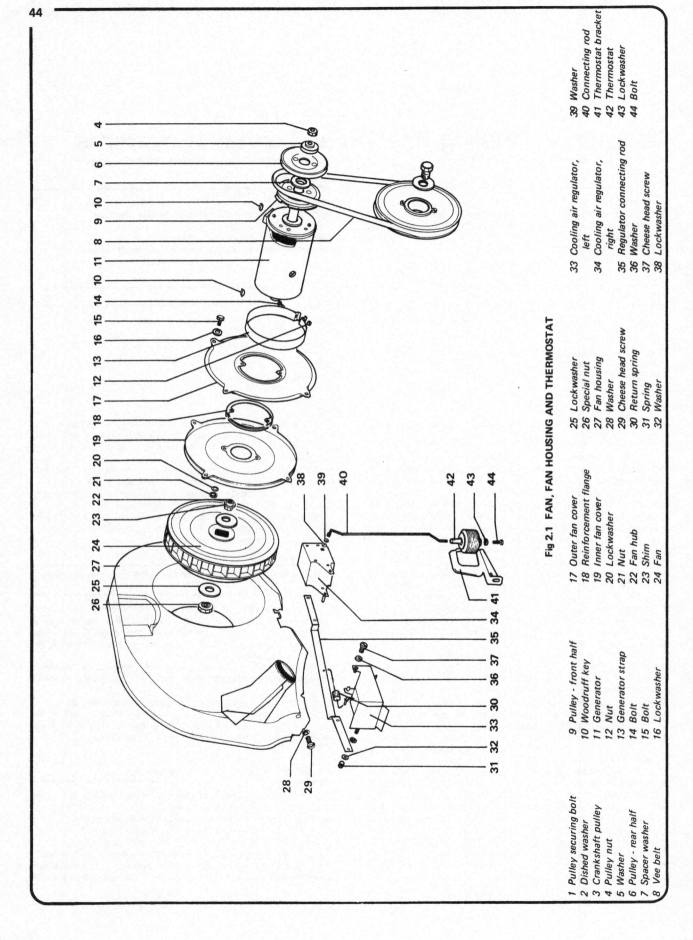

**Fig 2.1 FAN, FAN HOUSING AND THERMOSTAT**

1 Pulley securing bolt
2 Dished washer
3 Crankshaft pulley
4 Pulley nut
5 Washer
6 Pulley - rear half
7 Spacer washer
8 Vee belt

9 Pulley - front half
10 Woodruff key
11 Generator
12 Nut
13 Generator strap
14 Bolt
15 Bolt
16 Lockwasher

17 Outer fan cover
18 Reinforcement flange
19 Inner fan cover
20 Lockwasher
21 Nut
22 Fan hub
23 Shim
24 Fan

25 Lockwasher
26 Special nut
27 Fan housing
28 Washer
29 Cheese head screw
30 Return spring
31 Spring
32 Washer

33 Cooling air regulator, left
34 Cooling air regulator, right
35 Regulator connecting rod
36 Washer
37 Cheese head screw
38 Lockwasher

39 Washer
40 Connecting rod
41 Thermostat bracket
42 Thermostat
43 Lockwasher
44 Bolt

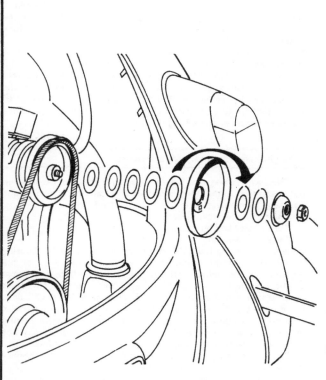

Fig 2.2 DIAGRAM OF SPLIT FAN BELT PULLEY AND SPACERS WHICH ARE MOVED FROM IN BETWEEN THE TWO PULLEY HALVES TO INCREASE BELT TENSION

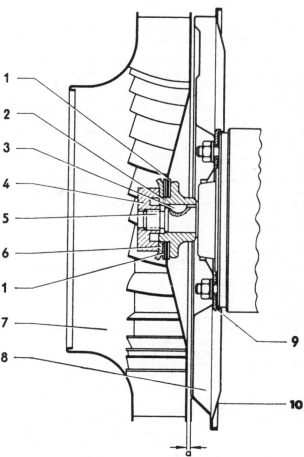

Fig 2.3 FAN ASSEMBLY — CROSS SECTION

1 Spacer washers
2 Fan hub
3 Woodruff key
4 Retaining nut
5 Generator shaft

7 Fan
8 Fan cover, inner
9 Reinforcement flange
10 Fan cover, outer
A   2 mm (0.080 in)

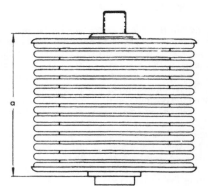

Fig 2.4 THERMOSTAT BELLOWS

A = 46 mm minimum at 65 - 70°C
(149 - 158°F)

Positioning pulley spacers (Sec 3.2)

one of more spacer rings. Spare spacers are fitted to the outside of the pulley.

3   The belt is correctly tensioned when firm thumb pressure on the belt midway between the two pulleys causes a deflection of 9 - 10 mm.

4   To remove the belt and split the pulley, lock the pulley first with a screwdriver in the edge of the inner flange against the top generator bolt. Remove the nut and clamp ring. The outer half of the pulley can then be separated from the inner half. To tighten the fan belt remove one spacer from between and then replace everything (with the moved spacer now on the outside of the pulley) and try the tension again. Take care when refitting the outer half of the pulley to get it square (photo). It helps if the engine is rotated. This will get the belt into its 'running' position. The engine is easily rotated with a spanner on the crankshaft pulley wheel. Continue removing spacers until the tension is correct. If all the spacers are out and the belt is still slack it is over-stretched and must be renewed.

5   Check the tension of a new belt after a few hundred miles running as initial stretch may need taking up.

## 4   Fan and dynamo - removal and replacement

1   The fan and generator have a common shaft and to separate them they must first be removed together from the engine. This involves:
a) Carburettor removal (see Chapter 3)
b) Raising the fan housing, which in turn requires removal of the thermostat as described in this chapter

2   Remove the fan belt (Section 3).

3   Disconnect the battery to prevent accidental short circuits and then disconnect the wires from the top of the generator. Tag the wires so that you know where to replace them (photo).

4   The generator is clamped to the pedestal by means of a metal strap. Undo the clamping bolt at the right and disengage the strap. If the engine is out of the car it is a good idea to slacken the fan nut before undoing this strap. The locking notch in the fan belt pulley can then be used to hold the shaft whilst the nut is slackened off. Put the fan belt pulley back on if you have already taken it off.

5   Undo the four bolts holding the fan cover plates to the fan housing.

6   Raise the fan housing (Section 5) and remove the generator and fan assembly from out of the fan housing and off the generator pedestal.

7   With the assembly out of the car, refit the fan belt pulley and clamp the generator body in a vice. The pulley is needed so that you can use the notch to lock the shaft whilst the fan nut is undone.

8   Once the nut has been removed the lock washer may be drawn off followed by the fan. Behind the fan is the thrust washer, spacer washers and fan hub which is keyed to the shaft.

9   The fan cover plates are held to the generator by two nuts on the ends of the generator through bolts. Note that the slot in the inner cover should face downwards when fitted to the generator, and the dished side goes into the fan housing. The purpose of the two covers is to provide a better suction point into the fan housing for cooling air drawn through the generator.

10  Reassembly and replacement should be done with care to ensure that the spacers and cover plates are correctly positioned.
a) Fit the outer cover plate onto the dynamo through bolts (photo).
b) Fit the stiffening plate (photo).
c) Fit the inner cover plate so that the peripheral slot will face the bottom of the fan housing when the generator is the right way up (photo).
d) Note the spacer ring on the dynamo shaft. If it is missing the fan hub will jam into the dynamo end cover (photo).
e) Fit the fan hub and spacer washers (photo).
f) Fit the fan to the hub (photo).
g) Replace the special lock washer and nut (photo).

11  Tighten the nut sufficiently to make sure that the hub is fully

home. Then measure the gap between the fan and the cover plate which should be 2 mm (0.080 ins). If any alteration is needed remove the fan from the hub and increase or reduce the number of shims. Keep spare shims behind the fan nut lock washer. Tighten the fan nut to the final torque of 43 lb ft.

12  Replacement of the generator/fan assembly is a reversal of the removal procedure. Take care not to distort anything and get the clamp strap and fan backplate bolts all in position before any are tightened. See that the strap fits the contours of the pedestal bracket as before. When all is tightened spin the fan to ensure that nothing is touching. If it is the fan housing is not seated correctly or something is bent.

## 5   Fan housing - removal and replacement

1   The fan housing may be removed with the engine installed but in addition to the items described in detail here the following must also be removed so that it may be lifted clear:
    Engine compartment cover and hinges
    Carburettor and air cleaner
    Generator and fan
Generally speaking the only reason for removing the fan housing completely with the engine in the car would be to get at the oil cooler or the thermostatically controlled air flaps in the base of the housing. It will be appreciated that the two oil cooler cover plates and the transverse flap control rod clip will have to be removed (and replaced) blind so make yourself familiar with the layout before starting. If the fan housing is merely being raised in order to take the dynamo/fan unit out it is not necessary to remove the engine compartment lid and hinges.

2   Slacken the dynamo securing strap and unscrew the thermostat bellows from the pull rod (details in next section).

3   Slacken the two screws at each side of the fan housing.

4   Remove the nut holding the upper part of the oil cooler outlet duct to the fan housing. Once the cover is pulled clear of the stud it can be lifted out (photo).

5   The lower outlet section is held by a screw (photo). Remove this and the whole piece can be drawn out of the hole in the vertical plate through which it fits (photo).

6   Remove the fan belt.

7   Unhook the return spring on the air flap link rod across the front of the fan housing and pull off the clip holding the left end so that it can be swung clear of the oil cooler when the fan housing is raised.

8   The fan housing may be lifted partially or completely off as required.

9   Whenever the fan housing is removed - for whatever reason - the opportunity should be taken to examine the condition and operation of the air flaps inside (photo). If these stick shut at any time the engine will overheat. If they are in a very poor condition and the expense of renewing them does not appeal, the best thing to do is remove them altogether. Their function is merely to shorten the warming up time and only in extremely low temperatures (well below freezing) is the engine likely to run over cold.

10  Replacement of the fan housing is the reverse of this procedure. If however, the engine is out of the car and being reassembled after an overhaul the following points should be noted.

11  Before putting the housing back onto the engine the cylinder top cover plates should be in position.

12  If the fan housing is being fitted together with the generator and fan attached, then the centre section of the inlet manifold should first be positioned. It cannot be manoeuvred between the housing and the generator pedestal afterwards (photo).

13  Continue with reassembly by carefully lowering the fan housing over the oil cooler. The pull rod for the thermostat control should go through the cylinder head aperture nearest the crankcase (photo).

14  The base of the fan housing should fit snugly inside the apertures of the cylinder cover plates. Make sure that the locating peg in the dynamo fits the recess in the pedestal.

Fitting outer half of fan belt pulley (Sec 3.4)

Disconnecting the rear dynamo connections. The second wire on the left hand terminal runs to a radio suppressor mounted on the other end of the dynamo (Sec 4.3)

Fitting the fan outer cover to the dynamo ... (Sec 4.10a)

... and the stiffening/spacer ring (Sec 4.10b)

On goes the inner cover plate (Sec 4.10c)

Note the spacer on the dynamo shaft (Sec 4.10d)

Fit the fan hub and shims ... (Sec 4.10e)

... followed by the fan (Sec 4.10f)

Secure with the lockwasher and nut (Sec 4.10g)

Removing the upper part of the oil cooler outlet duct (Sec 5.4)

Removing the screw holding the lower half of the cooler outlet duct (Sec 5.5a)

Lifting the duct from the vertical plate (Sec 5.5b)

Looking at the underside of the fan housing showing the thermostatically controlled air baffle plates (Sec 5.9)

Lowering the fan housing assembly into position ... (Sec 5.12)

guiding the thermostat rod through the cylinders (Sec 5.13)

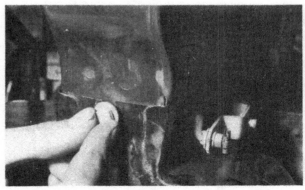

Tightening fan housing side screws (Sec 5.15)

Front plate being positioned (Sec 5.16)

Replacing the connecting rod for the fan housing baffle plates (Sec 5.17a)

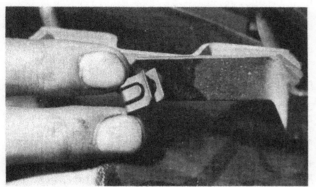
Securing the special clips ... (Sec 5.17b)

... and return spring (Sec 5.17c)

Removing the warm air duct hoses (Sec 6.3)

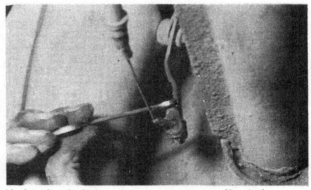
Unclamping the heat exchanger control cables (Sec 6.4)

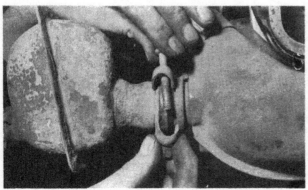
Undoing the heat exchanger rear exhaust clamp (Sec 6.6a)

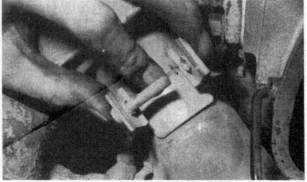
Undoing the heat exchanger sleeve clip (Sec 6.6b)

15 Replace and tighten the dynamo securing strap and then tighten the screws at each side of the fan housing (photo).

16 If the engine is out of the car the vertical front plate should be positioned before the two oil cooler cover plates are refitted (photo). When refitting the upper oil cooler cover a little pressure will be needed to get the fixing hole over the stud.

17 Reconnect the flap connecting lever and clip. Refit the return spring (photos).

18 Refit the fan belt ensuring that it is tensioned correctly.

19 Replace the carburettor and air cleaner, and adjust the accelerator cable.

## 6 Heat exchangers - removal and replacement

1 Remove both the air hoses from the fan housing at the lower ends and take out the screws securing the semi-circular plate round the inlet manifold pre-heater pipe. Take off the air cleaner pre-heater hose at the lower end.

2 Remove the securing screws and lift out the pulley cover plate followed by the engine rear cover plate.

3 Disconnect the warm air duct hose from the front of the heat exchanger underneath the car (photo).

4 Disconnect the control wire from the operating lever by undoing the clamping screw in the toggle (photo). This will probably be rusty and dirty so use plenty of penetrating oil otherwise you could break something which would just add to your repair list.

5 Take off the lower duct plate between the engine and the heat exchanger.

6 The front exhaust pipe flange should then be released by undoing the two nuts and the rear exhaust connection by undoing the clamp (photo). The heat exchanger inlet duct is clipped to the main exhaust silencer unit also as this has a small heat exchanger section on it. Undo this clip (photo).

7 By moving the heat exchanger forward off the front exhaust studs (photo) it will then be possible to lower and remove it.

8 Before replacing a heat exchanger it should be examined carefully for signs of splits. If it is damaged due to impact but otherwise sound it might be worthwhile having it straightened and/or welded. Otherwise fit a new one. Make sure also that the faces of the exhaust pipe flanges are perfectly flat. If they are distorted, steps must be taken to remedy the situation. Always fit new gaskets (photos).

9 The replacement of the heat exchanger is a reversal of the removal procedure. Make sure that when it is offered up all the joints fit true and flush before the nuts and clamps are tightened. If the nuts and clamps have to be used to force the unit into position, rather than hold it in position, stresses will be set up and something will break sooner or later. Certainly sooner than it would normally.

10 After reconnecting the control wire operate the lever to ensure that the arm moves through its full range.

## 7 Thermostat and controls - removal, replacement and adjustments

1 The thermostat controls flaps which restrict the air flow but do not completely obstruct it. If it should fail to operate therefore the engine will only be noticeably overheated in extreme conditions of high temperatures or hard use. The only indications of overheating are either a noticeable fall off in performance of the oil warning light indicating an exceptionally low oil pressure. It is essential to stop immediately either of these conditions appear as the engine will already have reached an undesirable state and will be seriously damaged if allowed to continue.

2 To check the operation of the flaps it is necessary to get access to the thermostat first. This is done by removing the right hand duct plate under the cylinders. Remove the screws holding it to the heat exchanger and crankcase. The thermostat is accessible once the right hand plate is removed. To set the flaps

first remove the bolt securing the bellows to the bracket (photo). Then make sure that the bellows is screwed fully on to the operating rod. Slacken the bolt which holds the bracket to the crankcase and then push the bellows unit upwards so that the flaps are fully open. The top of the bracket loop should now just touch the top of the bellows and the bracket bolt may be tightened. Then replace the bolt securing the bellows to the bracket (which will involve pulling the bellows down and closing the flaps if the engine is cold). If the thermostat is suspected of malfunctioning a check can be made on its length (excluding the projecting screwed bosses at each end) which should be at least 46 mm (1.8 inch) at a temperature (in water) of 65—70°C (150—158°F) or more. If you wish to set the thermostat so that the flaps are always open (i.e. if the bellows do not work and you have no immediate replacement) push the bellows and bracket up together into the 'flaps open' position and clamp the bracket at the raised position.

6 If the flaps themselves are suspected of jamming or being out of position on their spindles then the fan housing must first be taken off as described in Section 5. Both flap housings can be removed from the fan housing together once the eight securing screws are removed and the return spring unhooked. Examine the flaps and spindles for security and ability to stay in position. Once again, if there should be some doubt and the flaps are likely to jam shut they can be removed completely.

## 8 Heater exchanger controls - checking and setting

1 As previously explained the car is heated by ducting hot air from exchangers surrounding the exhaust pipes. When hot air from the exchanger is required the flap is opened so that the air pressure from the fan housing will carry it into the car. The warm air from the cylinder cooling fins has nothing to do with the heating system.

2 Should the heater efficiency drop the first thing to check is the operation of the flap control wires. These are connected to the flap operating arm on the side of the heat exchanger by means of a ferrule on the end of the wire clamped into a clevis. If the wire is broken on either side undo both. The clevis pin clamp screws are usually rusty so lubricate them well beforehand.

3 Once slackened the ends may be pulled out. Remove the plugs from the guide tubes. Inside the car remove the nut securing the right hand operating lever, remove the friction washers and pull the lever away. Then disconnect the hooked ends of the control wires and pull them out.

4 When fitting new cables grease them first and replace them in the reverse order of removal, note that the longer of the wires goes in the lower of the two guide tubes. Replace the sealing plugs securely in the guide tubes.

5 Having clamped the cable ends onto the flap operating levers make sure that they operate through their full range.

6 Details of the control wires and flaps for the heater outlets in the rear footwell are similar in principle to the heat exchanger flaps except that the cables are joined together where they are attached to the left hand control lever and cannot be replaced separately.

7 Access to the rear ends of the cables is by removing the rear seat and the vertical kick board in front of it. The cable end clamps can then be disconnected.

## 9 Exhaust system - removal, inspection and replacement

1 The Volkswagen exhaust and silencer is a complex unit made of heavy gauge material, which is expensive to replace. The silencer and tail pipe assembly is connected at five points on each side. These are:

a) To the exhaust pipes coming from the front of the cylinder heads through the heat exchangers (clamps).

b) To the exhaust ports on the rear of the cylinder heads (flanges).

c) To the inlet manifold pre-heater pipes (flanges).

Drawing the heat exchanger off the front mounting studs (Sec 6.7)

Fitting a new clamp gasket on the rear of the heat exchanger (Sec 6.8a)

Fitting a new gasket on the front exhaust port connection for the heat exchanger (Sec 6.8b)

Slackening the thermostat bellows mounting screw (Sec 7.2)

Fitting gasket for exhaust manifold flange on rear of cylinder heads (Sec 9.6a)

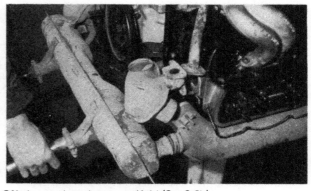

Offering up the exhaust manifold (Sec 9.6b)

The lower stud also carries the warm air intake pipe bracket for the carburettor air cleaner (Sec 9.6c)

Do **not** use any pre-heater pipe gasket with a small hole (Sec 9.6d)

d) To the heat exchangers (sleeve clips).
e) To the air inlet hoses from the fan housings (clips).


The exhaust manifold incorporates a small heat exchanger shrouding the upper pipes.

2   To remove the exhaust/silencer unit first remove the rear engine cover plate and the nuts, bolts and clamps which attach the assembly at the ten locations. If some of the underside nuts and bolts are badly rusted buy new ones before attempting to get the old ones off. It is quite usual for them to break or need cutting. A complete set of the gaskets should also be acquired (two exhaust flange, two inlet manifold flange, two clamp rings) before disturbing the unit.

3   Once all the connections are loosened the silencer can be drawn backwards off the studs of the cylinder head rear exhaust ports and lowered to the ground.

4   Depending on the reason for removal subsequent inspection and repair will have to be judged in the light of the seriousness of deterioration. The unit is made of heavier gauge material than more conventional exhaust systems. Thus small holes or cracks in the silencer may be patched and welded in the knowledge that the repair will last longer than on some other systems. This does not apply to the actual pipes leading into the silencer. If these are unserviceable repair is likely to be less successful. The flanges and connection to the other pipes must be examined for pitting, distortion or fractures. The mating faces of the flanges can be filed flat if necessary. The gaskets are thick enough to take up minor variations.

5   Before replacing the unit offer it up into position so that the line up of all the connecting points can be made without having to strain anything. If strain is necessary to make any connection then the likelihood of a fracture developing is greatly increased. It is worthwhile taking some trouble to heat and straighten any twisted parts.

6   Replacement of the system is a reversal of the removal procedure. First put new gaskets over the studs at the rear exhaust ports (photo). Offer up the unit (photo). Put the nuts on the studs enough to prevent it falling off. The lower stud on the right hand mounting also secures the hot air intake pipe which warms the air for the carburettor (photo). Then assemble the lower gasket rings and clamps loosely - but sufficiently tight to prevent them becoming dislodged. Then fit the pre-heater pipe gaskets in position and replace the bolts loosely. Note that the gaskets for each end of the pre-heater pipe may be different, one having a smaller central hole than the other (photo). If this is the case replace it with one the same as the larger hole. This modification was recommended in April 1971 as part of other changes to deal with progression (flat spot) problems. See Chapter 3 for those problems referred to in more detail.

7   The pipe clamp and flange bolts and nuts should not be progressively tightened a little at a time until fully tight. Do not overdo the tightening on any of them. Finally tighten the heat exchanger clips. After running the engine for some miles, so that it has had the opportunity to heat up and cool down a few times, recheck the connections for tightness.

## 10   Fault diagnosis

It is difficult to detect heating systems faults in a rear engined air cooled car because the tell-tale head of steam is not there to show and no temperature gauges are used. The first indications over heating are a falling off in power and a flickering of the oil pressure warning light. When this occurs the car must be stopped immediately.

Over cooling is a rare experience in anything but sub-zero temperatures, even if the thermostat control was to be stuck wide open.

Possible causes of overheating and heater inefficiency are tabled below.

| Symptom | Reason/s | Remedy |
|---|---|---|
| Overheating | Slack or broken fan belt | Renew if necessary and re-adjust tension. |
| | Insufficient engine oil | Top up as necessary and check for leaks. |
| | Engine ignition timing incorrect | Reset ignition timing. |
| | Thermostat and/or control flaps in fan housing stuck in closed position | Check operation and free as necessary. |
| | Oil cooler blocked | Remove, have tested and renew if necessary. |
| Heater ineffective | Air hoses from fan housing to heat exchanger insecure or damaged | Check hoses and secure or renew as needed. |
| | Air hoses from heat exchanger to car interior insecure or damaged | Check hoses and secure or renew as needed. |
| | Heat exchanger flaps operating control arms and/or wires jammed, broken or disconnected | Check operation of control cables and operating arms and that arms are moving the flap spindles properly. |

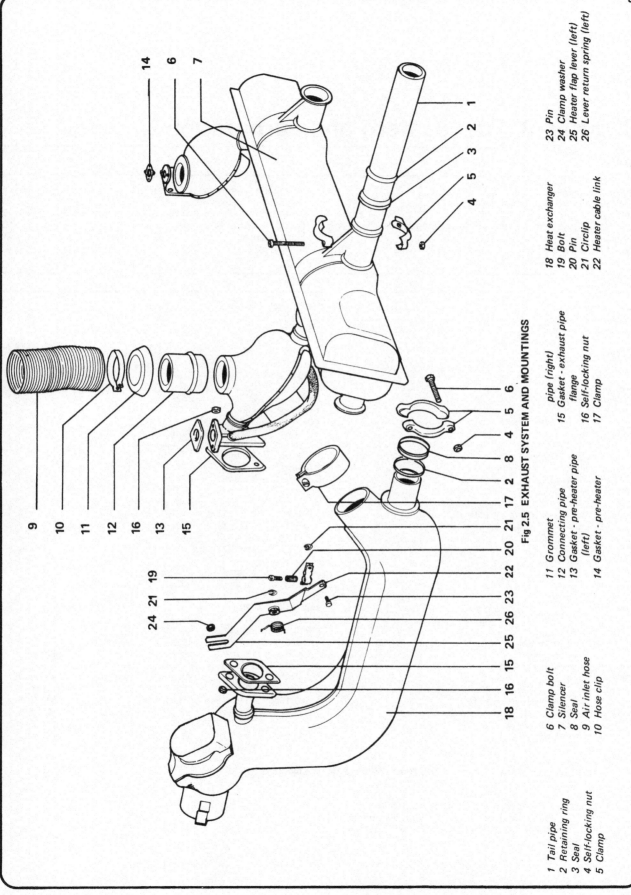

**Fig 2.5 EXHAUST SYSTEM AND MOUNTINGS**

1 Tail pipe
2 Retaining ring
3 Seal
4 Self-locking nut
5 Clamp

6 Clamp bolt
7 Silencer
8 Seal
9 Air inlet hose
10 Hose clip

11 Grommet
12 Connecting pipe
13 Gasket - pre-heater pipe (left)
14 Gasket - pre-heater

15 Gasket - exhaust pipe flange
16 Self-locking nut
17 Clamp

pipe (right)

18 Heat exchanger
19 Bolt
20 Pin
21 Circlip
22 Heater cable link

23 Pin
24 Clamp washer
25 Heater flap lever (left)
26 Lever return spring (left)

# Chapter 3 Fuel system and carburation

## Contents

## Specifications

**Fuel pump**  ... ... ... ... ... ... ... ... ... ...  Mechanical - Pierburg.
   Delivery rate (min) ... ... ... ... ... ... ...  400 cc/minute
   Pressure (maximum)  ... ... ... ... ... ... ...  3½ lbs/sq in

**Carburettors**
   Make  ... ... ... ... ... ... ... ... ... ... ...  Solex

1285 cc engine    31 PICT–3

|                                      | (a)        | (b)        | (d)          |
|--------------------------------------|------------|------------|--------------|
| Venturi diameter                     | 25.5       | 25.5       | 25.5         |
| Main jet                             | 145        | 130        | 130          |
| Air correction jet/emulsion tube     | 170        | 110        | 110          |
| Pilot jet/air drilling               | 60/120     | 55/120     | 52.5/130     |
| Auxiliary jet/air drilling           | 50/130     | 50/130     | 45/130       |
| Needle valve diameter                | 1.5 mm     | 1.5 mm     | 1.5 mm       |
| Needle valve washer thickness        | 1.5 mm     | 1.5 mm     | 1.5 mm       |
| Float weight                         | 8.5 gms    | 8.5 gms    | 8.5 gms      |
| Fuel level                           | 19.5 mm    | 19.5 mm    | 19.5 mm      |
| Relief drilling                      | —          | —          | 1.4/1.4 mm   |
| Accelerator pump stroke capacity     | 1.5+0.15cc | 1.5+0.15cc | 1.45+0.15cc  |
| Power fuel jet                       | 100/100    | 100/100    | 100/100      |
| Ignition setting (f)                 | 5º ATDC    | 5º ATDC / 7½º BTDC(g) | 7½º BTDC |

1584 cc engine    34 PICT–3

|                                      | (a)        | (b)        | (c)        | (d)         | (e)         |
|--------------------------------------|------------|------------|------------|-------------|-------------|
| Venturi diameter                     | 26         | 26         | 26         | 26          | 26          |
| Main jet                             | 145        | 130        | 127.5      | 130         | 127.5       |
| Air correction jet                   | 130        | 60         | 75         | 60          | 75          |
| Pilot jet/air drilling               | 65/147.5   | 65/147.5   | 60/147.5   | 55/120      | 55          |
| Auxiliary jet/air drilling           | 42.5/90    | 42.5/90    | 42.5/90    | 42.5/90     | 42.5/90     |
| Needle valve diameter                | 1.5 mm     | 1.5 mm     | 1.5 mm     | 1.5 mm      | 1.5 mm      |
| Needle valve washer thickness        | 0.5 mm     | 0.5 mm     | 0.5 mm     | 0.5 mm      | 0.5 mm      |
| Float weight                         | 8.5 gms    | 8.5 gms    | 8.5 gms    | 8.5 gms     | 8.5 gms     |
| Fuel level                           | 18 mm      | 18 mm      | 18 mm      | 18 mm       | 18 mm       |
| Accelerator pump stroke capacity     | 1.6+0.15cc | 1.6+0.15cc | 1.6+0.15cc | 1.45+0.15cc | 1.45+0.15cc |
| Power fuel jet                       | 100/100    | 85/85      | 100/100    | 85/85       | 100/100     |
| Relief drilling                      | —          | —          | —          | 1.55/1.55mm | 1.2/1.2mm   |
| Ignition setting (f)                 | 5º ATDC    | 5º ATDC / 7.5ºBTDC (g) | 5º ATDC | 7.5º BTDC | 5º ATDC  |

(a) Standard up till June 1971
(b) Sweden and Japan only till June 1971 and thereafter standard to November 1971
(c) US and Canada only to November 1971
(d) Standard, November 1971 on
(e) US and Canada (incl California) November 1971 on
(f) Ignition set at idle speed 800 - 900 rpm with distributor
    vacuum hoses off for 7½º BTDC and on for 5º ATDC
(g) June 1971 on

Additional Note:  All engines Serial B are set at 0º, with a single vacuum hose off or two vacuum hoses on.

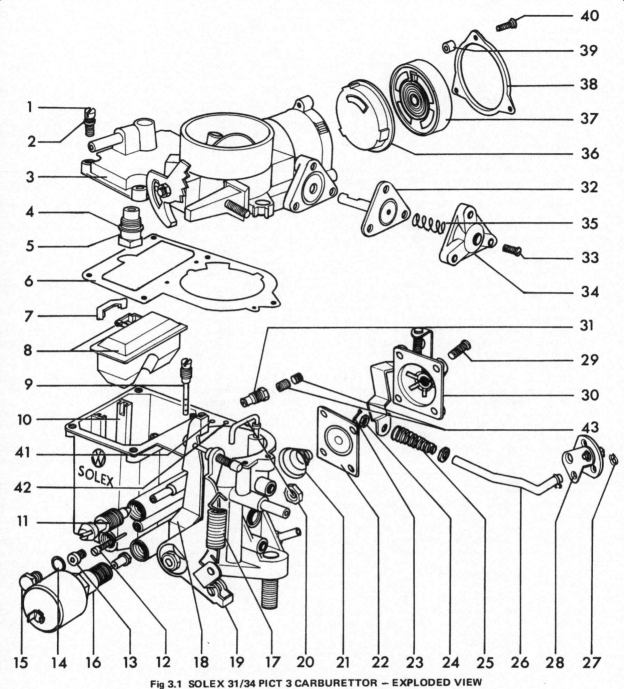

**Fig 3.1 SOLEX 31/34 PICT 3 CARBURETTOR – EXPLODED VIEW**

*Difference between the two types is in pilot jet position – angled on the 31 PICT 3*
*(Sec 3)*

| | | |
|---|---|---|
| 1  Cover screw | 12 Idle mixture control screw | 23 Split pin | 35 Spring |
| 2  Spring washer | 13 Main jet | 24 Washer | 36 Protection cap |
| 3  Top cover | 14 Washer | 25 Spring | 37 Heater coil and insert |
| 4  Needle valve washer | 15 Plug | 26 Connecting link | 38 Retaining ring |
| 5  Needle valve | 16 Electromagnetic cut off valve | 27 Circlip | 39 Spacer |
| 6  Gasket | 17 Return spring | 28 Bell crank lever (adjustable) | 40 Screw |
| 7  Float pin bracket | 18 Fast idle lever | 29 Countersunk screw | 41 Pilot air jet |
| 8  Float and pin | 19 Throttle lever | 30 Pump cover | 42 Auxiliary air jet |
| 9  Air correction jet and emulsion tube | 20 Injection pipe from accelerator pump | 31 Pilot jet | 43 Auxiliary fuel jet and plug |
| 10 Carburettor lower housing | 21 Diaphragm spring | 32 Vacuum diaphragm | |
| 11 By-pass air screw | 22 Accelerator pump diaphragm | 33 Countersunk screw | |
| | | 34 Diaphragm cover | |

## 1 General description

The Volkswagen fuel system is conventional in principle.

A fuel tank is mounted in the front luggage compartment and fuel is fed to the carburettor by a mechanically operated diaphragm pump which is driven by a pushrod actuated by a cam on the distributor drive shaft.

The carburettor is a fixed single choke downdraught type which incorporates a strangler, electrically operated, and an accelerator pump of the diaphragm type. The feed from the accelerator pump can also operate as a subsidiary fuel supply jet under certain conditions. With the automatic choke a diaphragm operated pushrod overrides the choke spring slightly as soon as there is vacuum on the engine side of the throttle flap.

Another device fitted to the carburettor is an electromagnetic cut-off valve which positively stops fuel from flowing into the inlet manifold. This is necessary because in certain high temperature conditions an over-heated engine can continue running on after the ignition is switched off.

As the 1302 series Beetle was introduced at a time when emission control was becoming the subject of legal control in many countries the question of modification arose in an otherwise 'established' engine — both 1285 cc and 1594 cc. Development had to continue during production. The variety of jet sizes and combinations which occurred will be apparent from a look at the specifications and these developments continue as this book goes to press. Details of the combinations of model options (internationally) and the permutation of the variety of changes they all enjoyed(?!) are beyond the scope of this volume. It is possible that some owners, particularly of the early models which went through a bad patch of progression (flat spot) difficulties may wish to make modifications to bring their cars in line with the later developments. It is strongly recommended therefore that the full implications of what is involved be first checked out with the VW agents. They will best be able to advise for your particular model.

## 2 Air cleaner - removal and servicing

1  To check the level of the oil in the filter bowl it is necessary only to undo the clips securing the top cover and lift it off. The oil should be in line with the mark. At the same time the sludge deposits can be ascertained by dipping a suitable probe into the oil. The oil should be no less than 4—5 mm deep above any sludge.

2  To remove the sludge the lower half of the unit should be removed from the carburettor.

3  To do this slacken the clip at the base of the cleaner and undo and remove the strap holding it to the carburettor mounting (photo). Then detach the hoses and lift the cleaner up and off (photo). Take care not to spill the oil and do not strain the neck of the lower half which fits on to the carburettor. This can easily be fractured with the result that oil will then leak out all over the carburettor.

4  Empty out the old oil and flush away the sludge with paraffin.

5  It will be noted that there are two flaps on the cleaner air intake.

6  The inner flap is controlled by a counter weight and at low speed it is shut so that the crankcase emission will be more readily drawn off through the vent pipe. At higher engine speeds the air stream opens the valve and the vacuum created in the intake pipe itself draws off the crankcase emission gases.

7  The other flap is thermostatically controlled and ensures that all air drawn into the cleaner comes from round No 1 and 2 cylinders via the pre-heat hose (photo). The cylinders warm up very quickly and as soon as the air temperature through the cleaner has reached 27.5ºC the flap will start to open admitting cool air in from the other inlet. At 32.5ºC the heated air supply is completely shut off. The operation of the flap can be observed when the engine is both hot and cold. Later models were fitted with a warm air inlet flap controlled by both temperature and inlet manifold vacuum (Fig 3.2). As the temperature of incoming air rises so the thermostatically controlled valve in the air cleaner opens the valve and permits manifold depression thereafter to control the air inlet flap by means of a diaphragm. This means therefore that the flap position may alter even after the engine has warmed up — the cooler air coming in at large throttle openings and the warmer air at small throttle openings.

8  In very dusty conditions the build-up of sludge will occur more quickly and may require more frequent cleaning out. The intake flaps will also tend to get caked with deposits also and the whole intake unit should be thoroughly flushed in paraffin.

## 3 Solex carburettor - description

The carburettor is basically a tube through which air is drawn into the engine by the action of the pistons and en route fuel is introduced into the air stream in the tube due to the fact that the air pressure is lowered when drawn through the 'tube'. A scent spray works on the same principle.

The main fuel discharge point is situated in the 'tube' - choke is the proper name for the tube to be used from now on - between two flaps which can block off the tube. One of these is the throttle flap. - operated by the accelerator pedal and positioned at the engine end of the choke tube. The other is the strangler - which is operated by an automatic device.

When the engine is warm and running normally the strangler is wide open and the throttle open partially or fully - the amount of fuel/air mixture being controlled according to the required speed.

When cold the strangler is closed - partially or fully and the suction therefore draws more fuel and less air, i.e. a richer mixture to aid starting a cold engine.

At idling speeds the throttle flap is shut so that no air and fuel can get to the engine in the regular way. For this there are separate routes leading to small holes in the side of the choke tube, on the engine side of the throttle flap. These 'bleed' the requisite amounts of fuel and air to the engine for slow speeds only.

The fuel is held in a separate chamber alongside the choke tube and its level is governed by a float so that it is not too high or low. If too high it would pass into the choke tube without suction. If too low it would only be drawn in at a higher suction than required for proper operation.

The main jet, which is simply an orifice of a particular size through which the fuel passes, is designed to let so much fuel flow at particular conditions of suction (properly called depression) in the choke tube. At idling speed the depression draws fuel from orifices below the throttle which has passed through the main jet and after that a pilot jet to reduce the quantity further.

Both main and pilot jets have air bleed jets also which let in air to assist emulsification of the eventual fuel/air mixture.

The strangler flap is controlled by an electrically operated bi-metal strip. This consists of a coiled bi-metal strip connected to the choke flap spindle. When the ignition is switched off the coiled metal strip is cold and the flap is shut. When the ignition is switched on current flows through the strip which heats up and uncoils - opening the choke flap after some minutes. If anything should go wrong with this electrical arrangement the flap will return to the closed position.

With the flap closed there are two features which partially open it immediately the engine starts. The flap spindle is offset so one side tends to turn around the spindle under the depression in the choke tube. Also there is a diaphragm valve connected to another rod attached to the flap spindle. Depression in the choke tube also operates this. If these devices did not exist no air at all would get through with the fuel. This would then flood the engine.

Finally there is another device - an accelerator pump. This is another diaphragm operated pump which is directly linked to the accelerator controls. When sudden acceleration is required

Air cleaner securing clamp screw. Note stay screw below (Sec 2.3a)

Disconnect the air cleaner preheater hose 'A' and the crankcase ventilation hose 'B' (Sec 2.3b)

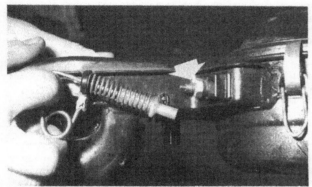
With the warm air flap control spring pulled off the thermostat unit (arrowed) is accessible (Sec 2.7)

Lifting the carburettor off the manifold (Sec 4.3)

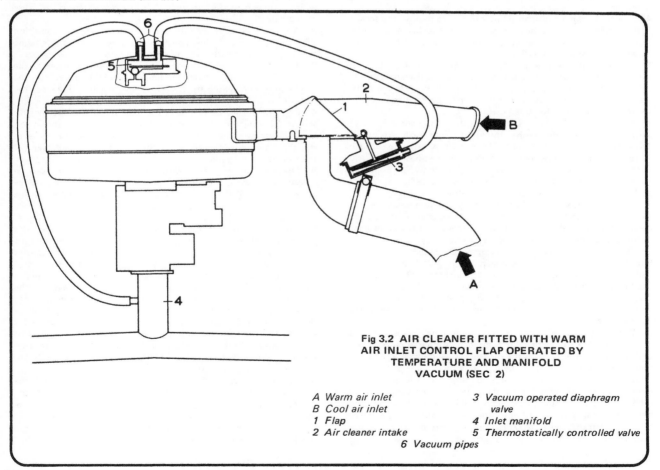

Fig 3.2 AIR CLEANER FITTED WITH WARM
AIR INLET CONTROL FLAP OPERATED BY
TEMPERATURE AND MANIFOLD
VACUUM (SEC 2)

A  Warm air inlet
B  Cool air inlet
1  Flap
2  Air cleaner intake
3  Vacuum operated diaphragm
   valve
4  Inlet manifold
5  Thermostatically controlled valve
6  Vacuum pipes

the pump is operated and delivers neat fuel into the choke tube. This overcomes the time lag that would otherwise occur in waiting for the fuel to be drawn from the main jet. The fuel in the float chamber is regulated at the correct height by a float which operates a needle valve. When the level drops the needle is lowered away from the entry orifice and fuel under pressure from the fuel pump enters. When the level rises the flow is shut off. The pump delivery potential is always greater than the maximum requirement from the carburettor.

Another device fitted is an electro-magnetic cut-off jet. This is a somewhat unhappy feature which is designed to positively stop the fuel flow when the engine is stopped. Otherwise the engine tends to run on - even with the ignition switched off - when the engine is hot.

## 4 Solex carburettor - removal, dismantling and replacement

1  The carburettor should not be dismantled without reason. Such reasons would be for cleaning or renewal of the float and needle valve assembly and, in rare circumstances, the jets. Partial dismantling would also be necessary for checking and setting the float chamber fuel level. Where statutory exhaust emission control regulations are in force it must be remembered that any disturbance of the carburettor (and ignition) settings may result in unacceptable exhaust gas emission. Such emissions will need checking with the proper equipment.
2  Remove the air cleaner and then detach the accelerator cable from the throttle control lever. Undo the screw which holds the cable end to the link, withdraw the cable and remove the link so that it does not fall out and get lost. Pull off the wire connection clips from the automatic choke and electro-magnetic cut-off.
3  Undo the two nuts which hold the carburettor to the inlet manifold and lift the carburettor off (photo). The exterior of the carburettor should be clinically clean before dismantling proceeds.
4  The first stage of dismantling should be to remove the screws holding the top to the base. Separate the two halves carefully and remove the paper gasket taking care to keep it from being damaged. It can be re-used (photo).
5  To clean out the float chamber, remove the float pin bracket and the float can then be taken out. Do not under any circumstances strain it in such a way that the pin or bracket are bent. When the float is removed the bowl may be flushed out and sediment removed with a small brush.
6  The needle valve is screwed into the top cover and when taking it out note the washer mounted underneath it (photo). The simplest way to check this for leaks is to try blowing through it. It should not be possible to do so when the plunger is lightly pushed in. If in doubt, then renew the assembly, as a leaking valve will result in an over-rich mixture with consequent loss of performance and increased fuel consumption.
7  The accelerator pump diaphragm may be examined when the four cover securing screws and cover have been removed. Be careful not to damage the diaphragm. Renew it if there are signs of holes or cracks which may reduce its efficiency.
8  The electric automatic strangler may be removed for cleaning but do not use petrol on the cover. If any part is suspected of malfunction the whole unit must be renewed. When refitting the bi-metal spring the looped end must be positioned so that it hooks over the end of the lever. Then the cover should be turned so that the notch lines up with the notch on the carburettor. Do not overtighten the securing screws.
9  The main jet is situated behind a hexagonal headed plug in the base of the float chamber. This can of course be removed without taking the carburettor off the car. Remove the plug and then unscrew the jet from behind it with a screwdriver. The pilot jet is fixed similarly in the body alongside the accelerator pump housing. When cleaning these jets do not use anything other than air pressure. Any poking with wire could damage the fine tolerance bores and upset the fuel mixtures. The electro-magnetic cut-off valve may be simply unscrewed from the carburettor body (photo). Do not grip the cylinder when doing

so — use a suitable spanner. Never clamp the valve or carburettor body in a vice.
10  The air correction jet and emulsion tube is mounted vertically in the body of the carburettor by the side of the choke tube. This too may be unscrewed for cleaning. Blow through the passageway in the carburettor also when it is removed.
11  Before reassembly check that the float is undamaged and unpunctured. It can be checked by immersion in hot water.
12  If the throttle flap spindle should be very loose in its bearings in the main body of the carburettor then air may leak past and affect the air to fuel ratio of the mixture. In such cases the easiest remedy is a new carburettor. An alternative is to drill and fit bushes to suit but this needs some expertise and time.
13  Reassembly is a reversal of the dismantling procedure but the following points should be watched carefully (photo). Do not forget the washer when replacing the needle valve. Make sure that the gasket between body and cover is correctly positioned. When refitting the accelerator pump cover, the screws should be tightened with the diaphragm centre pushed in. This means holding the operating lever out whilst the screws are tightened. Do not bend or distort the float arm when replacing it into the float chamber. When reconnecting the accelerator cable take heed of the procedure given at the end of the next section.
14  If a throttle valve positioner is fitted read about the details in Section 10 on emission control.
15  Do not forget to replace the air cleaner stay bracket.

## 5 Solex carburettor - adjustments

1  It must be emphasised that if the engine is running smoothly and performance and fuel consumption are satisfactory there are no adjustments that will materially improve any of these conditions beyond the manufacturers' specifications. If the engine is not performing as it should, be sure to check the ignition system before assuming that the carburettor is the cause of the trouble.
2  Assuming all components are clean and in good condition there are only two adjustments that can be made - these being the fuel level in the float chamber and the slow running speed.
3  To check the fuel level the carburettor must be fitted to the engine. The car should be standing on a level surface. Run the engine and then switch it off and remove the fuel line from the carburettor.
4  Remove the air cleaner assembly and then take out the five screws securing the upper half of the carburettor to the lower. Put a finger over the fuel inlet pipe (to prevent the little fuel in the top cover coming out when the top is lifted) and take off the top cover and gasket.
5  The level of the fuel - with the float in position - can be measured by using a depth gauge or by placing a straight edge across the top of the float chamber and measuring down with a suitable rule. Do not measure too near the edge as capilliary action up the side of the chamber could cause a false reading. If the level is incorrect it may be altered by fitting a washer of a different thickness under the needle valve which is screwed into the top cover. Washers are available in a range of thicknesses from ½ to 1½ mm (it can be seen that the fuel level measurement has to be taken fairly accurately to be of any use in deciding whether alteration is necessary). If the level in the chamber needs raising a thinner washer should be fitted and vice versa. If you are tempted to try and alter the level by bending the bracket on the float - forget it. It cannot be done accurately enough to be of any use and more often than not the result of such attempts is either breakage or distortion. In the latter case the net result is a sticking float which gives you more problems than you had to start with.
6  Whilst the cover is removed it would be as well to check the condition of the needle valve as described in the previous section.
7  Reassemble the top cover with the gasket the correct way round, reconnect and clip the fuel line and replace the air cleaner. If wished the level may be checked again once any adjustment has been made but it should not be necessary

Lower half of carburettor showing gasket (Sec 4.4)

Upper half of carburettor. Note needle valve 'A' and strangler flap 'B' (Sec 4.6)

Electro magnetic fuel cut off valve unscrewed from carburettor body (Sec 4.9)

Reassembling the two halves of the carburettor (Sec 4.13)

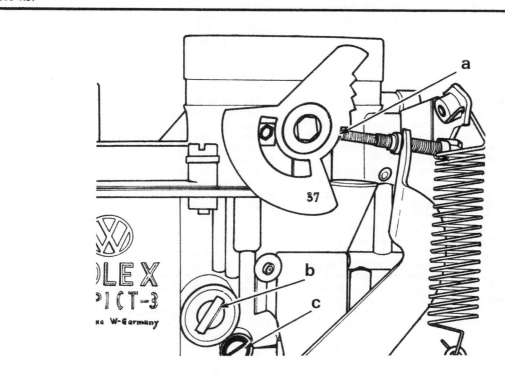

**Fig 3.3 CARBURETTOR ADJUSTMENT POINTS (SEC 5)**

A  Throttle stop screw on strangler cam in open position
B  By-pass air screw
C  Idle mixture adjustment screw

provided the needle valve is in good order and the measurements were accurately taken.

8    Slow running adjustment is only carried out when the engine is warm and the strangler flap fully open.

9    The first thing to be understood is that the slow running speed is NOT to be adjusted by use of the throttle stop screw. This screw has (or should have) a little plastic cover on the tip which will remind you. The only reason for touching this screw is if it is incorrectly set in relation to the fast idle cam. When the strangler flap is open the tip of the throttle stop screw should just touch the cam (see Fig 3.3), when the throttle flap is completely closed. This means in effect that with the accelerator pedal up the throttle is shut. Usually the throttle stop screw needs adjustment only after the accelerator cable has been disturbed.

10    The idling speed should be set to 800—900 rpm by turning the by-pass air screw, which is the larger of the two recessed screws in the side of the carburettor body above the electromagnetic cut-off valve. The idling mixture screw should not be touched.

11    If the correct idling speed cannot be achieved with the by-pass air screw then it is most likely the ignition timing is incorrect and this should be reset. It is of course assumed that the engine is in good condition and the valve clearances are correctly set. Another source of potential upset in timing is also the inlet manifold connecting hoses. These must be intact and secured properly with the clips.

12    The volume control screw should be touched only if there is a clear reason, such as a new carburettor or a replacement screw fitted. Normally it is set using a CO meter to give 4% in the exhaust gas. If this is not used the screw should be screwed in as far as possible - with great care so as not to damage the needle seat when it is fully home - and then backed off between 2½ and 3 turns. Then adjust the idle speed with the by-pass air screw to approximately 900 rpm. Then once again adjust the volume control screw until the rpm reach their maximum and then screw it in a little so that the speed drops 20—30 rpm. Then finally set the idling speed to 800—900 rpm with the by-pass air screw.

13    If the accelerator cable connection has been disturbed it is most important that it is correctly set to provide both maximum opening of the throttle and at the same time not cause any strain at the fully open position. An assistant will be needed to do this. First disconnect the throttle lever return spring and move the lever to the fully open position and then come back about 1 mm. With the accelerator pedal on the floor connect the cable into the clamp. This is done in such a way that no tension can ever exist due to the cable trying to pull on a fully open throttle. Then check that the throttle returns to the fully closed position and that the stop screw is set as described in paragraph 9 of this section.

## 6  Fuel pump - cleaning filter and checking

1    The pump cannot be dismantled other than for removal of the top cover to clean the filter screen (photo). This is done simply by removing the screw lifting off the cover and blowing the screen out with air. The carburettor does not have to be removed for this purpose. If the carburettor is suspected of malfunction first pull off the pipe from the carburettor and hold it into a container whilst the engine is turned on the starter. Fuel should come out. If it does not the cut-off valve may be out of order so disconnect the pipe from the pump outlet (the lower one) and connect another piece of pipe so that fuel can be collected in a container and repeat the procedure. Whichever item is not working should be renewed.

## 7  Fuel pump - removal and replacement

1    The fuel pump is mounted on the crankcase below the carburettor.

2    To remove the pump, first disconnect both fuel pipes. If the fuel tank is very full petrol may come out of the pipe leading from the tank, in which case it must be blocked with a pencil or similar suitable cylindrical article which can be pushed in. There is a separate fuel cut-off valve fitted in the fuel line system (incorporated in the pump itself in the latest models). This need not be disturbed. Its purpose is to prevent any fuel from passing from the pump to carburettor when the engine is stationary. A spring loaded valve in it only opens when the fuel pump pressure forces it open.

3    The two nuts holding the pump to the crankcase should be undone and the pump lifted off (photo). The mounting stud of the carburettor prevents the pump being lifted clear of its studs so the carburettor must be raised sufficiently to enable the pump to be brought out.

4    Pull out the pushrod and remove the gasket from between the pump and the plastic intermediate flange. It is not necessary to disturb the intermediate flange but if you do stuff a piece of rag into the crankcase as if anything drops down it could be extremely difficult, if not impossible, to get it out (photo).

5    If you are suffering from persistent fuel pump trouble of one sort or another (starvation of fuel or regularly punctured diaphragms) it is possible that the pushrod is not functioning correctly. Turn the engine until the rod protrudes the maximum amount above the intermediate flange. The normal gasket should be fitted under the intermediate flange. The rod should project 13 mm above the flange. It is possible to vary this by putting more or less gaskets under the intermediate flange. If the rod projects too much the diaphragm will be strained and may be punctured.

6    Before replacement the base of the pump should be packed with grease and a gasket, preferably new, fitted between pump and flange. Refit and tighten the nuts. After connecting the fuel lines run the engine to confirm that there are no fuel leaks.

7    If the cut-off valve has been disturbed it is important that the connections are made correctly. The one pipe which is not parallel to the other three is the outlet to the carburettor. The other end of this pipe connects to the outlet (lower) pump connection. The valve outlet pipe next to the angled pipe is connected to the fuel tank (photo).

## 8  Fuel tank and gauge sender unit

1    The fuel tank is mounted in the front luggage compartment. An electrically operated sender unit controlled by floats in the tank is mounted in the top.

2    Access to the tank is obtained by first removing the fibre board trim.

3    If the fuel gauge is not working first bridge the two terminals on the tank unit. If there is a reaction on the dashboard gauge then the tank unit is faulty. Otherwise the gauge is faulty or the wires leading to it are broken.

4    To remove the sender unit disconnect the two wires, grip it firmly and turn anticlockwise to release the bayonet fitting (photo). By manoeuvring the unit round it can be taken out complete with the two floats (photo).

5    If the floats are punctured or the contact wiper blade on the rheostat is not making contact it may be possible to rectify the trouble but do not expect to be able to buy individual parts. Improvisation will be needed otherwise the whole unit should be renewed.

6    The fuel tank is provided with twin vent pipes at each side which lead into an activated carbon filter unit behind the ventilation duct inlet (photos). This is designed to filter out the harmful elements of evaporating fuel.

7    If the tank is to be removed for any reason the level of fuel should first be low enough to prevent any fuel leakage when the vent pipes are disconnected. If necessary it can be siphoned out from the filler neck. With the vent pipes and filler neck disconnected remove the four holding down screws (photo). Lift the tank a little so that the flexible outlet pipe connection is accessible. This can then be pulled off and held whilst the tank is taken off. The rest of the fuel can then be drained off.

Fitting the air cleaner stay bracket (Sec 4.15)

Removing the fuel pump cover to clean the filter (Sec 6.1)

Removing the fuel pump (Sec 7.3)

The fuel pump actuating rod (Sec 7.4a)

The fuel pump intermediate flange (Sec 7.4b)

Fuel pump and external cut off valve connections. 'A' from the fuel tank and 'B' to the carburettor (Sec 7.7)

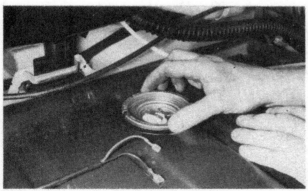

Removing the fuel gauge tank unit (Sec 8.4a)

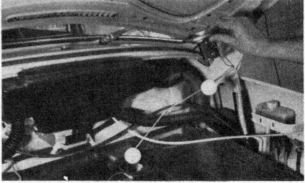

Lifting out the tank unit and floats (Sec 8.4b)

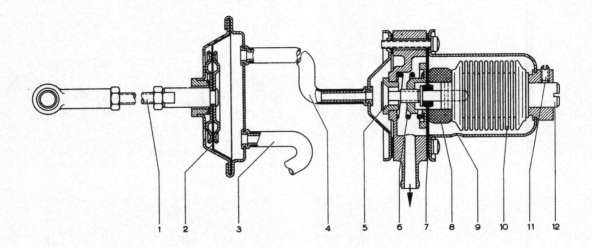

**Fig 3.4 EMISSION CONTROL — THROTTLE VALVE POSITIONER DEVICE (SEC 9)**

1 Pull rod
2 Operating diaphragm
3 Hose to carburettor
4 Hose to control unit
5 Valve
6 Spring
7 Control diaphragm
8 Plastic foam filter
9 Drilling
10 Altitude corrector
11 Setscrew
12 Adjusting screw

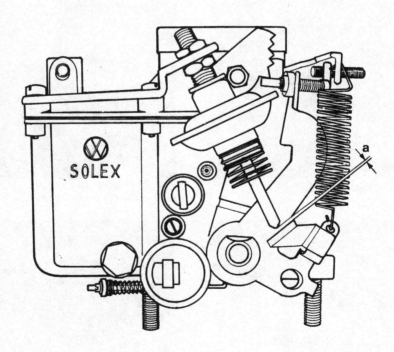

**Fig 3.5 EMISSION CONTROL — THROTTLE VALVE RETURN DAMPER DEVICE (SEC 9) (a = 1 mm)**

There are vent pipes at the left upper corner ... (Sec 8.6a)

... and the left corner and filler neck (Sec 8.6b)

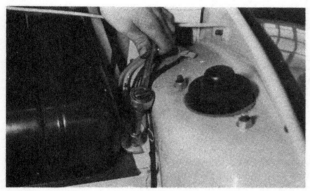

Undoing a tank mounting bolt (Sec 8.7)

Inlet manifold centre section being positioned (Sec 9.3)

The manifold outer sections are held by the cylinder head studs (Sec 9.4)

Inlet manifold aluminium gasket (Sec 9.6)

The sections of inlet manifold are joined by rubber boots and clips ... (Sec 9.7a)

... which must be carefully positioned and not overtightened (Sec 9.7b)

## 9  Inlet manifold - removal, inspection and replacement

1  The inlet manifold is in three sections. Each outer section fits inside the ends of the centre section and there is a rubber sealing boot over each connection held by hose clips. The outer sections are each twin branch leading to the twin port head.

2  It is not practicable to remove the inlet manifold either in part or in whole with the engine installed in the car.

3  When removing the inlet manifold with the engine removed from the car the fan housing will have to be taken off before the centre section can be taken out (photo). There is no way to get it out from between the fan and generator pedestal. It is secured by a lug to the crankcase.

4  The end sections are held to the cylinder heads by two nuts on studs (photo).

5  It is important that the mating faces of the flanges to the cylinder head are smooth and undistorted. Also there should be no signs of cracks or holes in the rest of the manifold. The rubber boots must be in perfect condition also.

6  When replacing the manifolds always use new gaskets for the cylinder heads (photo). See that the joining surfaces are quite clean. Jointing compound must not be used.

7  Reassembling all three sections loosely at first and get the rubber boots in position over the joints (photo). Tighten down the end sections - taking care not to overtighten and then clamp the centre section. Finally tighten the rubber connector clips (photo).

## 10  Emission control equipment

1  Pollution of the atmosphere from fumes released by both burnt and unburnt fuel and gases from the internal combustion engine is understandably becoming a topic of international concern. The state of California in the U.S.A. having suffered most, is in the forefront of legislative moves to control such emissions at a level which will not render the atmosphere harmful to humans. As the export of VW's to the States is a very significant percentage of their total output, and many seem to get to the West Coast it is natural that VW activity in the emission control field has been intensive and comprehensive in the few years since 1969 which happened to coincide with the introduction of the 1302 Beetle.

2  As development in this field is still continuing and the rate of official documentation must lag behind physical developments this section can only give an indication of the moves made so far and show the primary areas and methods used to clean up emissions.

There are four main areas to deal with. These are:

1  Burning of the fuel in all engine running conditions to keep unburnt hydrocarbons to a minimum.

2  Recirculating of exhaust gas to deal with unacceptable levels of emission dependent on the efficiency of the first stage.

3  Recirculation of crankcase fumes into combustion chambers.

4  Filtration of raw petroleum vented fumes from fuel tanks.

In general items 3 and 4 are the simplest to deal with. All modern cars - regardless of official regulations are now fitted with devices which re-circulate crankcase fumes to the inlet manifold. On the VW there is a flexible pipe from the oil filler neck to the intake duct of the air cleaner for this purpose. The fuel tank is vented through an activated filter unit as already described.

Fuel combustion relative to power output is notoriously inefficient in the internal combustion engine and is the main cause of the noxious emissions - being as they are unused components of the fuel. The fixed choke carburettor as fitted to the VW is much more difficult to modify than the variable choke variety in terms of fuel/air mixture control throughout the full range of engine speeds and load requirements. One of the principle objectives is to weaken the mixture which is always too rich in over-run situations when the throttle is shut. This is the reason for the air by-pass system which enables more air to be introduced when manifold depression is high and the throttle is closed. Coupled with these carburettor modifications are ignition timing changes which positively retard the spark to aid combustion also under these conditions. The changes over the two year period 1970–1972 have been considerable and have resulted in difficulties because of effects on performance known as 'progression' problems - better known as flat spots. This manual does not go into the detail of the modifications involved because they have not yet been fully concluded. Any owner who may not be satisfied with a car's performance should refer to a VW dealer who will be able to advise the most up to date and suitable remedies. Finally there is a cooling coil device that cools part of the exhaust gases themselves and re-circulates them via the combustion chambers. This has a beneficial effect on the resulting exhaust gas emission. It is fitted to those models where regulations are set to certain emission levels. Similarly there is a vacuum controlled throttle valve positioner fitted to certain models in conjunction with the by-pass air system already referred to.

The crankcase gas recirculation and the carbon filter for the fuel tank venting have already been referred to earlier. The air by-pass system in the carburettor is standard on all models and is an integral part of the carburettor.

During 1970 two forms of throttle valve controllers fitted to certain cars destined for the U.S. Fig 3.4 is a schematic drawing of one which maintains an independent control of the throttle under conditions of deceleration. It is dependent on the manifold depression under certain sets of circumstances. Later a dashpot was fitted in addition which acts as a damper to the return action of the throttle giving time for the throttle positioner to operate correctly (Fig 3.5).

The exhaust gas recirculation device designed to reduce emission of nitrogen oxide is fitted to stickshift models in California. A portion of the exhaust gases is cooled, filtered and metered back through the combustion chambers. Fig 3.6 gives an indication of the general layout.

## 11  Fault diagnosis

In addition to the more basic faults which may occur in any vehicle fuel system there are some peculiarities to the 1302 Beetle series as a result in the changes and modifications needed in connection with exhaust emission control - Early models in particular of both 1285 cc and 1594 cc engined versions were plagued with 'flat spot' or progression troubles and a series of changes were made over a period of time which were designed to improve both performance and fuel economy. These changes were not the same for all models and were not confined to the carburettor. Distributors were changed as well giving different advance curve characteristics. It is not within the scope of this manual to go into all the detail of which modifications have been made and when. Furthermore, to attempt to summarize them in shortened form would only cause misunderstandings by leading people to think that the remedy was simply a matter of changing jets or whatever. The different details shown in the Specifications show when the modifications were incorporated in production. To bring earlier models up to these specifications is possible but should be done through a VW agency. The point is that progression difficulties which may be experienced are not necessarily peculiar to one particular car.

Provided the ignition, valves and carburettor are all correctly set up and the inlet manifold joints are leakproof flat spot problems should be taken to a VW dealer for modifications to be made.

Before acting on the fuel system it is necessary to check the ignition system first. Even though a fault may lie in the fuel system it will be difficult to trace unless the ignition is correct. The table below therefore, assumes that the ignition system is in order.

| Symptom | Reason/s | Remedy |
| --- | --- | --- |
| Smell of petrol when engine is stopped | Leaking fuel lines or unions<br>Leaking fuel tank | Repair or renew as necessary.<br>Fill fuel tank to capacity and examine carefully at seams, unions and filler pipe connections. |
| Smell of petrol when engine is idling | Leaking fuel line unions between pump and carburettor<br>Overflow of fuel from float chamber due to wrong level setting or ineffective needle valve or punctured float | Check line and unions and tighten or repair.<br>Check fuel level setting and condition of float and needle valve and renew if necessary. |
| Excessive fuel consumption for reasons not covered by leaks or float chamber faults | Worn jets<br>Sticking strangler flap | Renew jets.<br>Check correct movement of strangler flap. |
| Difficult starting, uneven running, lack of power, cutting out | One or more jets blocked or restricted<br><br>Float chamber fuel level too low    or needle valve sticking<br>Fuel pump not delivering sufficient fuel<br><br>Intake manifold gaskets leaking, or manifold fractured | Dismantle and clean out float chamber and jets.<br>Dismantle and check fuel level and needle valve.<br>Check pump delivery and clean or repair as required.<br>Check tightness of mounting nuts and inspect manifold connections. |

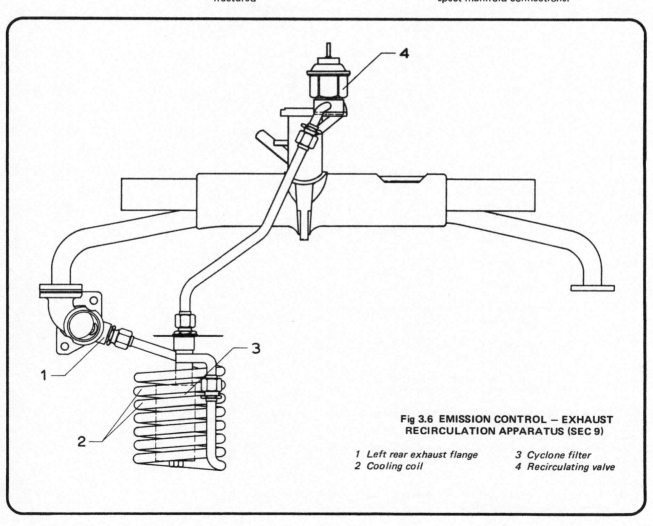

**Fig 3.6 EMISSION CONTROL – EXHAUST RECIRCULATION APPARATUS (SEC 9)**

1  *Left rear exhaust flange*      3  *Cyclone filter*
2  *Cooling coil*                  4  *Recirculating valve*

# Chapter 4  Ignition system

## Contents

## Specifications

**Spark plugs**

| | |
|---|---|
| Type ... ... ... ... ... ... ... ... ... ... ... ... ... ... ... ... ... ... | Bosch W 145 TI |
| | Champion L88A |
| Electrode gap ... ... ... ... ... ... ... ... ... ... ... ... ... | 0.7 mm/0.028 in |

**Distributor**

| | |
|---|---|
| Type and voltage ... ... ... ... ... ... ... ... ... ... ... ... | Bosch 12 volt |
| Firing order ... ... ... ... ... ... ... ... ... ... ... ... ... | 1 4 3 2 |
| Contact points gap ... ... ... ... ... ... ... ... ... ... ... | 0.4 mm/0.016 in |
| Dwell angle maximum limit ... ... ... ... ... ... ... ... | 42° — 58° |
| Automatic advance ... ... ... ... ... ... ... ... ... ... ... | Centrifugal and vacuum |

**Coil**

| | |
|---|---|
| 12 volt ... ... ... ... ... ... ... ... ... ... ... ... ... ... ... ... | Bosch 311 905 115A |

**Ignition timing**

| Engine type and serial | | Firing point setting | See Notes |
|---|---|---|---|
| 1285 cc | AB0,000,000,1 - 0,313,345 ... ... ... ... ... ... | 5° ATDC | (1) |
| | AB0,313,346 on ... ... ... ... ... ... ... | 7.5° BTDC | (2) |
| 1584 cc | B6,000,001 - 6,440,900 ... ... ... ... ... ... | 0° | (3) |
| | AD, AE, AF, AH ... ... ... ... ... ... ... ... | 5° ATDC | (4) |
| | AD ... ... ... ... ... ... ... ... ... ... ... ... | 7.5° BTDC | (5) |

Notes  (1)  Vacuum hoses on

(2)  Vacuum hose off

(3)  Vacuum hose off for manual transmission and
on for stickshift automatic

(4)  For models with two vacuum hose connections
which should be both on

(5)  For models with single vacuum hose
connection which should be off

General —  Study text for details of ignition timing setting requirements

**Timing marks**
V notch in belt pulley at firing point setting at 800 - 900 rpm (stroboscope setting)

**General note**
With continual development going on in connection with exhaust emission control production settings and
variations can alter without notice.

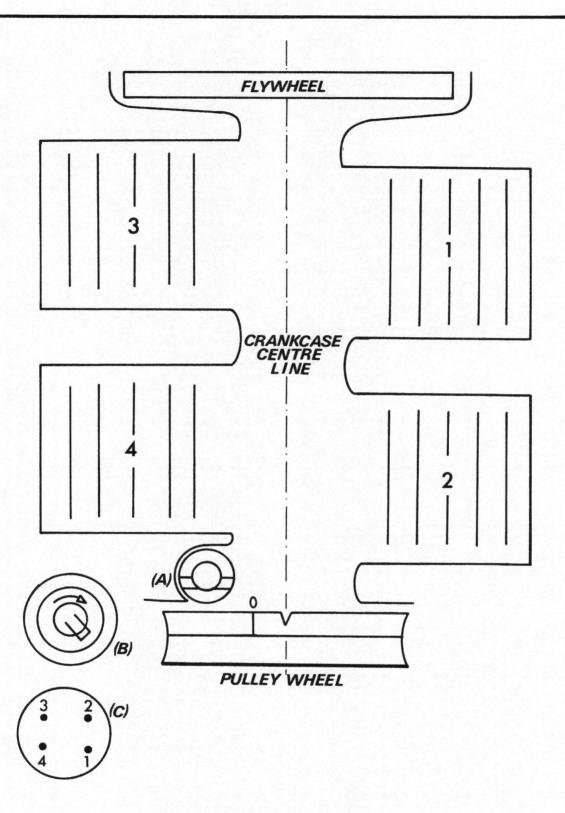

**Fig 4.1  IGNITION TIMING (SEC 6)**

A  Distributor drive shaft eccentric slot position for No 1 cylinder at firing point
B  Rotor in position to the notch in distributor body
C  HT lead positions in distributor cap

## 1 General description

Ignition of the fuel/air mixture in the Volkswagen engine is conventional in that one spark plug per cylinder is used and the high voltage required to produce the spark across the plug electrodes is supplied from a coil (transformer) which converts the volts from the supply battery to the several thousand necessary to produce a spark that will jump a gap under the conditions of heat and pressure that obtain in the cylinder.

In order that the spark will occur at each plug in the correct order and at precisely the correct moment the low voltage current is built up (into the condenser) and abruptly discharged through the coil when the circuit is broken by the interrupter switch (contact points). This break in the low voltage circuit, and the simultaneous high voltage impulse generated from the coil, is directed through the selector switch (rotor arm) to one of four leads which connect to the spark plugs. The condenser, contact points and rotor arm are all contained in and operated at the distributor.

Due to different spark timing requirements under certain engine conditions (of varying speed or load) the distributor also has an automatic advance device (advancing the spark means that it comes earlier in relation to the piston position).

The spark timing is altered by two methods. One is by centrifugal force acting on bob-weights attached to the distributor cam. As these move out so the cam position is altered in relation to the distributor shaft. The second method - in addition to the first - is by vacuum from the induction manifold. Engine speed governs the centrifugal advance. Throttle opening governs the vacuum advance.

Recent developments in the field of exhaust emission control have resulted in changes in carburettor design. The traditional methods of setting up and turning the engine are somewhat changed also and it is important to understand that the settings of both carburettor and ignition timing are even more interdependent than they were before. Previously if one or the other was fractionally adrift no serious symptoms were apparent. This is not now the case and flat spots, poor performance and excessive fuel consumption can result if everything is not spot-on.

## 2 Contact breaker points - adjustment, removal and replacement

1  Volkswagen service procedures check the contact points by measuring the cam dwell with special equipment. All else being equal the correct cam dwell gives a points gap of .4 mm/.016 ins. To check the gap, first remove the distributor cap by undoing the two retaining clips, and pull off the rotor arm (photos).
2  Push back the moving contact point against the spring just enough to see whether the surfaces of both contacts are clean and flat. If dirty clean them with a piece of dry clean cloth. If one contact has a peak and the other a pit, it will be impossible to set them with a feeler gauge and they should be removed (as described later on) for renewal or temporary renovation until a new set can be obtained.
3  Having established that the contact faces are clean and flat turn the engine (use a spanner on the crankshaft pulley nut) until the cam follower on the spring contact is resting on the highest point of one of the four cam lobes (photo).
4  Place a feeler gauge of the correct thickness in the points gap and if it is either tight or slack the points need adjustment. To do this slacken the screw holding the fixed point on to the mounting plate (photo). Then use the screwdriver blade in the notch to lever the fixed point plate either way as needed. It is best not to have the screw too loose when doing this. The feeler blade should slide between the two contacts, touching both but not forcing them apart.
5  When set tighten the securing screw and check the gap again to ensure the gap has not altered.
6  Replace the rotor arm and distributor cap.

7  If the points have to be removed take out the securing screw completely. Pull off the wire at the single terminal connector clip. The points assembly complete may then be lifted off the pivot post. Although it is not necessary, it is as well to understand the circuitry of the contact points, otherwise the fault tracing procedures described later are somewhat meaningless. The fixed contact is the earth side, so it is mounted, and in contact with the distributor body itself via the base plate. The moving contact is the 'live' side and when assembled it must be insulated from earth. The current travels from the L.T. wire on the coil to the spring arm to the contact or condenser. The spring contact (and the wires connected to it) must be insulated from the distributor. Similarly the pivot point of the spring contact must be insulated from earth. If this is borne in mind there should be no problem. When finally assembled the two contact breaker surfaces should line up.
8  The points may be removed completely by removing the adjusting clamp screw and disconnecting the lead at the connection (photo). The whole assembly lifts out.
9  If the points are being cleaned it is best to separate the two pieces of the assembly.
10  To clean up the faces of the contacts use a very fine oil stone. Stone the two faces flat ensuring particularly that the 'peak' is completely removed. If the pit in the other contact is very deep do not try and grind it right out. The points can be adjusted once the peak is removed. Make a note to get a new set at the earliest opportunity.
11  Reassemble the two halves if separated and replace the assembly over the pivot post. Put back the securing screw but do not fully tighten it down.
12  Reconnect the wires at the connector blade terminal.
13  Having re-adjusted the gap on one cam lobe it is advisable to check it on the other three also. Also check that there is no sideways play in the distribution shaft which could cause gap setting variations.

## 3 Distributor - removal and replacement

1  The distributor should be removed only if indications are such that it needs renewal or overhaul.
2  Take off the distributor cap and pull the L.T. wire which runs to the coil off the coil terminal. Detach the pipes which fit to the vacuum advance unit.
3  The distributor is held in position by a clamp which grips the lower circular part of the body. The clamp itself is held to the crankcase by a single bolt. If the bolt is removed the distributor and clamp together may be lifted out of the crankcase.
4  It must be realised that if the bolt which secures the clamp to the distributor is slackened - and the relative positions of distributor and clamp altered - then the static ignition timing is upset.
5  The lower end of the distributor drive shaft has a driving dog with offset engagement lugs. These engage into corresponding slots in the distributor drive shaft. Being offset it ensures that the shaft cannot be inadvertently set 180° out of position when the distributor is replaced.
6  It is a good idea to renew the rubber 'O' ring in the annular exterior groove of the body if possible. This seal prevents oil from creeping up on the outside of the body.
7  Replacement of the distributor is a reversal of the removal procedure. See that the offset drive shaft dogs are correctly aligned otherwise they will not engage and the body will not go fully home.

## 4 Condenser - testing, removal and replacement

1  The condenser or capacitor as it is sometimes called, functions as a storage unit for the low tension current which flows into it when the points are closed. When the points open it discharges and sends a boost through the L.T. circuit to the coil. If the condenser does not function correctly the current shorts

Removing the distributor cap ... (Sec 2.1)

... and rotor (Sec 2.1)

Contact points ready for gap check (Sec 2.3)

Checking the points gap with a feeler blade and undoing the clamp screw to enable the fixed point to be moved (Sec 2.4)

Disconnecting the points lead (Sec 2.5)

Undoing the condenser clamp screw (Sec 4.3)

to earth across the contact points. This causes arcing and rapid deterioration of the points and also causes the spark producing properties of the coil to malfunction or cease entirely. If, therefore, persistent misfiring and/or severe burning and pitting of the contact points occurs, the condenser is suspect and should be tested right away.

2  To make a simple check on the condenser remove the distributor cap and turn the engine until the contact points are closed. Then switch on the ignition and push open the points with something non-metallic. If there is a considerable spark then this confirms that the condenser is faulty. Normally there should be a very mild spark - almost invisible - across the points.

3  The condenser is mounted on the outside of the distributor and is easily removed and replaced (together with the wires and connectors) by undoing the securing screw.

## 5 Distributor - inspection and repair

1  Provided the component parts are kept in good order there should be little need to take the distributor apart except in cases of neglect or very high mileages. One of the indications is when the measured gap of the contact points is difficult or impossible to set accurately and consistently. This is due to wear of the shaft or shaft bushes or, more rarely, wear on the cams. When the shaft or bushes are worn the movement can be felt when sideways rocking pressure is applied to the top of the shaft.

2  In either case the only solution is to remove the distributor and renew the shaft. Alternatively one may find it simpler to renew the whole assembly. This might be necessary as the trend among manufacturers nowadays is generally this way. Check first that you can obtain the parts you may need.

3  Having removed the distributor, take out the contact points as described earlier.

4  The next job is to remove the driving collar from the bottom of the shaft but before doing this it is important to note which way it is fitted. See which way the driving dogs are offset in relation to the rotor arm notch in the top of the shaft. The notch and the offset of the dogs should face the same way.

5  When the relative position is noted clamp the collar in a vice and punch out the retaining pin. The collar may then be drawn off the shaft followed by the shims which control the endfloat of the shaft in the body.

6  Carefully unhook the pull rod from the vacuum unit to the contact breaker mounting plate and after removing the screws take off the vacuum unit. Then remove the mounting plate and shaft taking note of the position of the thrust washers.

7  If the shaft is obviously badly worn it must be renewed, but before buying a new one it is essential to check that the bushes in the distributor are not also worn. If they are, then the whole distributor should be renewed as it is not practicable to fit new bushes in the existing body.

8  Do not wash the bushes in paraffin or other solvent and make sure they are well lubricated before reassembly.

9  New distributor shafts when in position may need a variation in the thickness of the shims fitted between the driving dog and the body.

10  Reassembly is a reversal of the dismantling procedure. Make sure the driving dog is fitted the correct way round and when the pin is fitted peen the ends so that it cannot drop out.

## 6 Ignition timing and distributor drive shaft

1  In the description section of this chapter it was pointed out that the ignition timing and carburettor setting was a little more critical than on earlier models. It is possible to set the engine up by the well tried method of adjustment and road testing to obtain the best performance. It is a good idea when this method is used to get hold of someone experienced who has some idea of what the idling speed (800—900 rpm) sounds like. Provided the carburettor is set correctly to start with (Chapter 3) pro-

gressive setting changes at the distributor will achieve the desired results. If you can obtain a strobe light and a tachometer for temporary hook up you will save a lot of time. You will also be sure that the settings are spot on first time. The main point to remember is that having set it all up stationary and being delighted when the engine starts first time there will almost certainly be further adjustments necessary. If the pull away through the gears seems a bit 'flat' nudge the distributor more to advance (anticlockwise). If the engine fluffs a bit in the lower revolutions and then zooms away as the revs increase then back it off a little.

These tips are given here because the setting procedures given in the following paragraphs are precise - only when they have been done should you carry out any final 'sweetening'. There should be little need to alter the timing except in cases of engine overhaul or distributor overhaul.

2  If the timing has to be reset from scratch the distributor should be removed first so that the distributor drive shaft position may be verified and set as required.

3  The distributor drive shaft may be removed and installed with the engine assembled and in the car provided that the distributor, fuel pump and fuel pump intermediate flange have first been removed. (The distributor drive shaft also drives the fuel pump pushrod from a face cam incorporated on the shaft). If the engine is being reassembled after overhaul the drive shaft should be refitted after the oil pump, lower cover plate and crankshaft pulley have been refitted.

4  To withdraw the drive shaft from the crankcase first set No.1 cylinder to firing position. This is done by setting the correct mark on the pulley wheel to the crankcase joint. The offset slot in the top of the shaft should then be parallel with and towards the pulley wheel. Remove the spacer spring. Before starting to lift the shaft out it must be understood that there are thrust washers underneath the lower end and with the engine installed in the car there are dangers of these being irretrievably moved out of position. In any case they can only be lifted out with a narrow magnet on the end of a stick (if the engine is installed). So — don't take out the drive shaft unnecessarily and if you do have to don't disturb the thrust washers underneath. The shaft may now be lifted up and out, rotating anticlockwise as it is lifted. The main problem is getting hold of it. If you do not have the special tool there are a variety of ways namely: jamming a piece of suitably sized wooden dowel into the centre hole, gripping the sides of the hole with a pair of long nosed expanding circlip pliers, jamming a piece of thin wooden batten into the slot.

5  If the thrust washers are removed for some reason they should be replaced by dropping them down over a suitable guide rod so that they lie flat and central in the bottom of the shaft housing bore (photo).

6  The engine should be set at the firing point for No.1 cylinder. (The firing point is either before or after T.D.C. on the compression stroke - see Specifications for details.)

7  To find the compression stroke with the distributor drive shaft removed is not easy because there are no reference points. The only sure way is to remove No.1 spark plug and turn the engine until compression is felt when the timing marks come into line. It is easy to feel the compression by placing a finger over the plug hole. If the right hand rocker cover is removed the compression stroke can also be pinpointed when both valves are closed.

8  The distributor drive shaft should now be lowered into the crankcase with the offset slot positioned slightly anticlockwise from its final correct position as detailed in paragraph 4 (photo). When it is lowered into mesh with the crankshaft worm gear it will turn slightly clockwise to the final correct position. Replace the thrust spring (photo).

9  With the engine and distributor drive shaft set and not moved from the position as described in the preceding paragraph the distributor may be placed in position with the shaft lined up so that the eccentric dogs engage the eccentric slots. Provided the clamp has been undisturbed no further adjustment is necessary after the clamp securing bolt has been replaced and tightened.

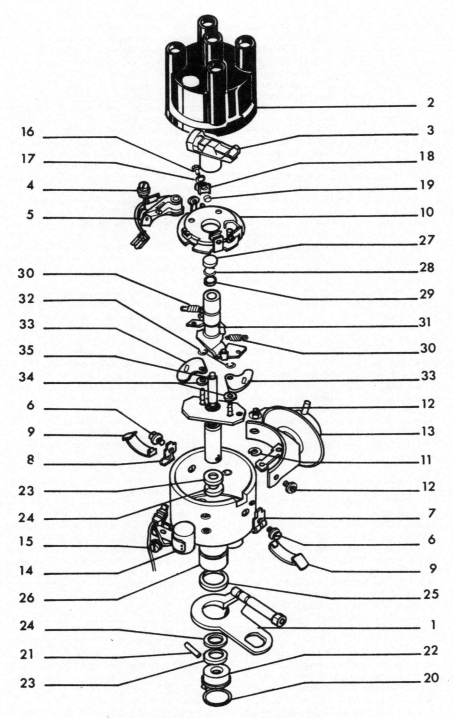

**Fig 4.2 DISTRIBUTOR WITH CENTRIFUGAL AND
VACUUM ADVANCE – EXPLODED VIEW
(SEC 5)**

| | | | |
|---|---|---|---|
| 1 Mounting clamp bracket | 10 Contact points mounting plate | 18 Retaining spring | 27 Felt washer |
| 2 Cap | | 19 Ball | 28 Circlip |
| 3 Rotor | 11 'E' clip for pull rod | 20 Circlip | 29 Thrust ring |
| 4 Contacts securing screw | 12 Screw | 21 Pin | 30 Return spring |
| 5 Contact points | 13 Vacuum unit | 22 Driving dog | 31 Cam |
| 6 Clip screw | 14 Condenser | 23 Shim | 32 Circlip |
| 7 Clip retainer | 15 Screw | 24 Fibre washer | 33 Bob weights |
| 8 Clip retainer | 16 Screw | 25 'O' sealing ring | 34 Washer |
| 9 Cap clip | 17 Spring washer | 26 Distributor body | 35 Drive shaft |

10 If the clamp ring has been slackened the body of the distributor should be turned so that the centre line of the rotor arm electrode matches up with the notch in the edge of the distributor body. This gives the near correct position. Final adjustment is made after the contact points have been checked and the gap set. With the crankshaft at the No.1 firing position the contact points should just be opening. To do this the distributor body should be first turned clockwise a fraction from the setting mark until the points are shut. The body is then turned anticlockwise until they are just open.

11 From now on the ignition timing is set with the engine running at idling speed (800—900 rpm). Having checked which type of distributor is fitted (see Specifications) the vacuum hoses are left on or pulled off as necessary (photo). The basic settings of the carburettor are checked as described in Chapter 3 and the engine is started, warmed up and set to run at the correct idling speed by using the by-pass air screw on the carburettor. Then stop the engine again.

12 Connect the strobe light into No.1 HT lead on the distributor cap. See also that the V notch in the crankshaft pulley wheel is clean and visible (paint it white if necessary). Start the engine again and shine the strobe light onto the pulley. The notch should line up with the crankcase joint. If it does not, slacken the distributor clamp and turn the body of the distributor one way or the other until it does. It is not necessary to tighten the distributor clamp each time an adjustment is made provided the distributor is held reasonably tight.

13 When an adjustment is made it is likely that the engine idling speed will alter so if it falls outside the specified limits adjust the by-pass air screw on the carburettor until it is once more correct. Then check with the stroboscope again.

14 When the mark lines up with the crankcase joint, clamp up the distributor. Reconnect the vacuum hoses as necessary.

15 With the timing set stroboscopically any performance problems with the engine will be due to incorrect carburettor or valve clearance settings. In cold climatic conditions malfunction of the inlet manifold pre-heater and the air intake pre-heater systems could also cause flat spots and poor performance, particularly during acceleration.

## 7 Spark plugs and HT leads

1 The proper operation of the spark plugs is essential to good engine performance and economy. They are also useful indications of engine condition and settings.

2 Make sure you use the correct plugs as listed in the specifications. Every type of engine has its own characteristics calling for a certain spark plug. A different type may be too 'cold' causing deposits to form on the electrodes which would normally burn off. This would result in poor sparking and eventual misfiring. Other plugs may be too 'hot'. These are much more dangerous as the electrodes would overheat and burn away and localised overheating could burn a hole in the piston.

3 Spark plugs today are generally very reliable and give no trouble in an engine which is in normally good condition. Official VW service routines no longer include plug cleaning and setting. They merely renew them every 12000 miles. However, occasion for removal can arise and they are of use in checking the running state of the engine. To remove the Volkswagen plugs it is best to use the special plug spanner supplied with the vehicle. This is quite conventional except that a rubber insert is fitted which grips the plug and enables you to lift it out through the top cover plate attached to the spanner. If the plug drops loose under the cover plate you can waste an awful lot of time fiddling about in order to get it out.

4 The colour of a normally operating plug is greyish brown and any deposits on it are usually light. Whitish deposits indicate weak fuel mixtures or overheating, whereas blackish deposits indicate over-rich fuel mixture.

5 If you are unable to have the plugs sand blasted and tested on a proper machine (you could if you carried a spare set) first clean off the deposits with a wire brush or by scraping. Considerable deposits may accumulate round the porcelain insulator of the central electrode. This can be scraped out with a fine pointed article (such as an old hacksaw blade ground to a point) but care must be taken not to damage the porcelain. If the porcelain is chipped or cracked anyway the plug must be discarded.

6 The actual electrodes must also be in good condition which means unburnt and comparable to the original length. The centre electrode must project above the end of the threaded body of the plug and the side electrode project across the full diameter of the centre one. The easiest way to assess deterioration is by comparison with a new plug. For cleaning the electrode the side one may be bent up a little to permit a fine file or emery to be used to face off the opposing surfaces of both electrodes. The surfaces should be flat. Then tap the side electrode down carefully with a feeler blade between the two. The correct gap is 0.6—0.7 mm (0.024—0.027 inch). Do not try to bend the centre electrode. The insulation will crack.

7 Do not soak plugs in petrol or paraffin. Even after the spirit is burnt off the residual deposits do more harm than good. If you get persistent problems with plugs oiling up you may have to wash them in spirit but when you get the engine put right buy a new set of plugs.

8 If the exterior insulation is damaged or loose the plug must be renewed. Streaky marks running up the insulation indicate a gas leak between body and insulation. Renew the plug under such circumstances.

9 When replacing the plugs use a new washer if possible - although most plugs nowadays are fitted with captive washers which makes it somewhat difficult. You are being persuaded to buy new plugs all the time. In any case try to make sure that the seating in the cylinder head where the plug fits is clear of grit or other things that could cause a poor seal. When cleaning the seats it is important to prevent bits dropping into the cylinder. As the Volkswagen plugs are less accessible than most the simplest way is to screw in the plugs a few threads and then direct as strong an air blast as you can find around the plug.

10 DO NOT OVERTIGHTEN PLUGS. The cylinder head is made of aluminium and apart from the risk of stripping the threads the overtightening of plugs can cause heat stresses to crack the head between the plug threads and the valve seat. There is a correct torque of 25 ft lbs/3.5 mkg but if this is not easy to measure then screw in the plug as far as the seat and then just give it a firm 'nip' with the plug spanner.

11 The leads for the plugs must be examined carefully along their length and at each end. The insulation should be clean, uncracked and undamaged in any other way. The metal ends should be free of corrosion. Everything should be dry. Renew any doubtful items and do not try to make do with repairs using insulating tape or such. It is not worth it.

## 8 Coil - testing

1 The coil serves to convert the battery current to the high voltage required to generate a spark at the spark plugs. It consists of a primary winding (low tension) and a secondary winding (high tension) which delivers the high voltage to the distributor rotor and thence to the plugs.

2 It is not normally tested separately, but during the tests applied to the whole ignition system in the course of diagnosing some fault. The testing involves checking that current flows through the primary windings and that the secondary winding delivers a high voltage. As this is most easily done with the coil in normal circuit no separate procedure is given for a coil which is taken out of circuit.

## 9 Fault diagnosis

1 Failure of the engine to start easily, misfiring and poor acceleration and fuel consumption can usually be attributed to

Fitting the distributor drive shaft thrust washer over a suitable guide rod (Sec 6.5)

Replacing the distributor drive shaft. Note fuel pump drive cam on the shaft (Sec 6.8)

Replacing the thrust spring (Sec 6.8)

Fig 4.3 DISTRIBUTOR DRIVE SHAFT (SEC 6)

1 Spacer spring
2 Fuel pump drive cam
3 Thrust washer

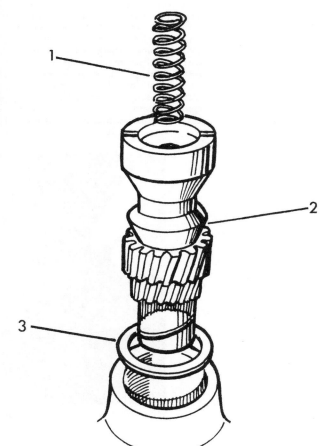

faults in the ignition system assuming, of course, that the engine is otherwise in reasonable condition. Volkswagen engines have a tendency to be fussy when starting hot. Do not attribute this to ignition until you have tried the hot start method of first pressing slowly the accelerator pedal right on the floor and holding it there before operating the starter motor. This overcomes the tendency to flood the warm engine with excess fuel. When starting from cold remember that an automatic choke is fitted. One quick depression and back of the accelerator pedal will ensure that the fast idle cam is set correctly. The pedal should not be touched after that until the engine fires. If the engine does not immediately fire, flooding is likely in which case the 'hot engine' procedure should be followed.

2  The table shows the logical progression to be followed in any circumstance where the ignition is being checked for correct operation. Do not by-pass any part of this procedure unless the fault is particularly obvious and rectification solves the problem. Such obvious faults would be broken or detached wires. It is assumed that the battery is in good condition and fully charged. It is impracticable to test the circuit otherwise. It also assumes that the battery is connected properly and that the starter motor turns the engine over normally.

the engine until the points are closed. Switch on the ignition. Hold the HT lead from the coil near a metal earth and open the points with a non-metallic article. If a spark now jumps from the end of the HT lead clean and reset the points to cure the trouble.

c) If there is no spark from the HT lead but a large spark from the points when opened as in para (b) the condenser is faulty. It should be renewed.

d) If there is no spark from the HT lead, and no spark large or small at the points when opened as in para (b) the winding of the coil has probably failed. Check that current is actually passing through the coil to terminal 1 from terminal 15. Do this by having the ignition switched on, the lead to terminal 15 connected and a test lamp or voltmeter from terminal 1 to earth. If there is no voltage then renew the coil.

**FAULT**

**No start or starts and misfires**

**CHECK**

1  Remove HT lead from centre of distributor cap and verify that spark jumps to earth when engine is turned. If it does, the fault lies in the rotor arm, distributor cap, plug leads or plugs which should be checked in that order.

2  If no spark from coil HT lead check the LT circuit in the following order:

a) Disconnect LT lead from terminal 15 of coil and check that current is coming to the end of the lead. Touch the lead to the coil terminal when a small spark will indicate current. Otherwise use a bulb or voltmeter. (The ignition must of course be switched on.) If no current indicated check the wiring from the ignition switch.

b) Remove the distributor cap. Turn

**Engine starts readily but the performance is sluggish, no misfiring.**

1  Check the contact breaker points gap.
2  Check the plugs.
3  Check the ignition timing.
4  Check the fuel octane rating.

**Engine misfires, runs unevenly, cuts out at low revolutions only.**

1  Check the contact breaker gap (too large).
2  Check the plugs.
3  Check the fuel system (carburettor).
4  Check wear in distributor shaft.

**Engine misfires at high revolutions.**

1  Check the plugs.
2  Check the contact breaker gap (too small).
3  Check the fuel system (carburettor).
4  Check the distributor shaft for wear.

Some distributors have two vacuum connections - both of which should be on when setting the timing by stroboscope (Sec 6.11)

White deposits and damaged porcelain insulation
indicating overheating

Broken porcelain insulation due to bent central
electrode

Electrodes burnt away due to wrong heat value or
chronic pre-ignition (pinking)

Excessive black deposits caused by over-rich
mixture or wrong heat value

Mild white deposits and electrode burnt indicating
too weak a fuel mixture

Plug in sound condition with light greyish brown
deposits

# Chapter 5 Clutch and operating mechanism

## Contents

## Specifications

| | |
|---|---|
| Type   ... ... ... ... ... ... ... ... ... ... ... ... | Single dry plate diaphragm spring |
| Operation   ... ... ... ... ... ... ... ... ... ... ... | Mechanical - cable |
| Diameter   ... ... ... ... ... ... ... ... ... ... ... | 200 mm |
| Pedal free travel ... ... ... ... ... ... ... ... ... ... | 10 - 20 mm/0.4 - 0.8 in |

**Torque wrench settings**

| | |
|---|---|
| Clutch cover to flywheel screws ... ... ... ... ... ... | 18 lb ft/2.5 mkg |

## 1 General description

The clutch is a single disc design and incorporates a driven plate (which carries the friction material on each side) and a pressure plate and cover assembly. The pressure plate is tensioned by a diaphragm spring incorporated in the cover assembly.

The clutch operating lever pivots in the forward end of the gearbox casing and a thrust bearing on the inner end bears on to the ends of the three release fingers when the arm is operated. The operating arm is moved by a cable from the clutch pedal.

As the friction surfaces of the driven plate wear so the clearance between the thrust ring and release fingers decreases. This clearance is reflected in the free play movement of the clutch pedal. The movement can be adjusted by altering the length of the cable. This is effected by turning the adjuster nut fitted to the clutch end of the cable.

## 2 Clutch cable - removal, replacement and adjustment

1   Clutch cables rarely break and do not stretch significantly so if you find that the clutch is slipping and further adjustment is not possible the cause is the clutch friction plate. Do not think that the cable is at fault.

2   To remove the cable jack up the rear of the car and remove the left hand wheel. Unscrew the cable adjusting nut from the threaded end (photo).

3   If the cable inner only is to be removed it is not necessary to disturb the outer sheath. If the outer is being taken off as well then the mounting bracket bolted to the transmission casting should be taken off. Reassembly will then be much easier.

4   Inside the car it will be necessary to detach the foot pedal cluster assembly. On right hand drive cars this requires care and patience and the procedure is given in Chapter 9. The front end of the clutch cable is fitted with a square loop which hooks on to a bracket of the clutch pedal inside the tunnel and is drawn out with the foot pedal.

4   Having unhooked the front end of the cable it can be drawn out of the guide tube. A new cable can be fed into the tube in the same manner although it may be a bit of a fiddle to get it started as you are working partly blind. Make sure the cable is well greased and try and keep the grease off the interior trim and seats. The real difficulty comes when hooking the end on to the lever and reassembling the pedal cluster. This is covered in Chapter 9.

5   Once the cable has been connected properly at the front, and after the pedal cluster has been reassembled replace the cable through the operating lever at the other end and refit the adjusting nut.

6   When adjusting the clutch, the pedal is the indicating factor. The top of the pedal should move forward ½ inch (12 mm) before firmer resistance is felt. If it moves more than this the adjuster needs screwing up to shorten the cable. If it moves less then slacken the adjuster. When the adjustment is taken up all the way and the free play is excessive then the driven plate is in need of replacement. Sometimes after replacing a cable it is found that the threaded rear end is too short to reach the operating lever easily. This is because the other end is not properly engaged in the hook recess. With luck a bit of waggling back and forth on the clutch pedal will settle it in position.

7   Stiff or uneven operation of the clutch could be due to several factors. One check worth making before doing anything too drastic is on the cable cover between the rear end of the tunnel and on the transmission casing. The outer sleeve should have a bend in it and the lowest point of this bend should be between 1—1¾ inches (25—45 mm) from an imaginary straight line between the ends of the sleeve. The latitude is generous so the measurement is easy enough. Should there be a variation outside these limits (a most unusual occurrence unless the sleeve has been disconnected and wrongly refitted) adjustments can be made. Disconnect the inner cable from the clutch operating lever, on the transmission casing and add or remove washers to the shoulder of the sleeve as required.

8   In late 1971 (model year 9172) a grease nipple was incorporated in the cable outer under the rubber boot at the tunnel end. If squeaks occur a few shots from a grease gun should be given. Another clutch modification at around the same time resulted in the bend in the cable sleeve being increased to 70 mm. If the cable breaks on one of these types obtain the parts which will reduce the bend to the limits given in para 7.

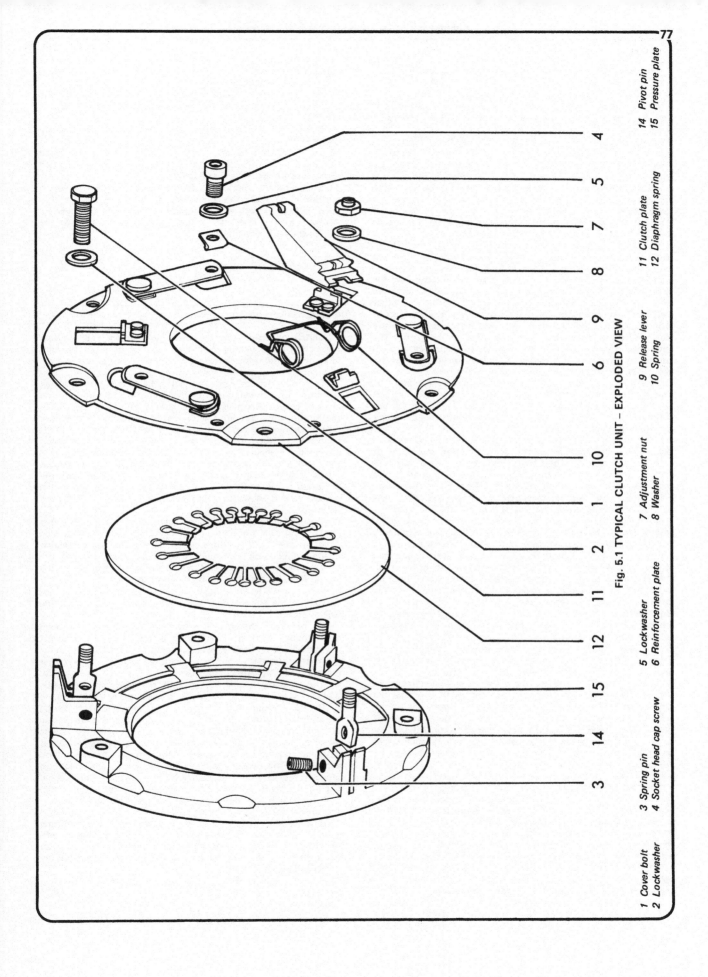

Fig. 5.1 TYPICAL CLUTCH UNIT – EXPLODED VIEW

1 Cover bolt
2 Lockwasher
3 Spring pin
4 Socket head cap screw
5 Lockwasher
6 Reinforcement plate
7 Adjustment nut
8 Washer
9 Release lever
10 Spring
11 Clutch plate
12 Diaphragm spring
14 Pivot pin
15 Pressure plate

## 3 Clutch assembly - removal, inspection and replacement

1   Remove the engine as described in Chapter 1.
2   Mark the flywheel and clutch cover with a punch so that they may be lined up on replacement if the old cover is being fitted again.
3   Working with a diagonal rotation slacken the six mounting screws which hold the clutch cover to the flywheel - slackening each one a little at a time until the tension is completely relieved. Lift off the cover and clutch driven plate.
4   The clutch driven plate should be inspected for wear and for contamination by oil. Wear is gauged by the depth of the rivet heads below the surface of the friction material. If this is less than 0.025 inch (0.6 mm) the linings are worn enough to justify renewal.
5   Examine the friction faces of the flywheel and clutch pressure plate. These should be bright and smooth. If the linings have worn too much it is possible that the metal surfaces may have been scored by the rivet heads. Dust and grit can have the same effect. If the scoring is very severe it could mean that even with a new clutch driven plate, slip and juddering and other malfunctions will recur. Deep scoring on the flywheel face is serious because the flywheel will have to be removed and machined by a specialist, or renewed. This can be costly. The same applies to the pressure plate in the cover although this is a less costly affair. If the friction linings seem unworn yet are blackened and shiny then the cause is almost certainly due to oil. Such a condition also requires renewal of the plate. The source of oil must be traced also. It will be due to a leaking seal on the transmission input shaft (Chapter 6 gives details of renewal) or on the front of the engine crankshaft (see Chapter 1 for details of renewal).
6   If the reason for removal of the clutch has been because of slip and the slip has been allowed to go on for any length of time it is possible that the heat generated will have adversely affected the diaphragm spring in the cover, with the result that the pressure is now uneven and/or insufficient to prevent slip, even with a new friction plate. It is recommended that under such circumstances a new assembly is fitted.
7   Although it is possible to dismantle the clutch cover assembly and, in theory, renew the various parts and levers the economics do not justify it. Clutch cover assemblies are available on an exchange basis. The component parts for their overhaul are held at the Central Reconditioning Depots and are not readily available at the Store Depots. It will probably be necessary to order an assembly in advance as most agencies other than the large Central Depots carry stocks only sufficient to meet their own requirements. However, it is possible to get assemblies from reputable manufacturers other than Volkswagen; Borg and Beck for instance.
8   If a new clutch cover is to be fitted make certain that there are no securing clips left in position. There may be no indications on the package so ask the supplier if any are fitted.
9   When replacing the clutch, hold the cover and support the friction disc on one finger through the centre. Be sure that the facing with radial lines goes towards the flywheel (the longer hub boss towards the cover), (photo). Position the cover so that the locating marks line up. If a new cover is being fitted it will be necessary to check whether there are any imbalance marks on either the flywheel or cover. On the flywheel this can be indicated by a 5 mm diameter countersunk hole or a white paint mark on the outer edge. On the clutch cover it would be indicated by a white paint mark on the outer edge. If only one (flywheel or cover) has an imbalance mark it does not matter how the cover is fitted. If both have marks make sure that they are 180° apart (ie, on opposite sides of the circle).
10 Replace the six securing bolts and screw them up evenly just enough to grip the friction plate but not enough to prevent it being moved. It is important to line up the central splined hub with the roller bearing in the counterbore of the flywheel locking bolt (photo). If this is not done it will be impossible to refit the engine to the transmission. It is possible to centralise them by

eye but a simple surer way is to select a suitable piece of bar or wooden dowel which will fit snugly into the flywheel nut and round which some adhesive tape can be wound to equal the diameter inside the friction plate boss. By inserting this the friction plate can be moved and centralised with sufficient accuracy.
11 Finally tighten up the six cover securing bolts evenly and diagonally a little each at a time to a final torque of 18 lb ft.
12 Before refitting the engine after a clutch overhaul check the transmission input shaft oil seal (Chapter 6) and the clutch release operating mechanism (see Section 5).
13 Before finally offering up the engine dust the splines of the gearbox input shaft (which should, of course, be clean and in good condition) with a little graphite or molybdenum powder. Also put a little molybdenum paste (not oil or grease) on the face of the release bearing.

## 4 Clutch release operating mechanism - inspection and repair

1   Clutch operation can be adversely affected if the release thrust ring and retaining springs are worn or damaged. Squeals, juddering, slipping or snatching could be caused partly or even wholly by this mechanism being worn.
2   Full examination is possible only when the engine has been removed and normally it is carried out when the clutch is in need of repair. The mechanism is contained in and attached to the transmission casing. Check first that the operating lever return spring mounted on the exterior of the shaft on the left hand side is not broken. If it is it can be renewed without removing the engine; once the lever has been disconnected from the cable and taken off the cross shaft. However, the damage which failure of this spring may have caused has probably occurred already. If you are going to examine the clutch anyway it will be easier to renew the spring after the engine is removed.
3   The clutch release bearing operates round a sleeve which is attached to the transmission casing. There is no thrust ring fitted in the centre of the clutch cover. The thrust bearing operates directly on to the ends of the three release levers.
4   With the engine removed examine the release bearing and the plastic face. It should spin silently and show no signs of wear or other damage. The retaining clips at each side must be a tight fit so that the bearing does not rattle about on the mounting forks (photo).
5   Do not wash the bearing in any cleaning fluid. It is sealed and although fluid may wash some grease out you cannot get any more in. If it needs renewal pull off the clips and lift it out.
6   When replacing the thrust release bearing fit the clips so that the ends point upwards (photo).
7   The cross shaft itself runs through the casing and should be freely moving and without any sign of slackness in the bushes.
8   If it is necessary to renew the bushes the cross shaft can be taken out after first taking the operating lever and return spring off the end of the shaft. Then remove the screw which locates the bush in the casing and remove all the components. When replacing the shaft lubricate well with molybdenum grease and ensure that the two concertina type grease seals are intact and properly seated inside the casing (photos). If one should come out on the inside of the casing make sure you get it put back. This bush takes considerable forces when the clutch is operated and should not be ignored or treated lightly.
9   When fitting a new return spring first remove the operating lever by undoing the circlip and taking it off the splined shaft. Fit the new spring so that the hooked end will eventually go round the lever and hold it back. Replace the lever and hook the spring end round it (photo).
10 Re-adjust the clutch pedal play after the engine has been replaced.

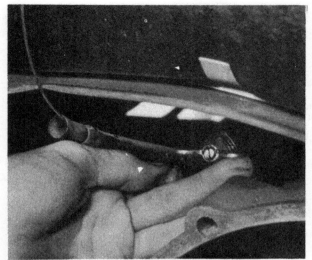
Clutch cable adjuster - engine is removed (Sec 2.2)

Replacing the driven plate and cover assembly (Sec 3.9)

Centre the clutch plate on the flywheel (Sec 3.10)

Clutch release thrust bearing (Sec 4.4)

View of thrust bearing attachment clips (Sec 4.6)

Fitting the clutch release shaft bush ... (Sec 4.8)

**5  Fault diagnosis**

| Symptom | Reason/s | Remedy |
| --- | --- | --- |
| Judder when taking up drive | Loose engine/gearbox mountings or over flexible mountings | Check and tighten all mounting bolts and replace any 'soft' or broken mountings. |
| | Badly worn friction surfaces or friction plate contaminated with oil carbon deposit | Remove engine and replace clutch parts as required. Rectify any oil leakage points which may have caused contamination. |
| | Worn splines in the friction plate hub or on the gearbox input shaft | Renew friction plate and/or input shaft. |
| | Badly worn roller bearings in flywheel centre for input shaft spigot | Renew roller bearings in flywheel gland nut. |
| Clutch spin (failure to disengage) so that gears cannot be meshed | Clutch actuating cable clearance too great | Adjust clearance. |
| | Clutch friction disc sticking because of rust on lining or splines (usually apparent after standing idle for some length of time) | As temporary remedy engage top gear, apply handbrake, depress clutch and start engine. (If very badly stuck engine will not turn). When running rev up engine and slip clutch until disengagement is normally possible. Renew friction plate at earliest opportunity. |
| | Damaged or misaligned pressure plate assembly | Replace pressure plate assembly. |
| Clutch slip - (increase in engine speed does not result in increase in car speed especially on hills) | Clutch pedal free play too little or non-existant resulting in partially disengaged clutch at all times | Adjust clearance. |
| | Clutch friction surfaces worn out (beyond further adjustment of operating cable) or clutch surfaces oil soaked | Replace friction plate and remedy source of oil leakage. |

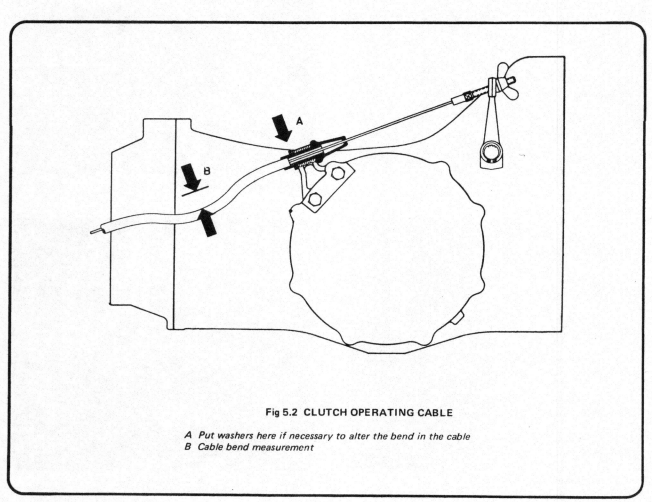

**Fig 5.2  CLUTCH OPERATING CABLE**

*A  Put washers here if necessary to alter the bend in the cable*
*B  Cable bend measurement*

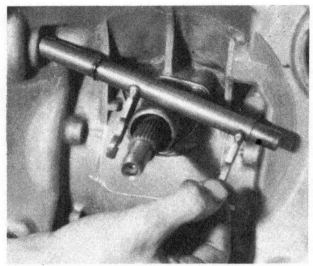

... followed by the shaft ... (Sec 4.8)

... and bearing sleeve and seals (Sec 4.8)

Make sure the bush and seal do not come out on the inside like this (Sec 4.8)

The locating screw for the bush and sleeve (Sec 4.8)

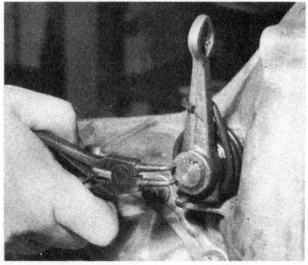

The release shaft operating lever showing circlip, splines and return spring (Sec 4.9)

# Chapter 6 Transmission and final drive

**Contents**

---

**Specifications**

---

**General**

Final drive and gearbox main casing is a one-piece tunnel type alloy casting

| | |
|---|---|
| Number of gears ... ... ... ... ... ... ... ... ... ... | 4 forward, 1 reverse |
| Synchromesh ... ... ... ... ... ... ... ... ... ... | Baulk ring on all forward gears |
| Oil capacity of casing ... ... ... ... ... ... ... ... | 3.0 litres/5.3 pints |
| Refill quantity ... ... ... ... ... ... ... ... ... ... | 2.5 litres/4.4 pints |

**Gear ratios**

| | |
|---|---|
| First ... ... ... ... ... ... ... ... ... ... ... ... | 3.80 : 1 |
| Second ... ... ... ... ... ... ... ... ... ... ... | 2.06 : 1 |
| Third ... ... ... ... ... ... ... ... ... ... ... ... | 1.26 : 1 |
| Fourth ... ... ... ... ... ... ... ... ... ... ... ... | 0.89 : 1 |
| Reverse ... ... ... ... ... ... ... ... ... ... ... | 3.61 : 1     3.80 : 1 from May 1972 |

**Final drive ratio**

| | |
|---|---|
| 1285 cc ... ... ... ... ... ... ... ... ... ... ... ... | 4.375 : 1 |
| 1594 cc ... ... ... ... ... ... ... ... ... ... ... ... | 4.125 : 1 |

**Torque wrench settings**

| | |
|---|---|
| Oil drain plugs ... ... ... ... ... ... ... ... ... ... | 14 lbs ft/ 2.0 mkg |
| Oil filter plug ... ... ... ... ... ... ... ... ... ... | 14 lbs ft/ 2.0 mkg |
| Transmission carrier to frame bolts ... ... ... ... ... | 166 lbs ft/23.0 mkg |
| Spring plate bolts/nuts ... ... ... ... ... ... ... ... | 72 lbs ft/10.0 mkg |
| Final drive cover nuts ... ... ... ... ... ... ... ... | 22 lbs ft/ 3.0 mkg |
| Gear change cover nuts ... ... ... ... ... ... ... ... | 11 lbs ft/ 1.5 mkg |
| Gear carrier to housing nuts ... ... ... ... ... ... ... | 14 lbs ft/ 2.0 mkg |
| Pinion bearing retainer ring ... ... ... ... ... ... ... | 108 lbs ft/22 mkg |
| Reverse lever guide screw ... ... ... ... ... ... ... | 14 lbs ft/ 2.0 mkg |
| Selector fork screws ... ... ... ... ... ... ... ... | 18 lbs ft/ 2.5 mkg |
| Pinion shaft round nut (ball bearings) ... ... ... ... ... | 87 lbs ft/12.0 mkg |
| (taper roller bearings) ... ... ... ... ... | 144 lbs ft/20.0 mkg |

---

## 1 General description

The gearbox and final drive is a one piece composite assembly housed in a single 'tunnel' type magnesium alloy die casting. Unlike the more orthodox design of gearbox which has an input and output shaft aligned on the same axis with a layshaft and gears below, the VW has an input shaft and output shaft only mounted alongside each other and each carrying a synchro

hub. This is because the input and output power is at the same end of each shaft. The output shaft incorporates the pinion gear which meshes with the crown wheel.

Synchromesh is used for all four forward speeds.

The whole assembly is mounted in the 'Y' of the floor frame — called the frame fork for obvious reasons — ahead of the engine. The differential unit and final drive, part of the assembly as already mentioned, come between the engine and the transmission gears.

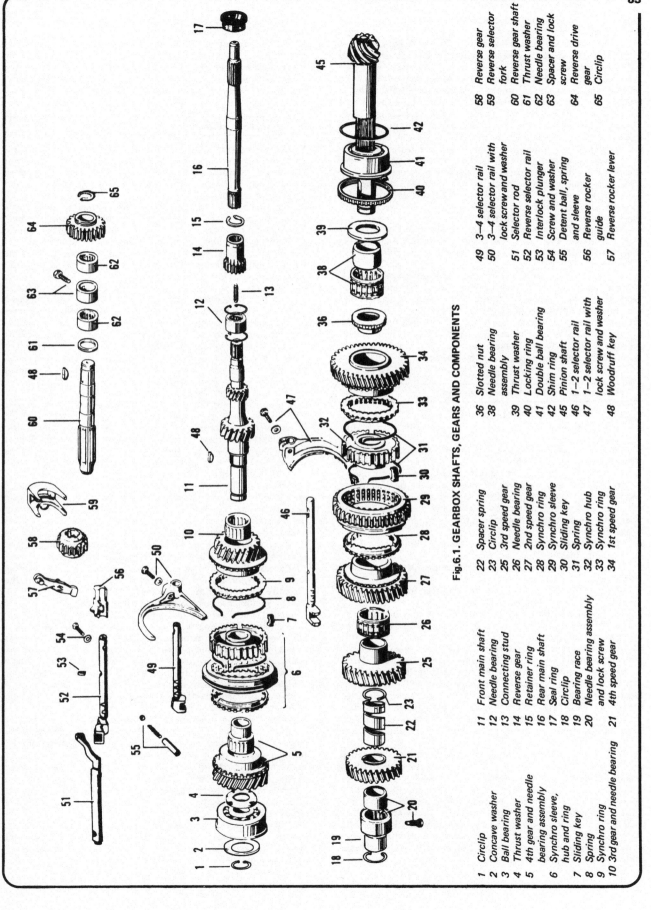

Fig.6.1. GEARBOX SHAFTS, GEARS AND COMPONENTS

1   Circlip
2   Concave washer
3   Ball bearing
4   Thrust washer
5   4th gear and needle bearing assembly
6   Synchro sleeve, hub and ring
7   Sliding key
8   Spring
9   Synchro ring
10  3rd gear and needle bearing

11  Front main shaft
12  Needle bearing
13  Connecting stud
14  Reverse gear
15  Retainer ring
16  Rear main shaft
17  Seal ring
18  Circlip
19  Bearing race
20  Needle bearing assembly and lock screw
21  4th speed gear

22  Spacer spring
23  Circlip
25  3rd speed gear
26  Needle bearing
27  2nd speed gear
28  Synchro ring
29  Synchro sleeve
30  Sliding key
31  Synchro hub
32  Synchro hub
33  Synchro ring
34  1st speed gear

36  Slotted nut
38  Needle bearing assembly
39  Thrust washer
40  Locking ring
41  Double ball bearing
42  Shim ring
45  Pinion shaft
46  1-2 selector rail
47  1-2 selector rail with lock screw and washer
48  Woodruff key

49  3-4 selector rail
50  3-4 selector rail with lock screw and washer
51  Selector rod
52  Reverse selector rail
53  Interlock plunger
54  Screw and washer
55  Detent ball, spring and sleeve
56  Reverse rocker guide
57  Reverse rocker lever

58  Reverse gear
59  Reverse selector fork
60  Reverse gear shaft
61  Thrust washer
62  Needle bearing
63  Spacer and lock screw
64  Reverse drive gear
65  Circlip

83

In order to dismantle the gearbox the differential must first be removed.

In view of the relative complexity of this complete unit, it is felt that a few words of warning should be given in order to let potential dismantlers fully realise what they may be letting themselves in for. First of all decide whether the fault you wish to repair is worth all the time and effort involved. Secondly, if the gearbox is in a very bad state then the cost of the component parts may well exceed the cost of a new replacement unit. Thirdly, remember that a basic knowledge of gearbox construction and function is a bare necessity before tackling this one. If you are doing one for the first time do not start on a Volkswagen!

Finally, two technical musts. You must be able to have access to the use of a press. So check this before you start. Make sure that you have made contact with an agent who is likely to be able to supply all the new gaskets and parts that may be required. It is not possible to work out exactly what may be required before you start but the minimum will be a gasket set, baulk rings and bearings so check that you can at least get these. The press is essential for dismantling the two shaft assemblies which is necessary if you want to replace the baulk rings.

If you have experience of earlier VW gearboxes there is another word of caution also. With the earlier models each gearshaft assembly was held together with a large locknut on the end of the shaft which was tightened to a specific torque. For production reasons these nuts have been replaced on later models by circlips used in conjunction with shims and special pressure washers which make assembly even more tricky. A selection of circlips and shims must be available.

## 2 Transmission - removal and replacement

1  Remove the engine as described in Chapter 1.
2  Detach the starter motor from the transmission casing if not already done.
3  Remove the cap screws securing the drive shaft inner flanges to the transmission on each side.
4  Remove the adjusting nut from the end of the clutch cable.
5  Lift up the back seat and remove the cover on the tunnel which is held by a single screw. Underneath will be seen a square headed screw securing the gear change rod to the gearbox lever. Cut the locking wire and undo the screw until the coupling is free (photo).
6  Undo the two nuts holding the transmission to the front mounting (photo).
7  Support the weight of the transmission, preferably on a trolley jack.
8  Remove the two large bolts at the rear which hold the transmission to the frame fork (photo).
9  Lower the transmission and draw it back and out (photo). Take care to support and balance it. If it drops heavily the casing could be damaged.
10  Replacement of the assembly is an exact reversal of the removal procedure. Note the following points. Refit the starter to the casing first (photo). When the unit is in position the mounting bolts at the rear should not be tightened until the nuts securing the flexible mountings have been slackened. Then tighten the two large bolts; next the two front mounting nuts and finally the four rear mounting nuts once more. This prevents distortion stresses being set up in the flexible rubber mountings.
11  The correct coupling of the gear shift to the shift operating rod is essential. Make sure that the point of the locking screw engages the dimple in the shaft exactly and re-lock the screw with wire. If it is found that gear selection is not quite satisfactory on completion it is in order to make minor adjustments to the position of the gear lever mounting. By slackening the two securing bolts the whole gear lever assembly can be moved a little in either a forward or rearward direction. If the assembly is moved forward engagement of 2nd and 4th gears is more positive. The same applies for the other two gears if it is moved

rearwards. This adjustment is intended to centralise the gear lever in the neutral position.
12  Do not forget to refill the transmission with the correct quantity and grade of oil. 5¼ pints are needed. This is more easily done from above before the engine is replaced. Make sure the two drain plug is tight and that the filler/level plug is slackened before putting the transmission back.

## 3 Transmission - dismantling

1  Before proceeding according to the directions given in this Section read the 'General description' Section first. Do not throw away gaskets when dismantling. They act as a guide when working out what new ones to use from the gasket set bought (see Reassembly Section).
2  Remove the sealing caps from the centres of the driving flanges by punching the blade of a screwdriver through them and levering them out.
3  Remove the circlip from round the splined shaft end. The flange can then be levered off the end of the shaft. Behind the flange is a spacer ring which may be taken off now or left until later (photo). Do the same on both sides.
4  Undo the nuts holding the cover on the left hand side and take it off. If necessary give it a few taps with a soft faced hammer to dislodge it. Do not use force. When the cover comes off the outer race of the taper roller side bearing race is moved from the side cover note that there are shims behind it which control the side bearing pre-load and pinion/crownwheel mesh.
5  If the casing is now turned over carefully the differential assembly can be taken out. Take care not to drop it and put it somewhere where it will not be damaged.
6  Remove the right hand cover from the casing.
7  From the front of the casing remove the three screws securing the sleeve round the input shaft.
8  Inside the differential casing release the circlip which locates the splined collar/reverse gear to the input shaft (photo). Slide it back along the shaft and slide the collar along behind it. The rear end of the shaft may now be unscrewed from the other half. Then take off the collar/gear and remove the circlip from the shaft also. The shaft may then be drawn out through the oil seal. It will be as well to replace this oil seal but if not take care not to damage it. (Note that this oil seal can be renewed with the transmission unit installed in the car. Access can be gained once the engine is removed.)
9  At the front of the gearbox remove the nuts holding the gear selector lever housing and remove the housing and lever.
10  Remove the nuts from the studs which secure the end casing (called the gear carrier) to the main casing and take off the braided earth strap at the same time.
11  The pinion shaft bearing is held into the casing by means of a castellated locking ring (see photo 3.8), (earlier gearboxes had four screws). This ring is normally undone with a special tool but careful use of a hammer and chisel can achieve the same results. First mark the position of the ring in relation to the casing so that you may re-tighten it to the same position. Then a couple of smart taps with the chisel against one of the castellations will slacken it enough to be unscrewed by hand. Be warned — if the chisel slips and chips a gear tooth then you are in the high price repair business!
12  Once the ring is removed the whole gearbox assembly is ready to come out of the casing. This can be achieved by using a heavy copper faced mallet and striking the end of the pinion. Another way is to insert a scissor jack shallow enough to fit between the pinion and the casing opposite (photo). Pad the head of the jack against the pinion and press it out. Be sure to support the gear carrier when the gear shafts come away. As soon as it is clear, be sure to collect any shim(s) from the pinion flange.
13  The main casing has two needle roller bearings still left in it. One has the reverse gear and shaft running in it. The gear and shaft may be removed together. They may be secured by a circlip or a locating screw through the casing.

Undoing the gearshift rod coupling screw (Sec 2.5)

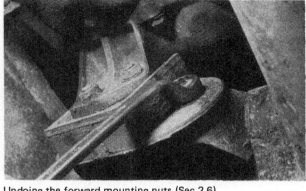
Undoing the forward mounting nuts (Sec 2.6)

Removing the rear mounting bolts (Sec 2.8)

Lowering the transmission on a trolley jack (Sec 2.9)

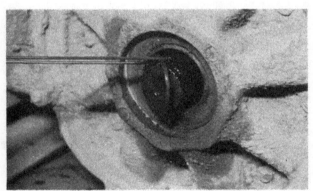
Hooking out the spacer ring with a piece of wire (Sec 3.3)

Releasing the circlip holding the reverse gear sleeve. Note locking ring for pinion bearing (arrowed) referred to in paragraph 11 (Sec 3.8)

Forcing out the pinion shaft with a scissor jack (Sec 3.12)

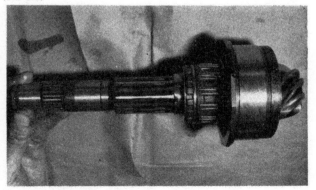
Pinion shaft (Sec 5b.1)

14 Similarly, the other needle bearing outer race (no spacer) is secured by a screw in the casing. Once this is removed the needle roller bearing race may be drifted out. (This bearing is the one that supports the rear end of the forward half of the input shaft.)

15 The large side bearings, which will be located on the differential, may remain where they care unless inspection indicates that they are worn and need renewal. They can be drifted off the differential.

16 So far, the dismantling process has been relatively straightforward. Now is the time to stop and reassemble if you are getting cold feet! The next step is to separate the two shafts with their clusters of gears from the gear carrier. To renew the baulk rings - which is one of the usual remedies for a less than perfect synchromesh action - this further dismantling is necessary.

17 Both gear shafts are held into their bearings by circlips. The bearings are a press fit in the carrier but not from the side. The input shaft bearing has to be taken out from the outside of the casing. The circlip retaining the shaft must therefore, be removed so that the shaft may be taken out of the bearing. This circlip is under tension from a dished thrust washer underneath and is liable to 'fly' when released from its groove. So take care and cover the end with a cloth when releasing it. The pinion shaft bearing will come out from either side after the locating bolt is removed.

18 Before moving the shafts from the carrier the selector forks must be taken off. Before any is moved in relation to their rails mark them carefully so that they can be refitted in exactly the same place. This setting is very critical and if wrong will cause selection problems and jumping out of gear.

19 Remove the small sliding gear and fork (reverse) from the pivot on the reverse lever.

20 Next loosen the clamping bolts which hold the two other selector forks to their respective rails. The fork for 1st and 2nd gear selection on the output (pinion) shaft can be lifted away after the rail has been drawn back sufficiently far. The other fork is shrouded by the gear carrier and is not lifted out at this stage. The rail for this one should be driven back far enough to free it from the fork. Do NOT drive the rails out of the gear carrier. If you do a lot of extra work will be caused, probably unnecessarily, because the detent balls and springs will be released.

21 The two shafts with their clusters of gears may now be removed from the carrier. It is a good plan to hold both together with a strong elastic band or a few turns of self-adhesive tape. Then, when the ends of the shaft are released, they will not fall about the place. Two pairs of hands are needed. One pair should hold the carrier - with the shafts hanging down whilst another person strikes the end of the input shaft with a soft faced mallet and supports the weight of the gear shafts as they are driven out. Do not let them drop down.

22 Once the shafts are clear of the carrier the bearings may be removed. The main (input) shaft front bearing is driven out from the inside of the carrier. This particular ball bearing is flanged on the outer race and will only come out in one direction.

23 To dismantle the input shaft first take off the thrust washer then 4th gear together with the needle bearing cage on which it runs. Remove the baulk ring. This leaves the inner race on the shaft. To get this off a press will be needed and the 'V' blocks should be suitably positioned to provide support behind the 3rd gear wheel. In this way there will be no danger of damage to the shaft or gears and the synchro hub assembly will be kept together. Make sure that all parts are supported and held whilst being pressed. 3rd gear may then be taken off together with its needle roller bearing. The 3rd gear bearing inner race need not be removed nor the key which locates the synchro hub. Keep the baulk rings with their respective gears for future reference - fix them with adhesive tape to prevent muddling.

24 The output (pinion) shaft should only be dismantled to a limited extent - which is sufficient to remove the gears, synchro hub and baulk rings. The pinion double taper roller bearing which is held by the notched locking nut should be left intact

as this requires the use of more special tools to which we do not feel most owners will have ready access. The services of a press may be required in order to carry out the partial dismantling necessary to remove the baulk rings although if properly supported the shaft may be driven out of the synchro hub with a heavy soft faced mallet.

25 First remove the circlip from the end of the shaft. The inner race of the needle bearing together with 4th gear may then be driven or pressed off together. Support the gear and then press or drive out the shaft.

26 Remove the spacer spring and then take off the other circlip round the shaft.

27 Third gear, the roller bearing, 2nd gears and 1st/2nd gear synchro hub and baulk rings may then be taken off in that order.

28 The synchro hub assemblies should be handled with care to prevent them coming apart inadvertently. It is important that if the centre hub and outer sleeve are separated that they be refitted in the same relative position. Some hubs have marks etched on each part to aid reassembly, so before anything else examine them on both sides for such marks. If none can be found make some of your own with a small dab of paint to ensure reassembly in the same position. To dismantle the hubs first lift out the spring retaining clip on each side. Then carefully slide the sleeve from the hub taking care not to drop and lose the three sliding keys.

29 Do not remove the selector fork rails from the gear carrier casing unless inspection indicates that there is something wrong with the detent balls and springs.

## 4 Inspection for wear in transmission components

1 As mentioned in the introduction to this Chapter the degree of wear in the components will to a large extent dictate the economics of repair or replacement with a new unit. If the crownwheel and pinion is obviously badly worn, resulting in noise and significant backlash, then it is possible that this may be repaired alone for approximately half the cost of a new unit provided that is the only major complaint. Such work is not within the competence of the average owner and this manual does not cover it.

2 Having been able to obtain the use of a simple mechanical press it is possible to remove all baulk rings for examination. The grooved taper face of the ring provides the braking action on the mating face of the gear wheel cone and if the ridges are worn the braking or synchro action will be less effective. The only way to determine the condition effectively is by comparison with new parts. As the parts are relatively cheap it is considered foolish not to renew them all anyway once the gearbox is dismantled. As a guide, when a baulk ring is fitted over its cone on the gear wheel there should be a minimum gap of 0.6 mm (0.024 inch) between the baulk ring and the gear teeth. The normal gap is 1.1 mm (0.043 inch) so it is obvious that if the gap is near the lowest limit new rings should be fitted. When obtaining new baulk rings make sure that you get the Parts Store to identify and mark each one according to its appropriate gear. Modifications have taken place and although the new ones will still fit and work they are not necessarily identical to the ones you take out. So if you muddle them up you could get problems. They are also not all the same in the set - some have wider cut-outs for example. So mark the new ones you get carefully.

3 Two types of bearings are fitted - ball and needle roller. As a rule needle roller bearings wear very little, not being subject to end thrust of any sort. Check them in position and if there are signs of roughness then they should be renewed. If any bearing should feel the slightest bit rough or show any sign of drag or slackness when revolved then it should be renewed. The double taper roller bearing should be similarly checked. If there is any sign of roughness or endfloat then this is a task for a specialist. If this bearing is needing renewal the condition of the

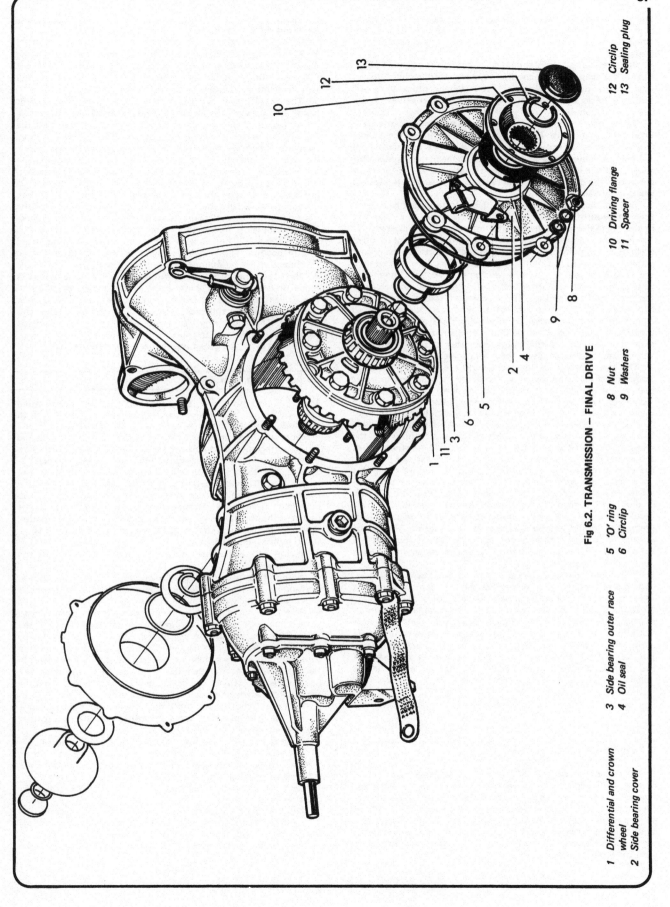

**Fig 6.2. TRANSMISSION – FINAL DRIVE**

1 Differential and crown wheel
2 Side bearing cover
3 Side bearing outer race
4 Oil seal
5 'O' ring
6 Circlip
8 Nut
9 Washers
10 Driving flange
11 Spacer
12 Circlip
13 Sealing plug

pinion gear and crownwheel must be very carefully examined. Once these need renewal then the setting of the whole box is altered and clearances and shims have to be re-calculated and changed.

4   The teeth of all gears should be examined for signs of pitted mating surfaces, chips or scoring. It must be appreciated that if one gear is damaged then its mate on the other shaft will probably be as bad and that one way or another a new pair of gears will be required.

5   The synchro hubs should be assembled for checking. It is important that there is no rock or backlash on the splines between the inner hub and outer sleeve. When the baulk rings are being renewed it is good policy to renew the three sliding keys and their locating spring rings as well. The keys fit into the cut-outs in the baulk rings and are subject to wear and the springs weaken with time.

6   One of the most critical parts of the Volkswagen gearbox is the operation of the selector forks. The two forks run in grooves in the outer sleeves of the synchro hubs and if the clearance of the forks in the grooves is excessive then there is a likelihood of certain gears jumping out. The clearance of the fork in the groove should not exceed 0.3 mm (0.012 inch). Clearance in excess of the maximum could be due to wear on the fork or in the groove or both. It is best therefore first of all to take the forks along to the spares supplier and ask him to compare their thickness with new ones. If the difference in thickness is not enough to compensate for the excess gap between fork and hub groove then the hub assembly will need replacement as well. This is an expensive item but as the gap is somewhat critical there is no alternative. Much depends on the total degree of wear.

7   The selector rails on which the forks are mounted need not be removed from the casing. A certain force is needed in order that they overcome the pressure of the spring loaded ball in the groove. This can be measured with a spring balance hooked on to the end of each selector fork. If the required pull is significantly outside the range of 15–20 kgs (33–44 lbs) then it is advisable to check the detent springs and balls. To do this push the selector rods right out of the casing. This will release the ball and spring but to get the springs out it is necessary to prise out the plastic plugs from the drillings opposite. Before doing this make sure you obtain some new plugs to drive in when re-assembling. Check the spring free length which should be 25 mm (1 inch). If less than 22 mm they should be changed. The balls should be free from pitting and grooves and the selector rods themselves should not be a sloppy fit in the bores. The detent grooves in the rails should not be worn. When the rails are removed do not lose the interlock plungers which fit between the selector rod grooves.

9   Examine all parts of the casing for signs of cracks or damage, particularly near the bearing housings and on the mating surfaces where the gear carrier and side bearing plates join.

10  It should not normally be necessary to completely wash all the gearbox components in fluid. Wipe components on clean cloth for examination. In this way the likelihood of dry spots during the first moments of use after reassembly are minimised. The casing itself should be thoroughly washed out with paraffin and flushed afterwards with water. Do not leave the needle roller bearings in position when doing this.

## 5  Transmission reassembly - general

Spend time in preparing plenty of clean, clear space and if your work bench is rough cover it with hardboard or paper for a good non-gritty surface. Do not start until you have all the necessary parts and gaskets assembled and make sure that all the ones you have obtained are going to fit. Gasket sets often contain items covering a variety of models so you will not need them all - this is why it helps to keep the old gaskets you take off until the job is eventually finished.

## 5a  Input shaft - reassembly

1   First reassemble the input shaft, beginning by putting the needle roller cage for 3rd gear in position on the shaft. Then put 3rd gear with its matching synchro ring onto the roller bearings with the cone towards the front end of the shaft.

2   The 3rd/4th gear synchro hub assembly goes on next. This has to line up with the key in the shaft. Once the keyway in the centre part of the hub is lined up with the key in the shaft the hub can be driven on using a suitable piece of tube and heavy hammer. There are three very important points to note when doing this. Make sure that the hub is on the right way round - some models have a groove in the outer sleeve 1 mm deep and this must be towards the front end of the shaft. If there is no indication then you may put the hub on either way round. Secondly, make sure that you only drive the centre part of the hub. Otherwise it will come apart and have to be reassembled. Thirdly, the slots in the baulk ring must be lined up with the keys in the hub. This is best done by someone holding the baulk ring in position with the keys whilst the hub is driven on the final amount. Be careful not to trap any fingers!

3   Next the inner race for the 4th gear needle roller bearing has to be driven on to the shaft in the same manner that the hub was driven on before it. Drive it right down to the hub. Then replace the needle roller cage followed by the baulk ring and 4th gear. The baulk ring also has three cut-outs which engage with the sliding keys in the hub.

4   Finally, place the thrust washer on the end of the shaft.

## 5b  Pinion shaft - reassembly

1   As pointed out earlier, the pinion shaft has been dismantled only as far as the pinion bearing which has been left in position (photo). If this bearing has been renewed then the gearbox and final drive will need resetting and this is a skilled job requiring special equipment and a selection of special shims to hand from which the necessary requirements are available.

2   The first 'loose' item therefore which goes behind the pinion is the shim (if any) controlling endfloat. The endfloat is measured by a feeler gauge after the 1st gear and synchro hub have been fitted. The measurement is between the face of the gear and the thrust washer which is locked in front of the pinion taper roller bearing. The measurement range is from 0.10 – 0.025 mm/0.004 - 0.010 ins.

3   If the gap is outside this range then the shims must be altered to suit.

4   Now put 1st gear (the largest one with helically cut teeth) in position on the needle roller bearings with the cone face of the synchro pointing away from the pinion gear (photo).

5   Select the 1st gear baulk ring and place it over 1st gear and then replace the 1st and 2nd gear hub over the splines on the shaft with the selector fork groove of the outer sleeve facing towards the front end of the shaft (photo). Make sure that the three cut-outs in the synchro ring engage with the sliding keys in the hub before pushing the hub fully home. Remember that the baulk rings for 1st and 2nd gears are slightly different. That for 1st gear has narrower cut-outs than those in the 2nd gear ring.

6   Now check the 1st gear endfloat as mentioned in paragraph 2.

7   Put the 2nd gear baulk ring in position in the hub so that the slots engage with the sliding keys.

8   Replace 2nd gear with the cone towards the hub (photo).

9   Third gear, which has a large bearing boss integral with it, should now be replaced with the needle roller bearing which fits together with 3rd gear, inside 2nd gear (photo).

10  Next fit the circlip on the shaft retaining third gear in position (photo).

11  The clearance between this gear and the circlip should be 0.10 – 0.25 mm/.004 – .010 ins. If the gap is outside this range then a circlip of different thickness is necessary to correct it.

12  Next fit the spacer spring, 4th gear and the inner race of the roller bearing (photo).

Fitting first gear on the pinion shaft (Sec 5b.4)

Fitting first/2nd gear clutch hub (Sec 5b.5)

Fitting 2nd gear and baulk ring (Sec 5b.8)

Fitting 3rd gear and roller bearing (Sec 5b.9)

Fit 3rd gear retaining circlip (Sec 5b.10)

Fitting the spacer spring, 4th gear and the bearing inner race (Sec 5b.12)

Driving on the bearing race with the circlip (Sec 5b.13)

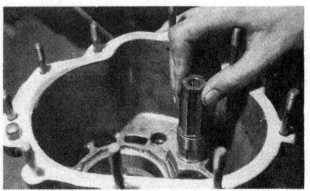

Installing reverse gear drive shaft (Sec 5c.1)

13 In order to drive the race and gear onto the shaft select a tube or socket of the required diameter. When the race is nearly fully on, put the circlip in position also and drive that on with it until it reaches the groove (photo).

### 5c  Main casing - installing needle bearings and reverse gearshaft

1  Two sets of needle roller bearings are fitted at the rear end of the main casing. One set comprises two roller cages and a spacer between and in this the reverse drive shaft runs. Drive one cage into the casing with a socket on an extension or suitable drift so that it is flush with one end of the bore. The metal face of the needle cage end should face inwards. The spacer should then be inserted with its slot so lined up that it will engage with the locking bolt which is screwed in through the side of the casing. Put the locking bolt in position and then drive the other needle roller bearing into the other end of the bore. Alternatively the bearings and spacer can be assembled to the shaft and put into the casing as an assembly (photo).
2  The gear may then be fitted to the other end and the circlip replaced (photo).
3  The other bearing supports the rear end of the input shaft front half. Fit the single needle roller cage into the bore so that the circular recess in the outer race will line up with the lock screw hole in the casing. Tap it into position and replace and tighten the lock screw. On later models the lock screw is dispensed with and a circlip retains the bearing at each end.

### 5d  Gear carrier - fitting bearings

1  The needle roller bearing for the forward end of the pinion shaft should be lined up so that the hole for the locking screw corresponds with the recess in the bearing (photo). Tap it into position and fit the locking screw.
2  The special ball bearing with the flange outer race should then be fitted into position from the outside of the carrier casing (photo).

### 5e  Gear carrier - refitting shafts and selector forks

1  It is assumed that the selector rails are in order (see Section 4, paragraph 7) and the forks are a correct fit in the hub sleeve grooves (Section 4, paragraph 6).
2  The first task is to fit the two shafts into the gear carrier. First of all place the two assemblies together and hold them with strong elastic bands or adhesive tape (photo).
3  As an alternative the input shaft can be placed in position by itself first, whichever method is used the selector fork for 3rd/4th gear must be fitted in position on the synchro unit. It cannot be fitted afterwards. Note that the curve of the fork shrouds the rear part of the hub (photo). When putting the shaft(s) in position the rail for the selector fork is engaged and care must be taken to see that the fork does not jam on the rail as it moves in.
4  If the pinion shaft is not put in together with the input shaft the bearing should be taken out of the casing. The shaft assembly may then be put in position (photo).
5  After that the bearing can be fitted in position round the shaft (photo).
6  With the shafts in position in the carrier the concave washer and circlip should be fitted to the end of the input shaft. Use a socket to drive the circlip against the washer and spring it into the groove (photo).
7  Next fit the selector pad and relay lever for reverse gear onto the rail (photo).
8  The fork for 1st/2nd gear may then be positioned (photo).
9  The selector forks setting is critical. If the wear between the fork and groove is outside the limit the possibility of a gear not being fully engaged and jumping out is increased. If you can get the unit set up in a Volkswagen agent's jig you would be well

advised to do so.
10  Provided you have clearly marked the fork positions on the rails there need be no difficulty either although if new forks or hubs have been fitted the markings may no longer apply.
11  If you have no marks and no jig facility handy proceed as follows. Start with the forks loose on the rails. Set all three selector rails in the neutral position, which is when the cut-outs in their ends all line up, and set the synchro hub outer sleeves also in neutral with the forks in position. Then tighten the fork clamp bolts sufficiently to prevent them slipping. Now push each selector in turn so that each gear is fully engaged. The outer sleeve of the appropriate synchro hub must move fully over the dogs of the baulk ring and gear in question. In each gear selected the fork must not bind in the groove. If difficulty is experienced in engaging a gear slacken the fork clamp nut and get the synchro hub sleeve fully into mesh and then retighten the fork clamp in position. Then move the selector back to neutral and into the opposite gear position. In all three positions there must be no semblance of pressure in either direction from the fork on to the groove in which it runs. When both forward speed selector forks have been correctly set tighten the clamp bolts to 18 ft lbs/2.5 mkg.
12  The sliding reverse gear and yokes can be attached to the relay lever next for setting purposes. It will tend to fall out of position because it is finally held by the reverse gear shaft in the main transmission casing.
13  To set this pinion first engage 2nd gear. Hold the pinion square and in this position it should be lined up midway between the straight cut teeth on the synchro sleeve and the helical teeth of 2nd gear on the input shaft (photo). Then move out of 2nd gear and shift into reverse. The reverse gears should mesh completely. Adjust as necessary by sliding the block along the selector rail. It is most unlikely that the relay lever pivot post is incorrect but as a check the distance from the centre of the eye to the face of the gear carrier should be 38.6 mm + or − 0.4 mm. On later models (from early 1972) this dimension altered to 40.6 mm (+ or − 0.4 mm).

### 5f  Gear carrier - assembly to main casing

1  The main casing should be ready with bearings and reverse gear shaft installed.
2  Fit the pinion setting shims in position on the face of the flange (photo). Put a dab of grease on the shim to prevent it falling off later.
3  Place a new gasket over the studs on the casing, having made sure that no traces of old gasket are left and that the two mating surfaces are quite clean and smooth
4  Make sure that the reverse sliding gear is not forgotten. It can be prevented from dropping out if reverse gear is engaged (photo).
5  It is best to fit the gear carrier to the casing with the casing standing upright. There are two points to watch:

a)  See that the pinion shims stay put.
b)  See that the splined reverse gear shaft lines up with and goes into the sliding reverse gear.

6  Provided the foregoing points are watched carefully the whole unit will drop into place quite easily and a few final taps with a soft mallet will butt the mating faces together. If for any reason something 'solid' is encountered while replacing the assembly stop and look. Do not force anything. Remember the points mentioned and take care with the lining up (photo).
7  When the assembly is fully home turn the casing on its side and refit the castellated locking ring (photo). The locking ring may be tightened with careful use of a hammer and suitable drift. Tighten it as far as the marks made prior to slackening it.
8  Replace the carrier nuts, noting that one carries the earth strap (photo). Tighten them all evenly to a torque of 14 ft lbs (2 mkg). Turn the shafts to ensure they turn freely and select all gears in turn.

Fitting the gear and circlip (Sec 5c.2)

Fitting the pinion shaft bearing into the gear carrier (Sec 5d.1)

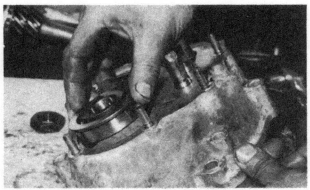

Fitting the input shaft bearing into the gear carrier (Sec 5d.2)

Hold both shaft assemblies together with tape (Sec 5e.2)

3rd/4th gear selector fork position (Sec 5e.3)

Putting the pinion shaft into the carrier (Sec 5e.4)

Fitting the pinion shaft bearing after fitting the shaft (Sec 5e.5)

Driving on the input shaft circlip against the concave washer (Sec 5e.6)

Reverse gear selector pad and relay lever (Sec 5e.7)

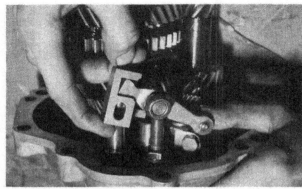

Position 1st/2nd gears selector fork (Sec 5e.8)

Assemble reverse sliding gear and yoke (Sec 5e.13)

Position the pinion setting shims (Sec 5f.2)

Reverse sliding gear held in engagement (Sec 5f.4)

Putting the gear carrier into the casing (Sec 5f.6)

Replace the castellated locking ring (Sec 5f.7)

Replace the nuts and braided earthing strap (Sec 5f.8)

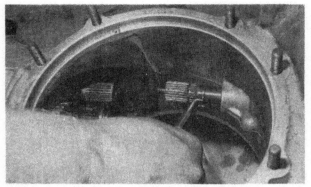
Putting the circlip on the input shaft (Sec 5f.10)

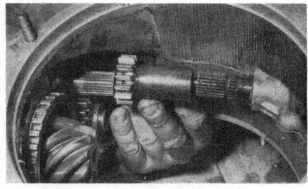
Putting the gear sleeve onto the splines (Sec 5f.11)

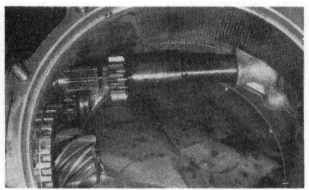
Screw the rear extension into the input shaft (Sec 5f.12)

Fit the sleeve over the input shaft extension (Sec 5f.13)

A new gasket for the gear shift housing (Sec 5g.1)

Engage the lever in the cut-outs ... (Sec 5g.4a)

.. and replace the housing (Sec 5g.4b)

Fit a new 'O' ring on the side covers (Sec 5h.3)

9  The front section of the input shaft is now ready for install-ation. Oil the land in the centre which will run in the oil seal and see that the small link stud is screwed into the end of the shaft. Then carefully insert the shaft through the oil seal from the rear of the main casing.

10  Once through, fit the circlip - preferably a new one - over the splines and past the groove onto the smooth part of the shaft (photo).

11  Put the reverse gear/splined sleeve onto the shaft, plain end first (photo).

12  Then screw the shaft stud into the end of the protruding input shaft (photo). Screw it in as far as it will go and then come back one spline in order to let the splined collar engage both halves of the shaft. Do not under any circumstances engage the sleeve with the ends of the shafts butted tight together. Move the sleeve forward so that the gears engage and then move the circlip back along the shaft so that it engages fully into the groove.

13  Replace the sleeve over the front of the shaft (photo).

## 5g  Gear shift housing - reassembly

1  Clean up the mating surfaces on the end of the gear carrier and shift housing and place a new gasket in position over the studs in the gear carrier

2  See that the gearbox is in neutral by checking that the cut-outs in the ends of the three selector rods are lined up.

3  The gear change lever in the housing should be an easy slide fit in the housing. If it is sloppy in any way it could cause jamming or other problems of changing gear.

4  Fit the housing over the studs, at the same time fiddling the lever so that the end locates in the cut-outs of the ends of the three selector rails (photos).

5  Replace the nuts and tighten to 11 ft lbs (1.5 mkg).

## 5h  Differential and side covers - replacement

1  Ensure that all parts are scrupulously clean.

2  If new bearings have to be fitted (necessitating driving the old ones off the differential casing and moving the outer races from the side covers) it should be borne in mind that the new bearings will require re-shimming in order to obtain the correct bearing pre-load and pinion gear backlash. It is most unusual for the taper roller bearings to need replacement other than as part of a complete rebuild. As mentioned earlier, the setting up of the differential to the correct clearances and pre-loads - which are essential if quiet running and long life are desired) is a skilled job requiring special measuring equipment designed for this particular transmission. It is assumed therefore, that the original bearings are being refitted.

3  The right hand bearing cover is fitted first. First fit a new 'O' ring (photo). Place the cover in position making sure that the mating faces of both cover and casing are perfectly clean and free from burrs. Do not use any gaskets (on the latest models this cover plate is no longer a separate item, being cast integrally with the casing).

4  With the cover securely in position carefully lower the differential casing into the transmission housing with the crownwheel teeth facing inwards (photo).

5  Replace the left hand cover - also fitted with a new 'O' ring (photo). No gasket should be used - the photo shows a gasket incorrectly placed.

6  Replace the spacer ring over the shaft (photo).

7  Put the driving flange onto the shaft (photo).

8  Fit the circlip over the end of the shaft and tap it into the groove using a socket of suitable diameter (photos).

9  Refit a new sealing plug (photo).

## 6  Synchromesh hub assemblies - dismantling, inspection and reassembly

1  Unless the transmission is the victim of neglect or misuse, or has covered very high mileages, the synchro hub assemblies do not normally need replacement. Until recently they could only be replaced as complete assemblies but it should be possible to obtain the inner or outer section as required.

2  When synchro baulk rings are being renewed it is advisable to fit new blocker bars (sliding keys) and retaining springs in the hubs as this will ensure that full advantage is taken of the new, unworn cut-outs in the rings.

3  When a synchro hub is dismantled, intentionally or acciden-tally, there are some basic essentials to remember:

a)  The splines of both parts wear into each other and provided neither is worn too far they should be kept matched if possible.

b)  Where the three sliding keys fit there is a recess in the centre of the spline on the outer sleeve (photo). It is essential, for correct operation, that these be lined up.

c)  Make sure that the sliding key retainer clips overlap on each side so that no key has the ends of both clips over it.

4  When examining for wear there are two important features to look at:

a)  The fit of the splines. With the keys removed, the inner and outer sections of the hub should slide easily with minimum backlash or axial rock. The degree of permissible wear is difficult to describe in absolute terms. No movement at all is exceptional yet excessive 'slop' would affect operation and cause jumping out of gear. Ask someone with experience for advice. If a new part is being fitted to a worn part check the fit in each  of the possible positions radially and also either way round to find the point of minimum play.

b)  Selector fork grooves and selector forks should not exceed the maximum permissible clearance of 0.3 mm (0.012 inch). The wear can be on either the fork or groove so it is best to try a new fork in the existing sleeve first to see if the gap is reduced adequately. If not, then a new sleeve is needed. Too much slack between fork and groove induces jumping out of gear. Where a hub also carries gear teeth on the outer sleeve these should, of course, be in good condition - unbroken and not pitted or scored.

## 7  Input shaft oil seal - removal and replacement

1  It is possible that clutch contamination may be caused by failure of the oil seal that goes round the input shaft in the transmission casing. During the course of transmission overhaul it would be automatically renewed but it is possible to fit a new one with the transmission installed. The engine must be removed first.

2  With the engine removed detach the clutch release bearing from the operating forks and remove the sleeve from round the input shaft by undoing the three nuts.

3  The seal surrounds the input shaft where it goes through the casing. It can be dug out with a sharp pointed instrument provided care is taken to avoid damaging the surrounding part of the transmission casing.

4  A new seal should be treated with sealing compound on the outside rim (taking care to prevent the compound getting anywhere else on the seal) and then placed in position with the inner lip of the seal facing into the transmission. Be careful not to damage the lip when passing it over the splines of the shaft and make sure it does not turn back when it reaches the part of the shaft on which it bears.

5  It should be driven into position squarely and a piece of tube is ideal for this put round the shaft (photo). If the seal should tip in the early stages of being driven in take it out and start again. Otherwise it may be badly distorted and its life will

Inserting the differential assembly (Sec 5h.4)

Replacing the cover. No gasket should be fitted, despite what shows in the photograph (Sec 5h.5)

Insert the spacer ring (Sec 5h.6)

Replace the driving flange (Sec 5h.7)

Put the circlip over the shaft (Sec 5h.8a)

Drive the circlip on with a socket (Sec 5h.8b)

Fit a new sealing plug (Sec 5h.9)

The indented splines in the sleeve must line up with the sliding keys (Sec 6.3b)

be shortened considerably.

6   The seal should be driven in until the outer shoulder abuts the casing.

## 8  Differential gears

1   The differential gear contained in the differential casing is not normally a do-it-yourself repair job. This is because failure is extremely rare and in circumstances of extreme wear as a result of either neglect or high mileages the whole assembly would need to be renewed anyway.

2   The function of the differential is to enable the driven wheels of the vehicle to rotate at different speeds when the car is turning and the outer wheel is obliged to travel in a wider area than the inner wheel. Each drive shaft has a bevel gear at the inner end and these are meshed constantly together with two bevel pinions. The shaft on which both pinions are mounted is fixed into the differential casing.

3   The crownwheel, which takes the drive from the gearbox, is bolted to the differential casing. When the drive rotates the differential casing, the pinion shaft is carried round with it and the pinion gears therefore rotate the drive shaft gears.

4   If either drive shaft is slowed down, or stopped completely, the differential pinions rotate on their own shafts due to the speed difference between the drive shafts.

5   Under such circumstances the power must be transmitted through the shaft offering least resistance. In cornering this would be the outer wheel. When you have one wheel in a ditch the power always goes to that wheel!

## 9  Limited slip differential (plate type)

Limited slip differential is fitted to cars where the terrain they have to cover requires both drive wheels to be able to give traction simultaneously.

Inside the differential casing there are two differential pinion shafts instead of one and these are not set in the casing direct. The casing transfers the drive to the pinion shafts by means of what is in effect a multiplate clutch. One set of plates is splined to the drive shaft gears and the others to the casing. The pinion shaft ends are sandwiched between two pressure rings which are recessed to accept them. The pressure rings are also splined to the drive shaft gears. If the drive shafts rotate at different speeds, therefore, the pressure rings ride up on the ends of the differential pinion shafts and, being forced apart exert pressure on the 'clutch' plates. This effectively locks both the drive shaft gears to the casing which then transmits the drive power equally to both.

It must be understood that there is some light pressure maintained at all times on the 'clutch' plates by inbuilt diaphragm spring plates. Also on normal road surfaces the locking mechanism will still operate on sharp turns, particularly if considerable power is used. This has a noticeable effect on handling which one has to get accustomed to.

A further point regarding vehicles fitted with limited slip differentials is that the differentials wear out more quickly. In all conditions where there is a difference between the driving wheel speeds the friction discs are working against each other to a certain extent. Thus their surfaces are subject to frictional wear.

Note also that a special oil is required for transmissions fitted with limited slip differential.

## 10  Fault diagnosis

It is sometimes difficult to decide whether it is worthwhile removing and dismantling the gearbox for a fault which may be nothing more than a minor irritant. Gearboxes which howl, or where the synchromesh can be 'beaten' by a quick gear change, may continue to perform for a long time in this state. A worn gearbox usually needs a complete rebuild to eliminate noise because the various gears, if re-aligned on new bearings, will continue to howl when different wearing surfaces are presented to each other.

The decision to overhaul therefore, must be considered with regard to time and money available, relative to the degree of noise or malfunction that the driver has to suffer.

| Symptom | Reason/s | Remedy |
| --- | --- | --- |
| Ineffective synchromesh | Worn baulk rings or synchro hubs | Dismantle and renew. |
| Jumps out of one or more gears (on drive or over-run) | Weak detent springs, or worn selector forks or worn gears, or all three | Dismantle and renew. |
| Noisy, rough, whining and vibration | Worn bearings, (initially) resulting in extended wear generally due to play and backlash | Dismantle and renew. |
| Noisy and difficult engagement of gear | Clutch fault | Examine clutch operation. |

Driving a new seal into position (Sec 7.5)

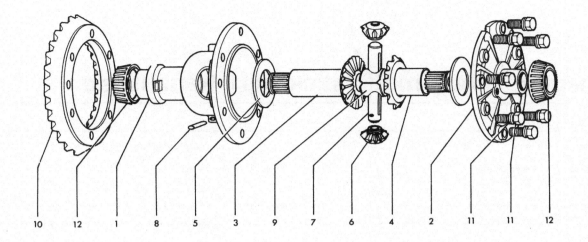

**Fig 6.3 DIFFERENTIAL — COMPONENTS**

1 Differential housing
2 Differential housing cover
3 Differential side gear (long shaft)
4 Differential side gear (short shaft)
5 Thrust washer
6 Differential pinion
7 Pinion shaft
8 Shaft locking pin
9 Spacer sleeve
10 Ring gear (crownwheel)
11 Screws and spring washers
12 Side bearing inner race

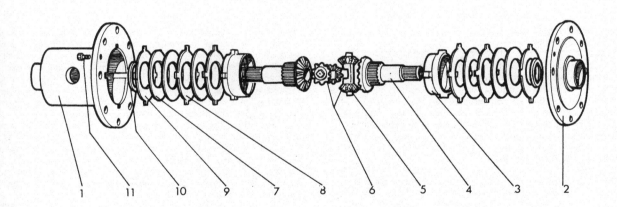

**Fig 6.4 LIMITED SLIP DIFFERENTIAL — PLATE TYPE**

1 Housing
2 Housing end plate
3 Pressure ring
4 Differential side gear
5 Pinion spindle
6 Differential pinions
7 Inner splined plates
8 Outer splined plates
9 Dished outer splined plates
10 Thrust washer
11 Socket head cap screw

# Chapter 7 Automatic stick shift transmission

## Contents

## Specifications

**Gear ratios**

| | |
|---|---|
| Low    ... ... ... ... ... ... ... ... ... ... ... ... ... ... ... ... ... | 2.25 : 1 |
| Medium   ... ... ... ... ... ... ... ... ... ... ... ... ... ... ... ... | 1.26 : 1 |
| High   ... ... ... ... ... ... ... ... ... ... ... ... ... ... ... ... ... | 0.89 : 1 |
| Reverse   ... ... ... ... ... ... ... ... ... ... ... ... ... ... ... ... | 3.07 : 1 |
| | |
| Stall speed - 1302 ... ... ... ... ... ... ... ... ... ... ... ... ... | 2000 - 2250 rpm |
| - 1302S ... ... ... ... ... ... ... ... ... ... ... ... ... | 1900 - 2100 rpm |
| Final drive ratio ... ... ... ... ... ... ... ... ... ... ... ... ... | 4.375 : 1 |
| Torque multiplication - 1302 ... ... ... ... ... ... ... ... | 2.1 |
| - 1302S ... ... ... ... ... ... ... ... | 2.5 |
| Converter oil capacity (dry) ... ... ... ... ... ... ... ... ... | 3.6 litres/7½ pints |
| Transmission/final drive oil capacity (dry) ... ... ... ... ... | 3.0 litres/6¼ pints |
| Converter oil pressure at 4000 rpm (80°C) ... ... ... ... ... | 38 - 52 psi (2.7 - 3.7 kg cm$^2$) |

**Torque wrench settings**

| | |
|---|---|
| Torque converter drive plate gland nut ... ... ... ... ... ... ... | 282 lbs ft/39 mkg |

## 1 General description

The automatic stick shift transmission is an optional extra, not currently available in the United Kingdom.

The system works as follows:

A 3-speed gearbox of conventional design, a clutch of conventional design and a torque converter are all married together. Gears are changed by a conventional gear lever. The gear lever, however, is connected to the clutch in such a way that as soon as the lever is moved longitudinally (i.e. in a gear selection direction) the clutch disengages.

The torque converter operates to transmit power when the engine is turning above idling speed and so therefore acts as a moving off clutch. It also acts as a form of 'slip' between engine and gear — In other words when engine load is higher — such as when moving from rest or uphill — the engine speed can increase to impart more power even though the vehicle remains in the same gear at the same speed. This enables the gearbox to manage with only 3 forward gears. These are the same as 2nd, 3rd and top of a conventional 4 speed manual gearbox.

If the torque converter is called upon to 'slip' too much — for example when driving up a long hill in top gear, the oil will overheat. When this happens a temperature sensitive warning light on the dashboard lights up and indicates that a lower gear should be selected. Lowest gear is adequate for all normal conditions and no warning light for the low range is installed.

The operation of the clutch is pneumatic via a control valve and servo. Vacuum is drawn from the engine intake manifold and there is also a vacuum tank. The control valve is fitted on the left side of the engine compartment and the vacuum tank under the left rear wing. The vacuum control valve is actuated by a solenoid switch and this in turn is actuated by a special switch incorporated in the gear lever base. As soon as the gear lever is moved forward or backwards the switch contacts close, and the solenoid operates. In addition there is a second switch. This acts as a starter inhibitor which avoids the engine being started with a gear engaged. It also prevents the clutch from engaging again during the brief period of lateral movement of the lever from one range to another through neutral.

The control valve also incorporates a device to regulate the speed with which the clutch engages. In accelerating circumstances (throttle open) the operation of the servo is quicker than would be possible with a foot pedal change. In decelerating conditions (throttle closed) the control valve controls the servo to operate less quickly. This enables the clutch to re-engage smoothly and without snatch.

Oil for the torque converter is circulated by a pump from the converter and through a reservoir tank which is mounted under the right rear mudguard. The pump is fitted on the end of the engine oil pump shaft. This oil circulation serves to cool the oil as well as maintain a constant pressure, (by means of a restriction in the return line). A relief valve is incorporated in the pump to limit maximum pressure.

## 2 Driving technique

1   The gear change lever looks and functions like a conventional floor change except that there are only 4 positions — 3 forward and 1 reverse. In order that the 'automatic' conventions are impressed on the driver the three forward speeds are referred to as 'L', 1 and 2, (even though they are 1st, 2nd and 3rd!). The change is through the conventional H pattern.

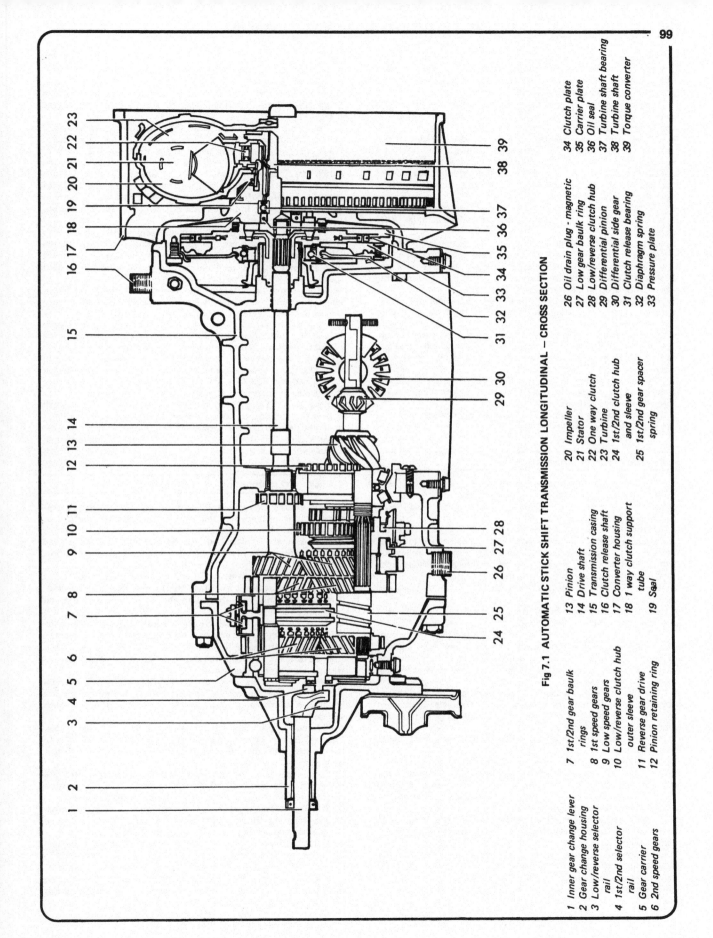

**Fig 7.1 AUTOMATIC STICK SHIFT TRANSMISSION LONGITUDINAL – CROSS SECTION**

1 Inner gear change lever
2 Gear change housing
3 Low/reverse selector rail
4 1st/2nd selector rail
5 Gear carrier
6 2nd speed gears
7 1st/2nd gear baulk rings
8 1st speed gears
9 Low speed gears
10 Low/reverse clutch hub outer sleeve
11 Reverse gear drive
12 Pinion retaining ring
13 Pinion
14 Drive shaft
15 Transmission casing
16 Clutch release shaft
17 Converter housing
18 1 way clutch support tube
19 Seal
20 Impeller
21 Stator
22 One way clutch
23 Turbine
24 1st/2nd clutch hub and sleeve
25 1st/2nd gear spacer spring
26 Oil drain plug - magnetic
27 Low gear baulk ring
28 Low/reverse clutch hub
29 Differential pinion
30 Differential side gear
31 Clutch release bearing
32 Diaphragm spring
33 Pressure plate
34 Clutch plate
35 Carrier plate
36 Oil seal
37 Turbine shaft bearing
38 Turbine shaft
39 Torque converter

2  The engine can be started only in the neutral position. When the engine is cold (and the automatic choke in operation) the idling speed is higher than when warm so before engaging a gear apply brakes, otherwise the car will creep forward.

3  For normal driving it is necessary to use only the top two gears (1 and 2). This is because the torque converter applies the engine power over a wider range.

4  To engage a gear whilst stationary move the lever into position 1. As soon as the lever starts to move, the clutch will automatically disengage. It is important that the engine speed is not above idling. Let go of the gear lever and depress the accelerator. The torque converter will take up the drive and the car will move off. Speed range 0—55 mph.

5  If starting on a steep slope or where tight manoeuvring is involved select 'L' for forward movement. Speed range 0—30 mph approximately.

6  Once the car is under way the gear change lever can be moved when required into the most suitable driving range.

7  If excessive load is placed on the torque converter in 1 and 2 ranges the oil temperature warning light will come on indicating the need to drop to a lower gear.

8  It is not necessary to disengage from the selected gear for temporary stops in traffic, but the brakes must be applied to prevent 'creep'.

9  When the car is parked the handbrake must be fully on. There is no transmission brake by selecting a gear because the torque converter effectively disconnects the transmission from the engine.

10  The vehicle can be tow started if the 'L' range is selected and a speed of more than 15 mph is attained. If less than that the torque converter will not 'bite'.

11  The car may be towed in case of breakdown or accident with the gear change lever in neutral.

### 3  Maintenance and adjustments

1  The automatic transmission fluid (ATF) level in the tank should be checked at 1000 mile or one month intervals. At the same time the converter, tank and all connecting hoses should be examined for signs of leakage.

2  If the ATF level drops, yet there is no sign of external leakage, check the engine oil level. If this has risen it indicates that there is probably a leak from ATF pump to engine oil pump. This must be attended to immediately otherwise both engine and converter could be ruined.

3  Every 6000 miles check the oil level in the final drive and gearbox.

4  Every 12,000 miles change the gearbox/final drive lubricant and clean the magnetic drain plugs.

5  Check shift clutch adjustment every 6000 miles. Indications of malfunction are slip or noisy engagement of reverse - assuming of course that the torque converter is operating correctly and engine revolutions are not too high at the time of gear engagement.

6  The clutch clearance can be checked by pulling the vacuum hose off the servo unit and then measuring the distance between the bottom of the adjuster sleeve and the upper edge of the servo mounting bracket (Fig 7.6).

7  If this measurement is more than 4 mm, the clutch needs adjustment.

8  To adjust the clutch, first slacken the adjuster sleeve locknut just enough to enable the adjuster to be turned. Then turn the adjuster away from the locknut until there is a gap of 6.5 mm between the two. Then move the locknut back to the end of the adjuster sleeve and tighten it once more.

9  If, as a result of adjustment the operating lever is found to be touching the clutch housing then it indicates that the clutch plate is worn out.

10  The control valve air filter will need cleaning at intervals depending on the condition in which the car is operating, 3000 miles is a suitable interval for normal conditions.

11  The filter is a mushroom shaped unit fitted to the side of the control valve (Fig 7.7). Simply unscrew it with a spanner on the hexagon shank of the mounting stud. Thoroughly flush it in petrol and if possible blow it dry completely with compressed air. It is important to avoid the possibility of any cleaning fluid being drawn into the system after it is refitted. Do not oil the filter.

12  Shift clutch engagement may need adjustment. As described earlier, the control valve governs the speed of clutch engagement. When changing to a higher gear it tends to be quick and slower from high to low. This prevents any undue snatch. To check the clutch try changing from 2 to 1 at about 45 mph without depressing the accelerator pedal. There should be a delay of about 1 second before the drive is fully taken up. If there is any snatch then it indicates that adjustment may be necessary — all other things being equal.

13  To adjust the speed of clutch engagement remove the cap from the top of the control valve to expose the head of the adjusting screw (Fig 7.7). To decrease the speed of engagement turn the screw ¼—½ turn clockwise. To increase engagement speed turn it ¼—½ turn anticlockwise.

14  After some time it may be necessary to clean, adjust or renew the switch contacts inside the gear lever which operates the shift clutch. Raise the rubber boot round the base of the lever and slacken the locknut at the bottom of the sleeve (Fig 7.5). Then screw the shift sleeve right off to expose the contacts when the top section of the lever comes off.

15  To set the contacts the sleeve must be screwed down until they just touch and then unscrewed ½ turn which gives a gap of 0.25 — 0.4 mm (0.010 — 0.016 inch). It is important that after this setting is made the elongated hole in the sleeve runs fore and aft. It is the slight movement of the lever in this slot which pushes the contacts together prior to shifting the gear. If the slot does not lie fore and aft within the setting limits then undo the other locknut on the threaded sleeve. The whole unit can then be turned into position.

### 4  Engine and transmission - removal and replacement

Due to the more complex nature of the automatic transmission it is not advised that the owner tries to overhaul or repair it himself.

Removal and replacement of the assembly may be carried out. The principles of removal are the same as for a conventional model.

The following additional points should be noted as well:

1  It will be necessary to detach the torque converter oil lines. The pressure line from the pump should be raised so that oil does not run out.

2  It is necessary to detach the torque converter from the engine flex plate. If the engine is rotated each of the four screws will appear through a hole in the transmission casing. When they have been removed the engine can be separated from the transmission in the usual way.

3  When the transmission unit is being taken off, first devise a way of keeping the torque converter from falling out of the housing, a simple metal strap fixed to two of the mounting studs will do this.

4  Detach the inner ends of the double jointed axle shafts. (See Chapter 6 for details.) Cover the inner joints with plastic sheeting to keep dirt out and hang them up to the underframe with wire.

5  Disconnect the oil hose banjo unions where they join the transmission casing, pull off the two wires to the temperature switches and unclip and pull off the hose from the servo unit.

6  Pull the three pin plugs from the temperature selector switch on the transmission case, and also the starter inhibitor switch on the gear change housing at the front of the transmission casing.

7  Replacement is a reversal of this procedure. When restarting the engine it is important to check that the converter oil is flowing back to the tank. If not after 2 or 3 minutes then there is probably an air lock in the system. Slacken the banjo joints on the transmission to bleed air out whilst the engine is running at

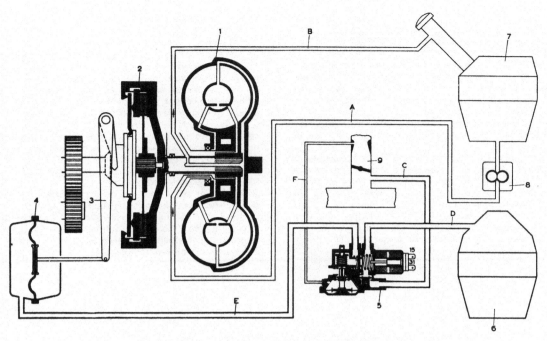

**Fig 7.2 SCHEMATIC LAYOUT OF TORQUE CONVERTER AND
AUTO—STICK SHIFT CLUTCH OPERATING SYSTEMS**

| | | |
|---|---|---|
| 1  Torque converter | 6  Vacuum tank | Vacuum lines |
| 2  Clutch | 7  Converter oil tank | C  Inlet manifold to control valve |
| 3  Clutch operating lever | 8  Converter oil pump | D  Tank to control valve |
| 4  Clutch servo | 9  Carburettor venturi | E  Servo to control valve |
| 5  Servo control valve | A  Oil pressure line | F  Control / reduction valve to venturi |
| | B  Oil return line | |

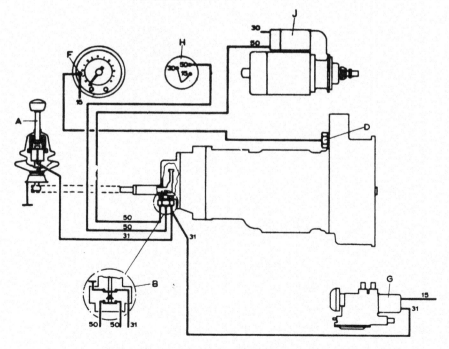

**Fig 7.3 ELECTRICAL CONNECTIONS FOR AUTO—STICK SHIFT**

| | | | |
|---|---|---|---|
| A  Shift lever and contact | D  Temperature switch (140 – | F  Warning lamp | H  Ignition switch |
| B  Starter inhibitor switch and |     150ºC) | G  Control valve | J  Starter motor solenoid |
|    neutral contact | | | |

idling speed.

## 5 Torque converter - stall speed test

1   The torque converter stall speed is that speed beyond which the engine will not turn when drive is engaged and the brakes are fully on. To carry it out it is necessary to be able to know the engine rpm. This involves temporary connection of an electric tachometer.

2   It is important that the engine be in proper tune for this test and thus developing its rated power output. The converter oil level must be correct.

3   With the engine warmed up and running, range 2 selected, and all brakes firmly on, increase engine speed to maximum possible and note the revolutions per minute. This must be done quickly and not continue longer than the time taken to read the instruments. Otherwise the converter oil will overheat seriously. If the stall speed exceeds specification (2300 rpm) it is indicative of a slipping gear change clutch. If it does not reach stall speed revolutions then the power output of the engine is down.

## 6 Engine differences

a)   Oil pump

The engine oil pump is elaborated to incorporate the converter fluid pump as well. Modifications to the crankshaft pulley wheel position allow the extra length to be accommodated.

The two pumps are separated by a plate and oil seals for the common lower gear spindle are incorporated in the plate. The same 4 studs provide the mounting for both pumps.

It is important, when checking both engine and torque converter oils to ensure that a drop in the level of either does not correspond with an increase in the level of the other. Such a condition could indicate faulty seals within the pump. Damage will occur if the two oils mix.

b)   Torque converter drive plate.

In place of the flywheel a drive plate is fitted to the crankshaft by a gland nut. This nut is tightened further than that for a flywheel. The torque setting is 282 lb ft. A special tool locked into the holes in the plate is normally needed to tighten the nut satisfactorily. Makeshift methods are likely to distort the plate which is then rendered unserviceable.

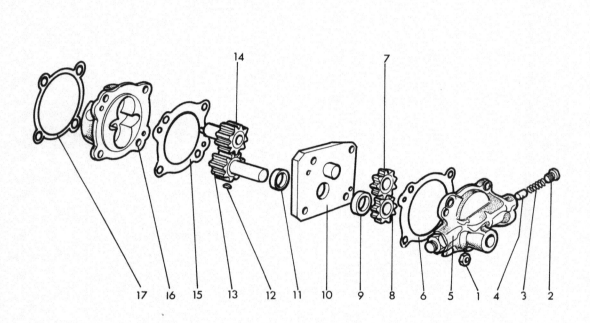

**Fig 7.4 TORQUE CONVERTER OIL PUMP**

| | |
|---|---|
| 1 Sealing nut | 6 Gasket |
| 2 Plug | 7 Converter oil pump - upper gear |
| 3 Spring | 8 Converter oil pump - lower gear |
| 4 Piston | 9 Plate oil seal |
| 5 Converter oil pump housing | |

| | |
|---|---|
| 10 Dividing plate | upper gear and shaft |
| 11 Plate oil seal | 15 Gasket |
| 12 Woodruff key | 16 Engine oil pump housing |
| 13 Engine oil pump - lower gear and shaft | 17 Housing gasket |
| 14 Engine oil pump - | |

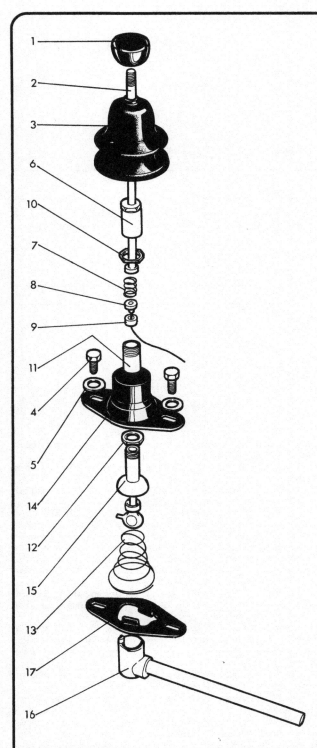

**Fig 7.5 AUTOMATIC STICK SHIFT — CHANGE LEVER ASSEMBLY — EXPLODED VIEW**

| | |
|---|---|
| 1 Grip | 10 Locknut |
| 2 Upper lever | 11 Threaded sleeve |
| 3 Boot | 12 Lower locknut |
| 4 Mounting bolt | 13 Spring |
| 5 Spring washer | 14 Mounting plate |
| 6 Shift sleeve | 15 Lower lever |
| 7 Spring | 16 Change rod |
| 8 Contact | 17 Reverse stop plate |
| 9 Insulating sleeve | |

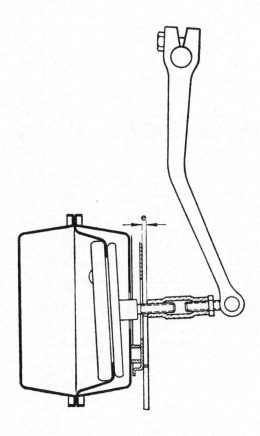

**Fig 7.6 CLUTCH/SERVO ADJUSTMENT**

*Dimension 'e' is 4 mm maximum*

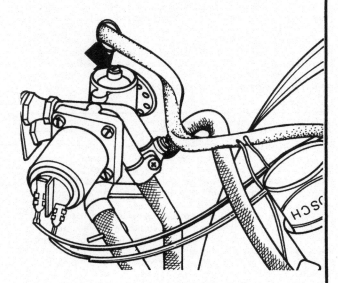

**Fig 7.7 VACUUM SERVO CONTROL VALVE MOUNTED IN ENGINE COMPARTMENT**

*Arrow indicates clutch engagement time regulating screw. Note perforated plate of air filter unit behind.*

# Chapter 8 Drive shafts and rear wheel shafts

## Contents

## Specifications

| | |
|---|---|
| Drive shaft length   ... ... ... ... ... ... ... ... ... ... ... ... ... | 415.5 mm |
| Drive shaft effective length (to ends of the joints)   ... ... ... | 405.3 mm |

**Torque wrench settings**

| | |
|---|---|
| Socket head cap screws for drive shaft flanges   ... ... ... ... | 25 lb ft/3.5 mkg |
| Wheel shaft nuts   ... ... ... ... ... ... ... ... ... ... ... ... ... | 253 lb ft/35.0 mkg |

## 1 General description

Unlike the swinging arm type of suspension fitted to the 1200 and 1300 models of 'Beetle', the drive shafts on the 1302 function solely to transmit the power from the final drive to the wheels and do not form part of the suspension system. The wheel shafts are mounted on the rear suspension trailing arms. The drive shafts are equipped with a constant velocity universal joint at each end and are coupled by flanges onto the axle shafts and transmission. Apart from the improved road holding this different design means that the axle shafts, wheel bearings and transmission may be removed for servicing separately with comparative ease. It should be remembered also that the rear wheel bearings are no longer lubricated by the transmission oil and require a lubrication service — although the intervals are well spaced (see Routine maintenance).

## 2 Drive shafts - removal and replacement

1  The drive shaft cap screws are best removed with a splined key to fit the socket. It is however, possible to use a hexagonal section key provided it is a dead fit and made of best quality hard steel (photo). If the screw sockets are damaged the greatest difficulty will be experienced in getting them out with any sort of key.

2  Before removing all the screws make sure that there are no accumulations of dirt around which could get into the joints. If any dirt gets in it will have to be cleaned out and the joints repacked with special molybdenum grease.

3  With all the screws removed the shafts may be taken away (photo).

## 3 Constant velocity joints - removal, repair and replacement

1  If the constant velocity joints have a noticeable amount of backlash they must be renewed completely. If the protective boot has split it is possible to dismantle and flush them, repack with grease and fit new boots.

2  First remove the drive shaft as described in the previous section.

3  It is not necessary to remove the rubber boot. Simply tap off the metal cover from the joint which is a press fit. Before going any further clean off the face of the joint and note any forge marks on each of the components or any other features which will enable you to ensure they all face the same way again on reassembly. If none is apparent scratch some marks of your own.

4  Remove the circlip from the end of the shaft. If the joint is now supported by vice jaws the shaft can be tapped out. Recover the concave washer from behind the joint on the shaft.

5  Flush the joint out thoroughly, let it dry and then repack it with approximately 60 grams of Castrol MS3 Grease, working it well in from both sides.

6  If the inner cage of the joint is dismantled or falls apart it must be correctly reassembled. First fit the splined hub inside the ball cage — it will only go in if two grooves are lined up (photo).

7  Then press the balls into the cage. They should be a snap fit unless the cage is worn badly (photo).

8  Place the ball and hub assembly into the outer cage so that the chamfered edge of the hub splines will be in a position against the shaft shoulder when the joint is eventually replaced on the shaft (photo). This means that it has to be the right way round in the outer cage because the outer cage goes on so that the protective boot assembly can be tapped back in position on the non-shouldered side.

9  Put the concave washer back on the shaft, concave side towards the joint (photo).

10  Put the joint back on the shaft (photo).

11  Refit the circlip (photo). In order to force the joint against the concave washer sufficiently to get the circlip in the groove support the shaft in a vice and drive the circlip down with a suitably sized socket (photo).

12  Having repacked the joint with grease tap the boot retainer plate back on to the joint. Use a screw to line up the holes in the joint and plate (photo).

Undoing a drive shaft cap screw with a hexagonal section key (Sec 2.1)

Taking the drive shaft away from the flange of the wheel shaft (Sec 2.3)

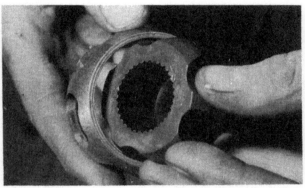
Constant velocity joint - placing the hub section in the cage (Sec 3.6)

Fitting the balls into the cage (Sec 3.7)

Fitting the hub, balls and cage into the outer section (Sec 3.8)

Fitting the concave washer on the drive shaft (Sec 3.9)

Placing the joint on the shaft (Sec 3.10)

Placing the circlip over the end of the shaft (Sec 3.11a)

Driving the circlip home (Sec 3.11b)

Tapping the boot retainer plate back onto the joint (Sec 3.12)

Removing the bearing retainer bolts (Sec 4.5a)

Taking the bearing retainer off (Sec 4.5b)

Removing the 'O' sealing ring (Sec 4.5c)

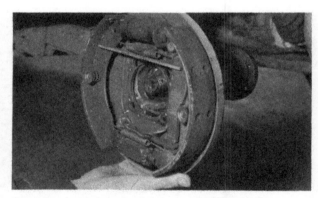

Removing the backplate and shoe assembly (Sec 4.5d)

Arm with inner ball bearing in position (Sec 4.10)

Packing the bearing with grease (Sec 4.11a)

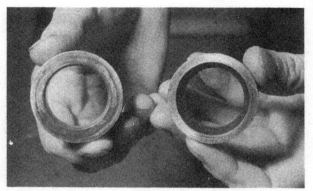

The inner spacer has a chamfered inner edge (right) (Sec 4.11b)

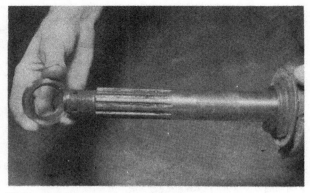

Fitting the inner spacer on the shaft (Sec 4.11c)

Fitting the spacer sleeve (Sec 4.12)

Driving the roller bearing on to the shaft (Sec 4.13)

Fitting the outer spacer (Sec 4.15a)

Replacing the wheel shaft nut (Sec 4.15b)

Tightening the axle shaft nut (Sec 4.16a)

Fitting a new axle shaft split pin (Sec 4.16b)

**4  Rear wheel shafts and bearings - removal and replacement**

1   Remove the nave plate from the wheel and take out the split pin from the axle shaft nut. With a socket and long bar slacken the nut. It is very tight.

2   Remove the drive shaft as described in Section 2.

3   Slacken the wheel nuts, jack up the car and remove the wheel and axle shaft nut.

4   Draw off the brake drum.

5   Remove the four screws holding the bearing cover to the arm and then take off the cover, 'O' ring and back plate (photos).

6   Using a soft faced mallet knock the wheel shaft out and remove the inner spacer.

7   Using a tyre lever take out the inner oil seal.

8   Remove the circlip behind the oil seal and then knock out the ball bearing from the other side using a suitable drift.

9   Remove the spacer sleeve and the inner race of the roller bearing. Drift out the outer race of the roller bearing from the arm.

10  Begin reassembly by first driving in the ball race. Then refit the circlip and oil seal with the lip facing inwards (photo).

11  Pack 60 grams of suitable grease (Castrol LM) into the hub centre working some of it into the ball bearing and onto the lip of the seal. Put the inner spacer onto the shaft so that the

chamfered edge will marry up with the radius on the shaft flange. Then drive the wheel shaft through the ball bearing until the flange just touches the inner race (photos).

12  Fit the spacer sleeve over the wheel shaft, grease the outer race of the roller bearing and drive it into position in the housing (photo).

13  The inner race has to be fitted over the shaft next and this is best done by using a suitable length of tube. A hammer can then be used to force it in (photo).

14  If necessary fit a new seal into the bearing cover and fill the double lip of the cover with grease.

15  Fit a new 'O' ring round the bearing and install the backplate and bearing cover. Replace the bolts and tighten them to 43 lb/ft. Refit the outer spacer, brake drum and hub and replace the slotted shaft nut which will be finally tightened when the wheel is replaced and the car is on the ground once more (photo).

16  The slotted wheel shaft nut has to be tightened to 253 lb ft/ 35.0 mkg. This needs a proper socket and an extension on the handle (photo). It should not be necessary to use a torque wrench because it will be simply a question of re-aligning the split pin holes with the castellations as before. The actual movement of the nut to increase the torque from, say, 150 lb/ft to 253 lb/ft is very little indeed. Always refit a new split pin and spread the split ends correctly (photo).

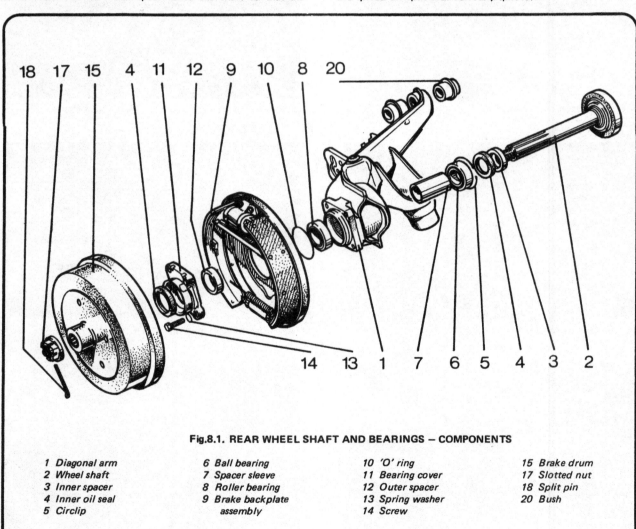

**Fig.8.1. REAR WHEEL SHAFT AND BEARINGS – COMPONENTS**

| | | | |
|---|---|---|---|
| 1  Diagonal arm | 6  Ball bearing | 10  'O' ring | 15  Brake drum |
| 2  Wheel shaft | 7  Spacer sleeve | 11  Bearing cover | 17  Slotted nut |
| 3  Inner spacer | 8  Roller bearing | 12  Outer spacer | 18  Split pin |
| 4  Inner oil seal | 9  Brake backplate | 13  Spring washer | 20  Bush |
| 5  Circlip |      assembly | 14  Screw | |

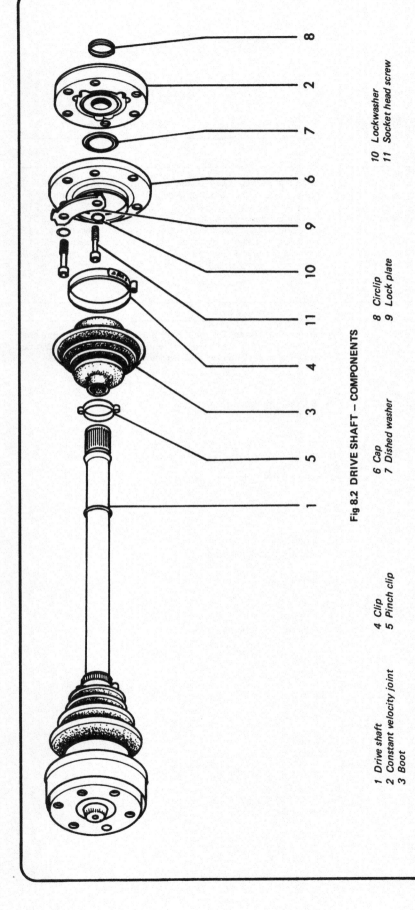

**Fig 8.2 DRIVE SHAFT – COMPONENTS**

1 Drive shaft
2 Constant velocity joint
3 Boot

4 Clip
5 Pinch clip

6 Cap
7 Dished washer

8 Circlip
9 Lock plate

10 Lockwasher
11 Socket head screw

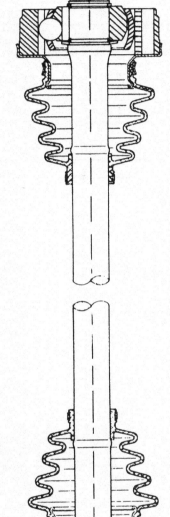

**Fig 8.3 DRIVE SHAFT – CROSS SECTION**

# Chapter 9 Braking system

## Contents

## Specifications

| | |
|---|---|
| Type ... ... ... ... ... ... ... ... ... | Hydraulically operated. Drums (1302) or discs (1302S) fitted to the front wheels. Drums fitted to rear wheels. Dual circuit hydraulic master cylinder. Parking brake operates via cables to rear wheels. |

**Discs**

| | |
|---|---|
| Diameter ... ... ... ... ... ... ... ... ... ... ... | 277 mm |
| Thickness ... ... ... ... ... ... ... ... ... ... ... | 9.5 - 8.5 mm (minimum) |
| Run out ... ... ... ... ... ... ... ... ... ... ... | 0.2 mm (maximum) |

**Calipers**

| | |
|---|---|
| Piston diameter ... ... ... ... ... ... ... ... ... | 40 mm |
| Friction pad thickness ... ... ... ... ... ... ... | 10 mm |
| Minimum pad thickness ... ... ... ... ... ... ... | 2 mm |
| Pad surface area (4 pads) ... ... ... ... ... ... | 72 cm$^2$/12.2 in$^2$     Later models 80 cm$^2$ |

**Front drums**

| | |
|---|---|
| Diameter ... ... ... ... ... ... ... ... ... ... ... | 248 mm |
| Lining width ... ... ... ... ... ... ... ... ... ... | 45 mm |
| Total lining area ... ... ... ... ... ... ... ... ... | 450 cm$^2$ |
| Lining thickness (new) ... ... ... ... ... ... ... | 3.8 - 4,00 mm |
| (oversize) ... ... ... ... ... ... ... | 4.3 - 4.5 mm (for skimmed drums) |

**Rear drums**

| | |
|---|---|
| Diameter ... ... ... ... ... ... ... ... ... ... ... | 230 - 231.5 mm (maximum) |
| Lining width ... ... ... ... ... ... ... ... ... ... | 40 mm |
| Total lining area ... ... ... ... ... ... ... ... ... | 358 cm$^2$ |
| Lining thickness (new) ... ... ... ... ... ... ... | 3.8 - 4.00 mm |
| (oversize) ... ... ... ... ... ... ... | 4.3 - 4.5 mm (for skimmed drums) |

**Tandem master cylinder**

| | |
|---|---|
| Bore ... ... ... ... ... ... ... ... ... ... ... | 19.05 mm |
| Stroke - front circuit drums ... ... ... ... ... ... | 17.5 mm |
| - front circuit discs ... ... ... ... ... ... | 14.0 mm |
| - rear circuit (with part drums) ... ... ... ... ... | 11.5 mm |
| - rear circuit (with part discs) ... ... ... ... ... | 14.0 mm |

**Wheel cylinders**

| | |
|---|---|
| Bore - front ... ... ... ... ... ... ... ... ... ... | 23.81 mm |
| - rear ... ... ... ... ... ... ... ... ... ... | 17.46 mm |

**Torque wrench settings**

| | |
|---|---|
| Brake backplate securing screws ... ... ... ... ... ... | 18 lb ft/2.5 mkg |
| Brake hose and pipe unions ... ... ... ... ... ... ... | 14 lb ft/2 mkg (maximum) |
| Stop light switch ... ... ... ... ... ... ... ... ... | 14 lb ft/2 mkg |
| Disc caliper securing bolts ... ... ... ... ... ... ... | 29 lb ft/4 mkg |
| Wheel cylinder to backplate screws ... ... ... ... ... | 20 lb ft/2.7 mkg |
| Caliper body screws ... ... ... ... ... ... ... ... ... | 15 lb ft/2.2 mkg |
| Wheel shaft nut (rear brake drum) ... ... ... ... ... ... | 253 lb ft/35 mkg |

# FRONT and REAR

**Fig 9.1 DRUM BRAKE ADJUSTMENT SHOWING LOCATION AND OPERATION OF NOTCHED ADJUSTER WHEELS (SEC 2)**

*Arrows indicate direction of turning to move shoes to drums*

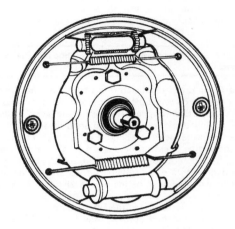

**Fig 9.2 FRONT DRUM BRAKE SHOES ASSEMBLY (SEC 3)**

**Fig 9.3 REAR DRUM BRAKE SHOES ASSEMBLY**

*Right hand side. (This illustration is mirrored for the correct arrangement for the left rear wheel (Sec 4)*

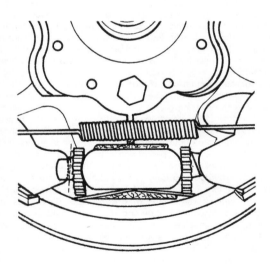

**Fig 9.4 BRAKE SHOE ADJUSTER SCREWS**

*Make sure the angled ends are correctly related (Sec 3)*

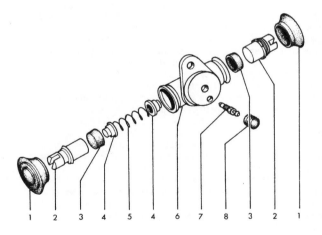

**Fig 9.5 HYDRAULIC WHEEL CYLINDER — COMPONENTS (SEC 6)**

1 Boot
2 Piston
3 Seal cup
4 Cup expander
5 Spring
6 Cylinder
7 Bleed valve
8 Dust cap

## 1 General description

On the 1302 models drum brakes are fitted to all four wheels. The operation of the brake shoes is by hydraulic pressure. Each pair of brake shoes is operated by a single cylinder which contains two opposed pistons, one operating each shoe in the drum. This means that there is one leading shoe only in each drum. Each shoe may be adjusted nearer to the drum by a screw type tappet and notched wheel mounted on each hydraulic piston.

A master hydraulic cylinder is operated by the foot pedal and generates the pressure which passes to the four wheel cylinders. The pipe lines are rigid metal except where they link from body to moving assemblies. The master cylinder is the tandem type which maintains the hydraulic pressure to either the front or rear wheels should the other fail.

The handbrake operates on the rear wheels only and the leverage from the handle is transmitted by two cables running in tubes inside the floor frame tube.

Hydraulic fluid level is maintained in the master cylinder by a reservoir located in the front luggage compartment behind the spare wheel.

On 1302S models the front brakes are discs and calipers, the rear brakes and handbrake being similar to the 1302.

The system operates when pressure on the foot pedal moves a piston in the master cylinder (in effect a pump). This pressurizes the hydraulic fluid in the pipe lines and forces the pistons outwards in the wheel cylinders. These in turn press the shoes against the drums. When pressure is relieved the shoes are drawn off the drums by retractor springs. The friction pads of the disc brakes are forced against the disc by hydraulic pistons also. When the pressure is relieved the piston seals flex sufficiently to permit the piston to retract fractionally. No springs are necessary.

The master cylinder piston is fitted with a spring loaded check valve which maintains a slight residual pressure in the fluid lines but not enough to actually move pads or shoes. This ensures instantaneous movement when the brake pedal is applied.

## 2 Brake adjustment (including handbrake)

1  It is possible to adjust the brakes without removing the wheels. Where discs are fitted the pads are self-adjusting. Remove the wheel caps and jack up each wheel in turn.
2  For the front wheels the two adjuster wheels are positioned at the bottom of the drum as you face the wheel. If the wheel is revolved they can be seen through the hole in the drum (photo). For the rear wheels the two adjusters are at the bottom of the drum, and access is through holes in the backplate.
3  Each adjuster should be moved in the appropriate direction (see Fig 9.1) with a screwdriver engaged in the notch until it can be moved no further and the wheel is locked. Then back off the adjuster one or two notches until the wheel revolves freely.
4  If any shoe(s) needs considerable adjustment (because they have been allowed to go unadjusted too long) then they will have to 'bed in' again to a different radius and this will call for further adjustment after a short interval. This is why regular brake adjustment is necessary to ensure top braking efficiency at all times. The linings will also last longer as it will ensure that the whole surface area is used evenly all the time.
5  When adjusting the rear brakes remember that when turning the wheels the drag of the transmission will be felt. Do not confuse this with binding brake shoes. The holes in the backplate through which the rear brake adjustments are made are normally covered with rubber plugs. These plugs are double — covering another hole through which the lining thickness may be seen (photo). If the plugs are missing replace them in order to keep out water and dirt.
6  Having completed adjusting one wheel it is good practice to operate the brake pedal once or twice and then adjust again. Sometimes the shoes can move fractionally off-centre during adjustment. The extra time required is well worth the trouble.

7  If a shoe still rubs against the drum a little even after being backed off more than 3 notches, leave it (provided it is only superficial). However, if the binding is quite severe then it is possible that the lining is very unevenly worn. In such instances remove the drum and have a look.
8  Once the rear brake shoes have been adjusted to the drums the handbrake may be checked. If both back wheels can be jacked off the ground together it will save some time. Pump the footbrake two or three times (to centralise the shoes) and apply the handbrake two notches. Pull back the rubber shroud at the base of the lever and slacken the locknut on the threaded end of each cable (photo). Then tighten each cable with the adjusting nut (holding the cable with a screwdriver in the slotted end) until an equal amount of drag can be felt on each rear wheel when it is turned. Pull the handbrake on four notches. At this it should not be possible to turn the wheels. Make sure any further adjustment is kept even between the two rear wheels.

## 3 Front drums and brake shoes - removal, inspection and replacement

1  The front brake drums form part of the wheel hub casting so they have to be taken off the stub axle. This involves releasing the front wheel bearings, details of which are given in Chapter 11. Before pulling the drum off it is a good idea to back the shoe adjusters off as far as they will go (Fig 9.2, page 111).
2  In the centre of each shoe a retaining pin, held in position by a spring loaded, slotted cup washer, must first be removed. This can be done with a pair of pliers, turning the washer so that the slot aligns with the head of the pin. Washer, spring and pin can then be removed.
3  Unhook the retractor spring which connects the two shoes nearest to the notched adjuster wheels. The end of one shoe can then be lifted out of the adjuster. Both shoes can then be disengaged quite easily from the hydraulic wheel cylinder. Immediately tie a piece of string around the wheel cylinder to prevent the pistons popping out. Do not apply pressure to the brake pedal either. If the pistons come out it will be necessary to bleed the hydraulic system.
4  The shoe lining surface should be not less than 0.5 mm (0.020 inch) above the rivet heads. Anything less and new linings should be fitted. If the linings have been contaminated with oil they will not work efficiently again and should be renewed. Great care should be exercised when handling brake shoes as oily or greasy hands can contaminate them significantly. The material is extremely absorbent. It is important to isolate the cause of contamination. If not the wheel cylinder, the only other source can be from grease flung out from the wheel bearing. Make sure the bearing grease seal is intact, renew it if necessary (see Chapter 11, which deals with front wheel bearings). Volkswagen supply linings and rivets to fit the original shoes. If you should contemplate renewing the linings yourself it is essential to have the proper punch tools for fixing the rivets. If you do not have these the simplest thing is to ask the supplier to fix them. Provided you have cut off the old linings and rivets it takes about two minutes per lining to fix the new ones, if you have the correct tools. One of the punches is clamped in the vice and the new lining, shoe and rivet head held over it whilst the end is belled over with the other special punch. Riveting should start from the centre and work outwards diagonally. Alternatively, other sources of supply may provide exchange shoes complete with linings fitted. Whatever you do it is important that the linings are all of the same make and type. It is best to fit a complete new set and make a proper job of it, or you will have uneven braking and trouble on wet road surfaces. Never try to renew the lining on one wheel only, always in pairs, and best in complete sets. Note also that the front brake shoes are wider than the rear ones and are not interchangeable.
5  Examine the friction surfaces of the brake drums. If they are in good condition they should be bright, shiny and perfectly smooth. If they show signs of deep scoring (due to over-worn brake linings) then they will need renewal. It may be possible

Adjusting a front brake shoe. The notched wheel may be seen through the hole in the drum (Sec 2.2)

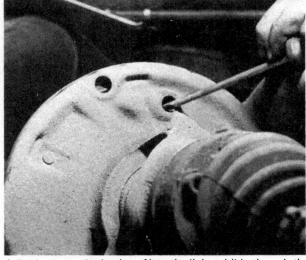

Adjusting a rear brake shoe. Note the lining visible through the other inspection hole (Sec 2.5)

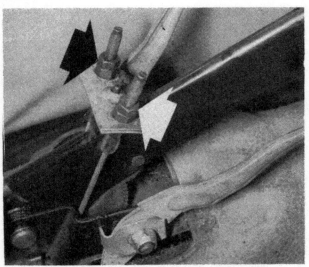

Handbrake cable adjuster and locknuts (arrowed) (Sec 2.8)

New lining ready to be fitted to the shoe (Sec 3.4a)

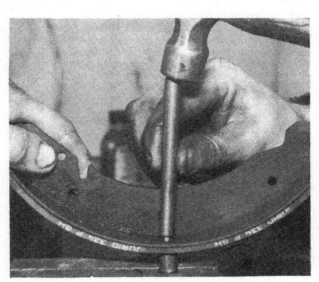

Rivetting a new lining to the shoe (Sec 3.4b)

Removing a rear brake drum (Sec 4.2)

to have them machined out on a lathe but if this is done it will be essential to fit oversize brake linings accordingly. This work should be carried out by a Volkswagen agent or an acknowledged brake specialist. It is a waste of time fitting new linings to work in scored drums (except when the scoring is only very light).

6  Before replacing the shoes the backplate should be thoroughly brushed off and the two adjusters removed and cleaned so that they can be freely turned. The threads may be treated with a very light touch of high melting point grease. Replace the adjusters; if the bottom one tends to fall out leave it until the shoes are refitted. Both adjusters should be screwed right in to the notched wheels. It is most important that the bottoms of the slots, which are angled, face the right way (Fig 9.4, page 111).

7  Examine the hydraulic cylinder. The rubber boots should be intact and there should be no sign of fluid leakage. If there is then the cylinders must be overhauled (see Section 6).

8  Assemble the two shoes together with the heavier of the two retractor springs engaged in the two holes nearest the cut-out slots on the inner radius of the shoe. These shoe ends should then be put into place in the slots in the ends of the pistons. Next fit the other ends of the shoes into the adjusters (replace the bottom one now) so that they fit properly in the adjuster slots. Then hook the other retractor spring into the holes in the shoes.

9  Reassemble the steady pins, springs and washers, turning the washers 90° across the pin heads to secure them. If you have dismantled all the brakes together note that the steady pins are different lengths so do not get them mixed up. This is because the front linings are wider than the rear - wider linings - longer pins.

10  Centralise the shoes. (otherwise you may have difficulty replacing the drum) and then refit the drum and wheel bearing, adjusting the bearings as described in Chapter 11. If the wheel cylinders have been overhauled bleed the hydraulic system (Section 11).

11  Adjust the shoes to the drums as described in the previous section. If new linings have been fitted further adjustment may be needed after a few hundred miles.

### 4  Rear drums and shoes - removal, inspection and replacement

1  Rear brake shoes tend to wear most on the front shoe at the adjuster end. If, however, brake adjustment has been neglected they will all wear more at the wheel cylinder ends of the shoes. In such cases the visual check of the brake lining material through the inspection hole could be misleading. There may be less material thickness at the other end of the shoe (Fig 9.3, page 111).

2  To remove the brake drum involves slackening of the wheel shaft nut as described in the previous chapter. This nut must be slackened with a proper socket and bar when the wheel is on the ground. The brake shoe adjusters should be slackened off fully. The drums should then draw off the splined shafts without difficulty (photo).

3  Remove the steady pins, springs and washers in the same fashion as for the front brake shoes.

4  Unhook the lower of the two retractor springs and then unhook the handbrake cable from the operating lever.

5  Disengage the ends of the two shoes from the adjusters and the two shoes together with the handbrake lever and plate may be lifted out.

6  Linings should be renewed if the surface is worn to within 0.4 mm (0.020 inch) or less of the rivet heads at any point. Also, if there is any indication of oil contamination the linings must be renewed. Details for relining may be found in the section dealing with front brakes.

7  If the shoes are to be changed remember to remove the handbrake operating lever by pulling off the clip which fixes it to the shoe.

8  When reassembling the two shoes prior to refitting, the spreader plate should engage in the two slots and the shoe with the lever attached goes to the rear with the lever notch facing the rear (photos).

9  Make sure that the adjuster wheels are free-moving and fully backed off before locating the ends of the shoes in the slots. The angled bottom of the slots should face the right way (Fig 9.4).

10  It must be emphasised that any leaks, either from the bearing or the hydraulic cylinder, should be dealt with to prevent further contamination or failure of the hydraulic system.

### 5  Disc pads - removal, inspection and replacement

1  Remove the front wheel.

2  There are two visual examinations to be made before dismantling anything. These are the thickness of the friction pad and the gap between the pad and disc.

3  Pad friction material thickness must not be less than 2 mm otherwise the pads should be renewed.

4  The residual clearance should not be more than 0.2 mm (0.008 inch) between disc and pad. This can be measured with a feeler gauge.

5  If the gap is greater it is probably due to a sticking piston. A simple remedy is given later on in this section.

6  If the pads are to be used again mark where they came from beforehand so they may be put back in the same position. Then drive out the retaining pins from the outside with a long nosed punch (photo). Lift off the spring retainer plate (photo).

7  Before removing the old pads it is best to force them away from the disc carefully, with a suitable flat metal lever. This will push the pistons back. Before doing this it will be necessary to remove some hydraulic fluid from the reservoir to prevent it overflowing when the pistons are pushed back. Do this with a suitable suction device such as an empty flexible plastic bottle.

8  Once the pistons are pushed back remove the pads and piston retaining plate (photo). Note that there is a cutaway portion on one side of the piston. Provided the piston is not rotated after the retaining plate is taken out there should be no cause for difficulty on replacement of the plate. For details of the correct position of the piston cut-out refer to Section 7.

9  Blow out the aperture in the caliper and examine the seal which should show no signs of cracking or brittleness. If it does it should be renewed (see Section 7).

10  Clean off the piston retaining plate and replace it together with the new friction pads. New pad retaining spring plates are normally provided with the pads and these should be used. The spring plates have a wide and narrow side. Put the wide side upwards. When replacing the retaining pins (from the inside) do not use a punch smaller in diameter than the pin. Preferably, use no punch at all otherwise there is a possibility of shearing the shoulder off against the split clamping bush.

11  Pump the brake pedal to bring the pads up to the disc and check the level of hydraulic fluid in the reservoir.

12  If the clearance between the disc and pad is too great after brake operation then this is an indication that the inner piston rubber seal is sticking somewhat and distorting more than normally. This retracts the piston more than usual when the pressure is taken off. Movement of the piston can usually cure this. Remove a brake pad and put in a block of wood no less than 6 mm thick. Pump the brakes to force the piston further out and then force it back again. Do this a few times and the problem should disappear. If not it will be necessary to check the piston seals and caliper cylinders thoroughly as described in Section 7.

### 6  Hydraulic wheel cylinders - renewal of seals and cylinders

1  If the wheel cylinders show signs of leakage, or of pistons being seized up, then it will be necessary to dismantle them and fit new seals. The procedure for front and rear cylinders are the same although the bores of the cylinders are different requiring different diameter seals. See Fig 9.5, page 111.

2  Remove the brake drum and the brake shoes and seal the cap of the fluid reservoir with a piece of plastic film to minimise loss of fluid from the system when the cylinder is dismantled.

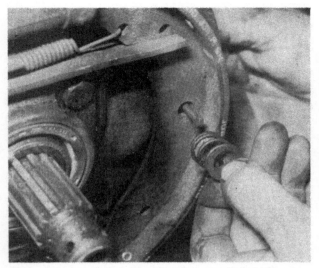

Fitting the steady pin, spring and washer whilst reassembling the right rear brake shoe assembly (Sec 4.8a)

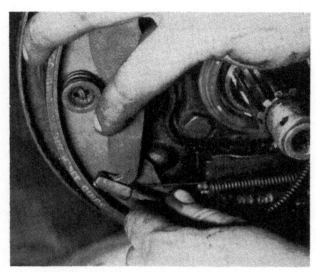

Hooking the handbrake cable to the lever on a right rear brake assembly (Sec 4.8b)

Taking out a pad retaining pin (Sec 5.6a)

Removing the spreader spring (Sec 5.6b)

Removing a disc pad (Sec 5.8)

Removing the caliper securing bolts (Sec 7.4)

3  Pull off the rubber boots from the ends of the cylinder, bringing the pistons and slotted ends with them. Behind the pistons are the seal cups and in the centre there is a spring with two 'cup expanders' which fit inside each seal and as their name implies force the seals outward into the cylinder bore under the pressure of the spring.

4  With the cylinder clear examine the bore surfaces for signs of ridging or scoring. Any residue stuck in the bore should be cleaned out with brake fluid or meths - if very stubborn a gentle rub with some No.400 wet and dry paper will clean it up. Any noticeable scores or ridges indicate that a new cylinder should be fitted. No attempt should be made to smooth them out as this will be unsuccessful.

5  To remove the cylinder undo the brake pipe union from behind the backplate. Cover the end of the pipe with the dust cap from the bleed nipple pro tem. Undo the two securing screws from the backplate and the cylinder may be lifted out. If a new cylinder is fitted the diameter of the bore must be exactly the same as the diameter of the one being replaced, otherwise the balance of the brakes will be upset.

6  With the cylinder perfectly clean lubricate the bore with brake fluid and insert the spring complete with seal cup expanders at each end.

7  Lubricate the new seals with fluid and put one in at each end of the cylinder with the lip facing inwards. Take great care not to turn the lip back whilst doing this.

8  Put a piston into the bore of the cylinder behind each seal and then fit the rubber boot over the cylinder and piston so that it engages in the grooves.

9  Absolute cleanliness of hands and parts is essential during reassembly.

10  If a new wheel cylinder is being fitted reconnect the brake pipe union taking care not to cross the thread, kink the pipe or overtighten the union.

## 7 Disc caliper pistons and seals - inspection and renewal

1  Before assuming that anything is wrong which requires removal of the caliper pistons make sure that the checks in connection with renewal of the friction pads as described in Section 5 have been carried out.

2  Discs may deteriorate, if left unused, due to corrosion. If this happens it is best to let a VW agency repolish them with special blocks which can be inserted in place of the friction pads. Discs which are badly scored or distorted must be renewed. It is possible to have them re-machined but the economics of this against fitting new parts should be examined.

3  The run-out of the disc can be checked only with a clock gauge micrometer. With the bearing properly adjusted the run-out should not exceed 0.2 mm (0.008 inch).

4  To renew a disc or repair piston seals, the caliper assembly must first be removed. It is held by two bolts from the back of the steering knuckle (photo). (If the disc only is to be removed it is not necessary to disconnect the hydraulic fluid hose. The whole assembly should be tied up onto the bodywork to prevent any strain on the hose.) If the pistons are to be removed from the caliper thought must first be given as to how pressure can be applied to force them out. Only one piston can be worked on at a time as the other piston must be installed and clamped in position so as to maintain pressure to force the other out. Pressure can be applied from a foot pump if you rig up a spare hydraulic pipe union and short length of pipe to which the pump connector will fit. One piston will have to be clamped in such a way that there will still be room enough for the other to come right out. Here again a tong-like clamp may have to be made up from some 1½ x 1/8 inch flat steel bar if you are unable to obtain a suitable tool.

5  Mount the caliper assembly in the vice padding the jaws suitably so that the flange of the caliper will not be scored or marked. The friction pads and retaining plates should be removed (see Section 5).

6  Prise out the spring ring from the outer seal using a screw-driver. Then, with a blunt plastic or wooden tool prise out the seal itself. Do not use sharp tools for fear of scoring the piston or cylinder.

7  Using a clamp to hold one piston force the other out under pressure as described in paragraph 4. To prevent damage in case the piston should come out with force put some cloth in the caliper to prevent it striking the piston and clamp opposite.

8  With the piston out the rubber sealing ring can be taken out of its groove in the cylinder; once again use only a blunt article to get it out.

9  With methylated spirits or hydraulic fluid, clean the piston and cylinder thoroughly. If there are any signs of severe scoring or pitting then renewal will be necessary. With the cylinder this involves renewing the whole caliper unit.

10  When renewing seals the spring ring and piston retaining plate must also be renewed. The VW service kit includes all the items needed. Use them. Before reassembly it is advantageous to coat the piston and new rubber seal with VW cylinder paste specially formulated for this job. Otherwise make sure they are thoroughly lubricated with clean hydraulic fluid. On no account use anything else.

11  Fit the rubber seal in the cylinder groove and then fit the piston into the seal. Great care must be taken to avoid misaligning the seal when doing this and the piston must be kept square while it is pushed in. The cut-out portion of the piston should lie at an angle of 20° from a line across the disc diameter facing in to the centre of the disc and against the direction of forward disc rotation.

12  Fit the new outer seal and spring ring.

13  Repeat the process for the other piston.

14  Refit the caliper to the knuckle, tightening the securing bolts to 29 lb/ft. Replace the piston retainer plates and pads as described in Section 5.

15  The disc itself may be removed after the caliper is taken off.

16  Remove the hub cap — (on the left wheel, this involves removing the 'C' washer securing the speedo cable). Undo the bearing nut clamp screw, remove the nut and pull off the disc which is an integral part of the wheel hub (photo on page 123).

17  Replace the disc in the reverse order and re-adjust the wheel bearing as detailed in Chapter 11.

18  Refit the caliper to the knuckle and tighten the two retaining bolts to the correct torque of 29 lb/ft/4 mkg.

19  It is rare that the caliper housing has to be split and this should not be done unless it is obviously leaking. Renewal of the interior 'O' rings on the fluid channels may then be needed. Undo the four socket head screws to separate the two halves. Remove the two 'O' rings and fit new ones. Re-align the two halves and replace the screws. Tighten them from the centre outwards in sequence to 7 lb/ft (1 mkg) and then again in sequence to a final torque of 15 lb/ft.

20  When the caliper is replaced reconnect the hydraulic fluid hose and bleed the system as described in Section 11.

## 8 Tandem master cylinder - removal, replacement and adjustment

1  The tandem master cylinder comprises a single cylinder in which there are two pistons one behind the other. Each circuit is supplied independently with fluid. If the pressure in one circuit should fail the other is not affected. Provided the slave cylinders and fluid lines are all in good condition and there is no air in the system then any softness or sponginess in the system will probably be due to worn seals in the master cylinder. As these are internal there will be no visible leak to indicate this.

2  To remove the cylinder assembly first jack up the car and remove the right hand front wheel (RH drive) or left as the case may be. The cylinder is bolted to the bulkhead alongside the floor tunnel (photo on page 123).

3  Have a suitable receptacle handy to collect the contents of the fluid reservoir - if possible siphon the contents out of the reservoir itself. Otherwise pull the pipes and plugs from the top

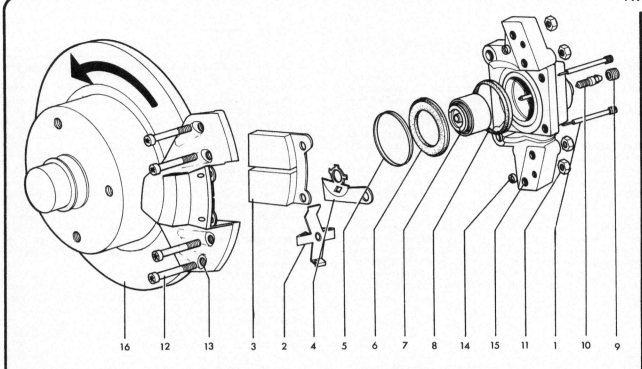

**Fig 9.6 DISC AND CALIPER — COMPONENTS**

1 Pad retaining pin (see note)
2 Spreader spring (see note)
3 Friction pad
4 Piston retaining plate

5 Clamp ring
6 Seal
7 Piston
8 Rubber seal

9 Dust cap
10 Bleeder valve
11 Hexagon nut
12 Cheese head screw

13 Caliper outer housing
14 Seal
15 Caliper inner housing
16 Brake disc

*Note: Arrow shows forward rotation of disc. Later models have modified
spreader springs and only 1 retaining pin (see photographs) (Section 7)*

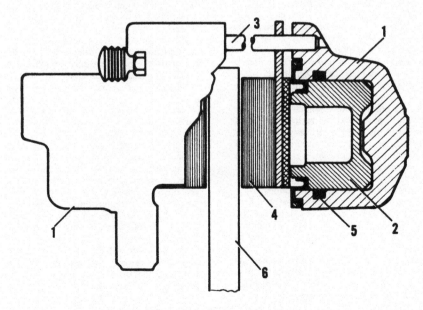

**Fig 9.7 DISC BRAKE CALIPER
CROSS SECTION**

1 Caliper
2 Piston
3 Pad retaining pin

4 Pad
5 Fluid seal
6 Disc

of the cylinder body and drain it into the receptacle there. Keep fluid away from paintwork.

4   Unscrew the rigid pipe unions from the body of the cylinder. It is not necessary to undo the brake light switches. Just disconnect the wires.

5   The two screws in the bulkhead behind the brake pedal should now be removed to release the assembly. Take care not to drop the washers or spacers off the screws into the space below or you may have a difficult job retrieving them.

6   Replacement is a reversal of the removal procedure. Make sure that the spacers are correctly refitted. As soon as the unions have all been reconnected and the system replenished with fluid and bled, see that the unions are all perfectly leakproof.

7   It is important that the pushrod which operates the plunger from the brake pedal is correctly set. In the rest position, the ball end of the pushrod should have a 1 mm clearance before it contacts the bottom of the recess in the piston. If this clearance is absent (and the piston cannot return fully) the operation of the system is seriously affected. To adjust the length of the rod slacken the locknut and screw the rod in or out as required. This adjustment will also be affected if the pedal cluster mounting plate is moved. It is important that the pedal stop is set far enough back so that if one brake circuit fails the pedal can move far enough to operate the other circuit before it comes up against the panel.

## 9 Tandem master cylinder - dismantling, overhaul and reassembly

1   Thoroughly clean the exterior of the unit before starting to dismantle. Then remove the piston stop screw located between the two fluid inlet ports (Fig 9.8).

2   Remove the boot from the rear of the cylinder and take out the internal circlip.

3   The two pistons and all their component parts may then be drawn out. Do this carefully, taking note of the order and position in which they come out.

4   All internal seals are fitted to the grooves in the pistons as indicated in Fig 9.8. They can be pulled off and fitted without special tools but care must be taken not to over-stretch them. The primary piston is fitted with three seals all the same size and shape. The front two face forward and the third to the rear. The secondary piston has two seals, both facing forwards. The front seal is the same as those on the primary piston but the rear one is the odd one out so do not confuse it with the others.

5   When reassembling the pistons into the cylinder first place the cup washer, cup seal, support washer, spring plate and spring, in that order over the nose of the primary piston (to which the new secondary cup and rear seal should have been already fitted). Hold the cylinder vertical with the open end downwards and feed the whole assortment back in so that the loose items do not fall off the piston.

6   The secondary piston primary cup is held in location by a support washer and spring plate also. These in turn are held firm by the stop sleeve and stroke limiting screw. By undoing the stroke limiting screw inside the stop sleeve all these component parts may be released. The new seal is then easily placed in position.

7   When replacing the secondary piston it should be pushed far enough forward to enable the stop screw to be put in so that it fits behind the rear end of the primary piston. This is most important. It must not be fitted so that it engages the recessed part in the shank of the primary piston.

8   Refit the stop ring, circlip and rubber boot over the end of the cylinder.

9   Some cylinders incorporate a pressure differential warning system. This consists of a single piston held centrally in balance by the equal pressure of the two circuits. To remove the piston with its equilibrium springs the switch must first be screwed out

of the body. Then the end plug can be removed and the internal components taken out.

## 10 Hydraulic fluid lines and hoses - examination, removal and replacement

1   Regular examination of the pipes which carry the pressurised fluid from the master cylinder to the four wheel cylinders is very important. Any sudden leak due to fracture or corrosion will result in loss of pressure and the front or rear brakes will be inoperative except for the handbrake which is inadequate for driving purposes.

2   Trace the routes of all the rigid pipes and wash or brush away accumulated dirt. If the pipes are obviously covered with some sort of underseal compound do not disturb it. Examine for signs of kinks or dents which could have been caused by flying stones. Any instances of this mean that the pipe section should be renewed but before actually taking it out read the rest of this section. Any unprotected sections of pipe which show signs of corrosion or pitting on the outer surfaces must also be considered for renewal.

3   Flexible hoses, running to each of the front wheels and from the underbody to each rear wheel should show no signs of external signs of chafing or cracking. Move them about and see if surface cracks appear. Also if they feel stiff and inflexible or are twisted they are nearing the end of their useful life. If in any doubt renew the hoses. Make sure also that they are not rubbing against the bodywork (photo on page 123).

4   Before attempting to remove any pipe for renewal it is important to be sure that you have a replacement source of supply within reach if you do not wish to be kept off the road for too long. Pipes are often damaged on removal. If a Volkswagen agency is near, you may be reasonably sure that the correct pipes and unions are available. If not, check first that your local garage has the necessary equipment for making up the pipes and has the correct metric thread pipe unions available. The same goes for flexible hoses.

5   Where the couplings from rigid to flexible pipes are made there are support brackets and the flexible pipe is held in place by a 'U' clip which engages in a groove in the union (photo). The male union screws into it. Before getting the spanners on, soak the unions in penetrating fluid as there is always some rust or corrosion binding the threads. Whilst this is soaking in, place a piece of plastic film under the fluid reservoir cap to minimise loss of fluid from the disconnected pipes. Hold the hexagon on the flexible pipe coupling whilst the union on the rigid pipe is undone. Then pull out the clip to release both pipes from the bracket. For flexible hose removal this procedure will be needed at both ends. For a rigid pipe the other end will only involve unscrewing the union from a cylinder or connector. When you are renewing a flexible hose, take care not to damage the unions of the pipes that connect into it. If a union is particularly stubborn be prepared to renew the rigid pipe as well. This is quite often the case if you are forced to use open ended spanners. It may be worth spending a little money on a special pipe union spanner which is like a ring spanner with a piece cut out to enable it to go round the tube (photo on page 123).

6   If you are having the new pipe made up, take the old one along to check that the unions and pipe flaring at the ends are identical.

7   Replacement of the hoses or pipes is a reversal of the removal procedure. Precautions and care are needed to make sure that the unions are correctly lined up to prevent cross threading. This may mean bending the pipe a little where a rigid pipe goes into a fixture. Such bending must not, under any circumstances, be too acute, otherwise the pipe will kink and weaken.

8   When fitting flexible hoses take care not to twist them. This can happen when the unions are finally tightened unless a spanner is used to hold the end of the flexible hose and prevent twisting.

9   After removal or slackening of a brake pipe union the hydraulic system must be bled.

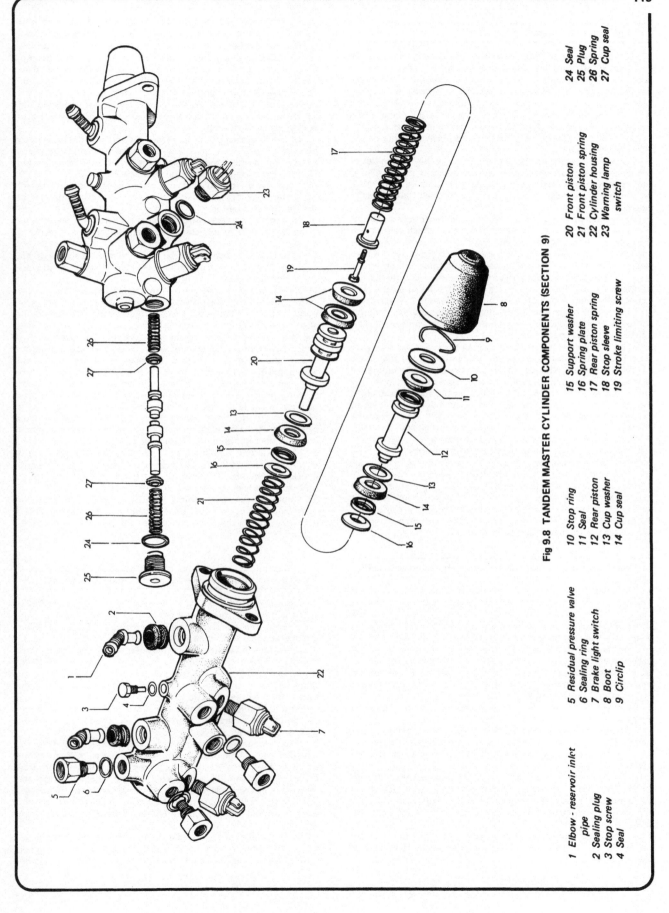

**Fig 9.8 TANDEM MASTER CYLINDER COMPONENTS (SECTION 9)**

1 Elbow - reservoir inlet
   pipe
2 Sealing plug
3 Stop screw
4 Seal

5 Residual pressure valve
6 Sealing ring
7 Brake light switch
8 Boot
9 Circlip

10 Stop ring
11 Seal
12 Rear piston
13 Cup washer
14 Cup seal

15 Support washer
16 Spring plate
17 Rear piston spring
18 Stop sleeve
19 Stroke limiting screw

20 Front piston
21 Front piston spring
22 Cylinder housing
23 Warning lamp
   switch

24 Seal
25 Plug
26 Spring
27 Cup seal

## 11 Hydraulic brake system - bleeding

1  The purpose of the process known as bleeding the brakes is to remove air bubbles from the hydraulic system. Air is compressible - hydraulic fluid is not. Bleeding should be necessary only after work on the hydraulic system has allowed air into the system. If it is found necessary to bleed brakes frequently then there is something wrong and the whole system should be checked through to find where the air is getting into the system. Cars left unused for a long time may also require brake bleeding before full efficiency is restored.

2  Normally, if work has been carried out at the extremities of the system - e.g. at wheel cylinders or adjacent pipes, then it should only be necessary to bleed that particular section. Work on the master cylinder, however would call for all four wheels to be bled.

3  Before starting, make sure you have an adequate supply of the proper fluid, a clean receptacle and a tube which will fit over the bleed nipple securely and which is conveniently long enough. A useful device is the tube which is fitted with a non-return valve. This avoids the necessity of keeping the other end of the tube submerged in liquid whilst bleeding is in progress.

4  Clean off the bleed nipple (or pull off the protective cap). Put about 1 inch depth of fluid in the receptacle (a salad cream jar is ideal and needs less fluid!). Connect the pipe to the nipple and put the other end in the jar and undo the nipple about half a turn - no more is necessary.

5  A second person is needed to operate the brake pedal at your instruction. The pedal should be depressed smartly one full stroke to the floor and allowed to return slowly. This should be repeated until no more bubbles emerge from the tube in the jar. Smart operation of the pedal ensures that the air is forced along the pipe rather than by-passed. Keep a watch on the level of fluid in the reservoir. If it gets too low it will let air into the master cylinder and then you will have to bleed all four wheels.

6  Once all the air is expelled, the best moment to tighten the bleed nipple is during the return stroke of the pedal.

7  Repeat the procedure for each wheel as necessary. Do not put fluid bled out of the system back in. Always use fresh.

8  It is considered by many a good idea to completely replenish the brake fluid, by bleeding, at regular intervals. Such intervals would be two years or 30,000 miles, whichever came first. Renewal of the wheel cylinder seals at the same time would be well worth the small cost and time involved.

## 12 Brake and clutch pedal cluster - dismantling and reassembly

1  The brake and clutch pedals are mounted on a common shaft which in turn is supported by two brackets (photo). One of these brackets (on RH drive cars) is fitted to the right of the brake pedal and is held to the floor by two bolts. The other is bolted to the left hand side of the floor tunnel. The shaft is hollow allowing the accelerator rod to pass through it. At the left hand end of the pivot shaft a bracket links to the accelerator cable. The clutch cable hooks onto a lug which is part of the pedal inside the tunnel. This section explains how to deal with all three items on the cluster (photo on page 123).

2  Remove the carpet from the left hand toe panel and pull out the panel.

3  Remove the two bolts holding the cover on the side of the tunnel. These two screws hold the bracket supporting the left end of the cross shaft as well so some movement will be noticed.

4  If only the accelerator cable is being renewed the split pin can be removed from the clevis pin, the cable eye released and the cable drawn out. If the cross shaft is being taken out then remove the lever from the accelerator rod by taking off the circlip.

5  At the other end of the shaft remove the clevis pin securing the brake master cylinder pushrod to the pedal. It is held in position by a circlip.

6  Then remove the large circlip on the end of the main cros shaft next to the mounting bracket. The two mounting bracke bolts can then be undone. When these bolts are being undon take precautions to ensure that the clutch pedal remains in a upright position - it does not matter about the brake peda which can fall back to the floor. This will ensure that the clutc cable does not get unhooked inside the tunnel. There is a separate plate also behind the pedals which has upturned lug acting as pedal stops. Do not disturb this although it will nee adjustment on reassembly.

7  Unclip the accelerator rod from the back of the accelerato pedal, remove the link and draw the brake pedal and accelerato rod out of the tube together with the brake pedal return spring Note the position of the intermediate washers.

8  If you wish to draw out the clutch pedal and cable detach the other end of the cable from the clutch operating lever or the transmission casing.

9  Now draw out the clutch pedal and shaft together, keepin the pedal as upright as possible so that the cable may be draw out with it.

10  A new clutch cable must be fed into the tube through th aperture in the tunnel. All that is needed is patience to guid the end into the tube.

11  Reassembly is a reversal of the dismantling procedure. The setting of the pedal stop plate requires some care, bearing in mind that the clutch pedal free play adjustment is affected and also the setting of the master cylinder pushrod. When replacing the clutch pedal the end of the cable has to be hooked on first and then the pedal manoeuvred into position without letting the end of the cable come loose or get snagged on the hook in the wrong position. It is best to get a second person to hold the other end of the cable and keep tension on it whilst the pedal is being positioned. If the cable appears to be too short after positioning, it is probably because the hook has slewed round. Waggle the pedal back and forth a few times - still with the other end of the cable being held, and it will probably straighten out. If it does not go back to square one.

12  Before finally tightening the mounting bracket bolts check that at the end of the return movement the rubber faces of both pedals are vertical. If they are not the stop plate has slotted holes to allow their adjustment to the vertical.

13  Finally check the master cylinder pushrod clearance (as described in Section 8 of this Chapter) and then check and if necessary, adjust the free play of the clutch pedal (as described in Chapter 5).

## 13 Handbrake cables and lever - removal and replacement

1  Slacken off the locknuts at the lever end of both handbrake cables and remove them together with the adjusting nuts.

2  Remove the rear brake drums and unhook the cable from the operating lever on the shoe.

3  Undo the bolt which holds the outer sleeve clip to the brake backplate where the cable passes through. Disengage the clip from behind the washer and spring on the cable and draw the cable out from the backplate. Then pull the cables out of the tube from the other direction.

4  Before fitting a new cable make sure that at the brake end the spring and washer are properly fitted between the eye of the cable and the outer sleeve.

5  It is necessary to remove the handbrake lever before the threaded ends of the cable can be reconnected to it. Remove one of the circlips from the end of the lever pivot pin and withdraw the pin. Keep the hands well clear of the ratchet button and then move the whole lever assembly forward so that it disengages from the floor plate. If the ratchet button is inadvertently pressed the ratchet will fall down. It must be put back before replacing the lever.

6  Put the cable through the backplate and then work the sleeve clamp through the hole in the backplate so that the spring and washer are on the inside of the slotted bracket of the clamp.

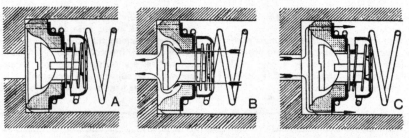

**Fig 9.9 TANDEM MASTER CYLINDER – FUNCTION OF RESIDUAL PRESSURE VALVE**

A  *At rest. Main valve seated on end of cylinder under main spring pressure and inner valve seated in centre of main seal under secondary spring pressure*
B  *Braking. Secondary valve opens under pressure of fluid which passes into system*
C  *Brakes released. Main valve opens under fluid back pressure until main spring overcomes pressure - keeping some pressure in system. Secondary valve stays seated.*

*Note: A residual pressure valve is incorporated in each fluid outlet on the master cylinder (Section 9)*

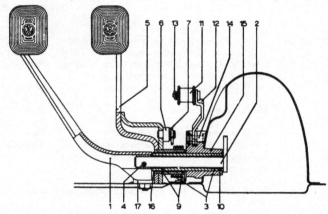

**Fig 9.10 BRAKE AND CLUTCH PEDAL CLUSTER LHD – CROSS SECTION VIEW (SEC 12)**

| | | | |
|---|---|---|---|
| 1 Clutch pedal | 5 Brake pedal | 10 Mounting tube | 14 Accelerator pedal lever pin |
| 2 Pedal shaft | 6 Master cylinder pushrod | 11 Accelerator pedal roller | 15 Mounting bracket |
| 3 Bush | 7 Pushrod lock plate | 12 Accelerator connecting lever | 16 Circlip |
| 4 Locating pin | 9 Bush | 13 Clip | 17 Stop plate |

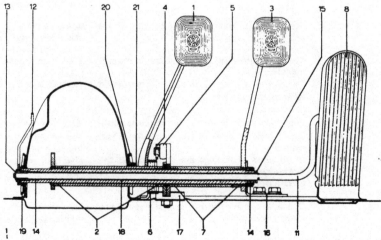

**Fig 9.11 BRAKE AND CLUTCH PEDAL CLUSTER RHD – CROSS SECTION VIEW (SEC 12)**

| | | | |
|---|---|---|---|
| 1 Clutch pedal | 6 Brake pedal return spring | 12 Accelerator connecting lever | 17 Stop plate |
| 2 Bush | 7 Bush | 13 Circlip | 18 Cross shaft |
| 3 Brake pedal | 8 Accelerator pedal | 14 Bush | 19 Mounting bracket |
| 4 Pushrod lock plate | 11 Accelerator pedal shaft | 15 Washer | 20 Cover plate |
| 5 Master cylinder pushrod | | 16 Mounting bracket | 21 Cover plate guide |

Replace the bolt into the back of the backplate and tighten it. Then hook the cable onto the lever.

7 Feed the threaded end of the cable into the tubes in the frame fork and finally see that the outer sleeve fits into position in the end of the tube. The threaded ends should appear inside the car under the handbrake lever mounting position. It may be necessary to hook them up with a piece of wire.

8 Making sure that they are not crossed, insert the cables into the two eyes in the base of the lever and then put the lever in position checking that the rear section engages properly in the floor section (photo). Once again be careful not to press the ratchet release button. Replace the pivot pin and circlip and screw on the adjuster and locknuts.

9 Adjust the handbrake as described in Section 3.

## 14 Fault diagnosis and remedies

Before diagnosing faults in the brake system check that any irregularities are not caused by:

| | | |
|---|---|---|
| 1  Uneven and incorrect tyre pressures | 3  Wear in the steering mechanism | 5  Misalignment of the bodyframe |
| 2  Incorrect 'mix' of radial and cross-ply tyres | 4  Defects in the suspension and dampers | |

| Symptom | Reason/s | Remedy |
|---|---|---|
| Pedal travels a long way before the brakes operate | Brake shoes set too far from the drums | Adjust the brake shoes to the drums. (This applies equally where disc brakes are fitted but only the rear drums need adjustment). |
| Stopping ability poor, even though pedal pressure is firm | Linings and/or drums badly worn or scored | Dismantle, inspect and renew as required. |
| | One or more wheel hydraulic cylinders seized resulting in some brake shoes not pressing against the drums (or pads against discs) | Dismantle and inspect wheel cylinders. Renew as necessary. |
| | Brake linings contaminated with oil | Renew linings and repair source of oil contamination. |
| | Wrong type of linings fitted | Verify type of material which is correct for the car and fit it. |
| | Brake shoes wrongly assembled | Check for correct assembly. |
| | One of the dual hydraulic circuits is leaking resulting in only front or only rear brakes in operation | Examine hydraulic system for signs of leaks. |
| Car veers to one side when the brakes are applied | Brake linings on one side are contaminated with oil | Renew linings and stop oil leak. |
| | Hydraulic wheel cylinder(s) on one side partially or fully seized | Inspect wheel cylinders for correct operation and renew as necessary. |
| | A mixture of lining materials fitted between sides | Standardise on types of linings fitted. |
| | Unequal wear between sides caused by partially seized wheel cylinders | Check wheel cylinders and renew linings and drums as required. |
| Pedal feels spongy when the brakes are applied | Air is present in the hydraulic system | Bleed the hydraulic system and check for any signs of leakage. |
| Pedal feels springy when the brakes are applied | Brake linings not bedded into the drums (after fitting new ones) | Allow time for new linings to bed in after which it will certainly be necessary to adjust the shoes to the drums as pedal travel will have increased. |
| | Master cylinder or brake backplate mounting bolts loose | Retighten mounting bolts. |
| | Severe wear in brake drums causing distortion when brakes are applied | Renew drums and linings. |
| Pedal travels right down with little or no resistance and brakes are virtually non-operative. (See note at end) | Leak in both hydraulic system circuits resulting in lack of pressure for operating wheel cylinders | Examine the whole of the hydraulic system and locate and repair leaks. Test after repairing each and every leak source. |
| | If no signs of leakage are apparent all the master cylinder internal seals are failing to sustain pressure | Overhaul master cylinder. |
| Binding, juddering, overheating | One or a combination of causes given in the foregoing sections | Complete and systematic inspection of the whole braking system. |

Note: Due to the safety feature of dual hydraulic circuits the possibility of both circuits failing simultaneously is very remote indeed.

Removing the disc (Sec 7.16)

Tandem master cylinder viewed from lower right. Note the stop light switch connections with leads removed (Sec 8.2)

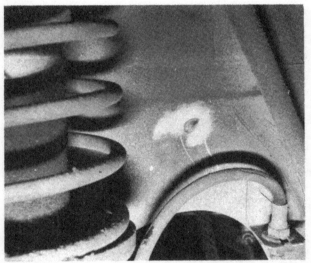

Signs of a brake hose rubbing against the body. The mounting bracket, lower right was bent to keep it clear (Sec 10.3)

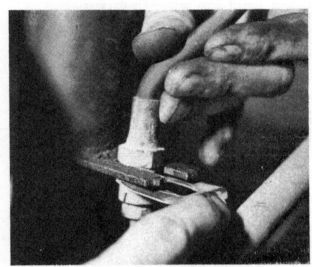

Flexible hose mounting bracket and clip (Sec 10.5)

Foot pedal cluster. Note pushrod to brake master cylinder (arrowed) (Sec 12.1)

Handbrake lever lifted out to install cables (Sec 13.8)

# Chapter 10 Electrical system

## Contents

## Specifications

**Battery**

| | |
|---|---|
| Type ... ... ... ... ... ... ... ... ... ... ... ... ... ... ... ... | 12 volt |
| Capacity ... ... ... ... ... ... ... ... ... ... ... ... ... ... ... | 36 amp/hours |
| Earth ... ... ... ... ... ... ... ... ... ... ... ... ... ... ... | Negative |

**Generator**

| | |
|---|---|
| Type ... ... ... ... ... ... ... ... ... ... ... ... ... ... ... | Bosch or VW  DC |
| Maximum current ... ... ... ... ... ... ... ... ... ... ... | 30 amps |
| Mean regulating voltage... ... ... ... ... ... ... ... ... ... | 14 volts |
| Nominal output speed ... ... ... ... ... ... ... ... ... | 2000 rpm |
| Cut in speed ... ... ... ... ... ... ... ... ... ... ... | 1450 rpm |
| Commutator minimum diameter ... ... ... ... ... ... ... | 32.8 mm |
| Segment insulation undercut ... ... ... ... ... ... ... ... | 0.5 mm |
| Brush length ... ... ... ... ... ... ... ... ... ... ... ... | Must be greater than length of holder |

**Regulator**

| | |
|---|---|
| Type ... ... ... ... ... ... ... ... ... ... ... ... ... ... ... ... | Bosch or VW - matched to generator |

**Starter motor**

| | |
|---|---|
| Type ... ... ... ... ... ... ... ... ... ... ... ... ... ... ... | Bosch or VW - pre-engaged |
| Nominal power ... ... ... ... ... ... ... ... ... ... ... ... | 12 volt .7 hp |

**Lamps**

| | |
|---|---|
| Headlamp bulb ... ... ... ... ... ... ... ... ... ... ... ... | 45/40w |
| Parking lamp bulb ... ... ... ... ... ... ... ... ... ... ... | 4w |
| Stop/tail lamp bulb ... ... ... ... ... ... ... ... ... ... | 21/5w |
| Turn indicator lamp bulbs ... ... ... ... ... ... ... ... ... | 21w |
| Rear number plate bulb ... ... ... ... ... ... ... ... ... | 10w |
| Interior light bulbs ... ... ... ... ... ... ... ... ... ... | 10w festoon |
| Warning lamp bulbs ... ... ... ... ... ... ... ... ... ... | 1.2w and 2w |
| Side marker bulb - US only ... ... ... ... ... ... ... ... | 4w |

**Fuses** ... ... ... ... ... ... ... ... ... ... ... ... ... ... ... ...

12 fuse holders are provided and the list below gives the basic circuits. For variations and additional items refer to the wiring diagrams. The fuse holder is mounted beside the steering column and No 1 fuse is at the left of the row.

| Fuse  1 | Parking lights front |
|---------|----------------------|
|         | Parking light rear right |
|         | Rear number plate light |
|         | Side marker lights (US only) |
| Fuse  2 | Parking light rear left |
| Fuse  3 | Headlamp main beam right |
|         | Headlamp main beam left (from August 1971) |
| Fuse  4 | Headlamp main beam left |
|         | Headlamp main beam right (from August 1971) |
| Fuse  5 | Headlamp dip beam right |
|         | Headlamp dip beam left (from August 1971) |
|         | Main beam warning light (from August 1971) |
| Fuse  6 | Headlamp dip beam left |
|         | Headlamp dip beam right (from August 1971) |
| Fuse  7 | Vacant |
| Fuse  8 | Emergency flashers |
| Fuse  9 | Headlamp flasher |
|         | Interior light |
| Fuse 10 | Brake lights |
|         | Horn |
| Fuse 11 | Windscreen wiper motor |
| Fuse 12 | Gauges and warning lights |

**Torque wrench settings**

| | |
|---|---|
| Generator pulley nut  ... ... ... ... ... ... ... ... ... ... ... ... ... ... | 43 lb ft/6.0 mkg |
| Fan nut  ... ... ... ... ... ... ... ... ... ... ... ... ... ... ... ... | 43 lb ft/6.0 mkg |

## 1 General description

The system is 12 volt comprising:
A battery with negative earth mounted in a carrier under the rear seat.

A D.C. generator mounted on a pedestal above the engine driven by a belt from the crankshaft pulley. The generator armature shaft also carries the cooling fan at the opposite end.

A voltage regulator and cut-out unit mounted under the back seat.

A starter motor of the pre-engaged type (one which meshes with the flywheel ring gear before the power is switched to the motor).

The battery provides the necessary power storage source for operating the starter and providing the current to operate the lights, accessories and ignition circuit. It is kept in a state of full charge by the generator. The regulator controls the generator output. This control automatically adjusts according to the state of charge of the battery, the electrical load demanded and engine revolutions in such a way that the generator is never overloaded and the battery never over or undercharged. It must be appreciated that indiscriminate additions of electrical accessories can upset this balance.

The starter motor is mounted on the transmission casing. Drive pinion engagement and switching is effected by a solenoid. The pinion is engaged by the solenoid before the same solenoid switches current to the starter motor itself. The pinion is driven through a one-way roller clutch to obviate any damage from over-run.

Later models are wired to accept a plug in diagnosis system, details of which are given in this Chapter.

## 2 Battery - removal and replacement

1 The battery is fixed under the rear seat which must first be lifted up and out.
2 There is a protective plastic cover over the top of the battery. On models with computer diagnosis there is a small lead to a connection for sensing the battery electrolyte level. Detach this.

3 Unclamp the battery terminals (earth [or negative] terminal first) and lift the battery out vertically to prevent electrolyte spillage.
4 When replacing the battery see that both terminals and terminal clamps are clean and free from corrosion or deposits of any sort. Smear them with petroleum jelly (not grease) before connection. Never replace the rear seat without the battery cover in position. The springs of the seat can short circuit the terminals and start a fire.

## 3 Battery - maintenance and inspection

1 Normal weekly battery maintenance consists of checking the electrolyte level of each cell to ensure that the separators are covered by ¼ inch of electrolyte. If the level has fallen, top up the battery using distilled water only. Do not overfill. If a battery is overfilled or any electrolyte spilled, immediately wipe away the excess as electrolyte attacks and corrodes any metal it comes into contact with very rapidly.
2 As well as keeping the terminals clean and covered with petroleum jelly, the top of the battery, and especially the top of the cells, should be kept clean and dry. This helps prevent corrosion and ensures that the battery does not become partially discharged by leakage through dampness and dirt.
3 Once every three months, remove the battery and inspect the battery tray and battery leads for corrosion (white fluffy deposits on the metal which are brittle to touch). If any corrosion is found, clean off the deposits with ammonia and paint over the clean metal with an anti-rust/anti-acid paint.
4 At the same time inspect the battery case for cracks. If a crack is found, clean and plug it with one of the proprietary compounds marketed by firms, such as Holts, for this purpose. If leakage through the crack has been excessive then it will be necessary to refill the appropriate cell with fresh electrolyte as detailed later. Cracks are frequently caused in the top of the battery cases by pouring in distilled water in the middle of winter after instead of BEFORE a run. This gives the water no chance to mix with the electrolyte and so the former freezes and splits the battery case.
5 If topping up the battery becomes excessive and the case has been inspected for cracks that could cause leakage, but none are found, the battery is being over-charged and the regulator will have to be checked.
6 With the battery on the bench at the three monthly interval

check, measure its specific gravity with a hydrometer to determine the state of charge and condition of the electrolyte. There should be very little variation between the different cells and if a variation in excess of 0.025 is present it will be due to either:

a)  Loss of electrolyte from the battery at some time caused by spillage or a leak, resulting in a drop in the specific gravity of the electrolyte when the deficiency was replaced with distilled water instead of fresh electrolyte.

b)  An internal short circuit caused by buckling of the plates or a similar malady pointing to the likelihood of total battery failure in the near future.

7  The correct readings for the electrolyte specific gravity at various states of charge and conditions are:

|  | Temperate | Tropical |
| --- | --- | --- |
| Fully charged | 1.285 | 1.23 |
| Half charged | 1.20 | 1.14 |
| Discharged | 1.12 | 1.08 |

## 4  Electrolyte replenishment

1  If the battery is in a fully charged state and one of the cells maintains a specific gravity reading which is 0.025 or more lower than the others, and a check of each cell has been made with a voltage meter to check for short circuits (a four to seven second test should give a steady reading of between 1.2 to 1.8 volts), then it is likely that electrolyte has been lost from the cell with the low reading at some time.

2  Top the cell up with a solution of 1 part sulphuric acid to 2.5 parts of water. If the cell is already fully topped up draw some electrolyte out of it with a pipette.

3  When mixing the sulphuric acid and water NEVER ADD WATER TO SULPHURIC ACID — always pour the acid slowly onto the water in a glass container. IF WATER IS ADDED TO SULPHURIC ACID IT WILL EXPLODE.

4  Continue to top up the cell with the freshly made electrolyte and then re-charge the battery and check the hydrometer readings.

## 5  Battery - charging

1  In winter time when heavy demand is placed upon the battery, such as when starting from cold, and much electrical equipment is continually in use, it is a good idea occasionally to have the battery fully charged from an external source at the rate of 3.5 to 4 amps.

2  Continue to charge the battery at this rate until no further rise in specific gravity is noted over a four hour period.

3  Alternatively, a trickle charger, charging at the rate of 1.5 amps, can be safely used overnight.

4  Specially rapid 'boost' charges which are claimed to restore the power of the battery in 1 to 2 hours are most dangerous as they can cause serious damage to the battery plates through over-heating.

5  While charging the battery note that the temperature of the electrolyte should never exceed 100°F.

6  Make sure that your charging set and battery are set to the same voltage.

## 6  Dynamo - routine maintenance

1  The main requirement is maintaining the fan belt at the proper tension as described in Chapter 2.

2  Both armature shaft bearings are sealed and additional lubrication is not possible as a frequent routine.

3  Keep an eye on the condition of the commutator and carbon brushes. These can be seen through the aperture in the casing once the cover at the fan belt end is loosened and moved back. The brushes should protrude from the upper ends of their

holders. If they do not then they are getting short and need renewal. The commutator should not show serious signs of discolouration and there should be no indication of a channel worn where the brushes track.

## 7  Dynamo - testing in position - general

1  If the ignition warning light does not go out when the engine is running at a fast tickover or only goes out at high revolutions it is usually due to a fault in either the dynamo or regulator. If checked and dealt with quickly it is often possible to avoid expensive repairs.

2  First examine the dynamo brushes and the surface of the commutator. If the brushes are worn or commutator dirty it is possible to deal with them without removing the dynamo from the car. Section 12 explains how to remove the brushes and clean the commutator.

3  In order to carry out further checks a voltmeter is required.

## 8  Dynamo - no load regulated voltage check

1  Disconnect the lead from terminal    B+ on the regulator (situated under the rear seat cushion at the left) and make sure the end cannot touch any nearby part and short to earth.

2  Connect the positive lead from the voltmeter to terminal B+ on the regulator and the negative lead to earth (Fig 10.1A).

3  Start the engine and increase speed slowly to a fast tickover. The voltmeter should rise to a reading of 13—14 volts and stay there. If there is no reading the fault is most likely in the generator. If the reading is incorrect then the regulator is most probably at fault. Nevertheless both could be faulty in either case.

## 9  Dynamo - no load unregulated voltage check

1  This check will tell you if the generator is at fault and must be done quickly or you could damage an otherwise sound generator.

2  Disconnect the leads from terminals DF and D+ on the generator (Fig 10.1B).

3  Connect the voltmeter + terminal to the D+ terminal on the generator and the voltmeter negative terminal to the D— terminal.

4  Start the engine. At a fast tickover - say 1500 generator rpm the voltage should be approximately 12 volts. At twice this speed the voltage should increase to 36 volts. Check quickly and switch off within a few seconds. If the voltage is nil or low then the generator is faulty.

## 10  Dynamo - current output check and reverse current check

1  The two previous tests have confirmed the presence or lack of voltage. This does not confirm the presence or lack of amps which are needed to charge the battery (even though the warning light may go out). For the current output check you will need an ammeter - with a range of 50 amps negative and positive. (If you have fitted an ammeter as an extra into the charging circuit already, this, of course, performs the function of this test and in fact tells you at all times whether the generator is doing its job properly.)

2  Disconnect the D+ cable from the generator and connect an ammeter in circuit (Fig 10.1C). Under no circumstances run the engine with the D+ connection out of circuit or the dynamo field windings will be damaged.

3  Start the engine. At low speed the ammeter should show a discharge although at very low idling speed it should move to zero when the regulator cut-out functions. At high engine speed the ammeter should show a positive reading. Try this with some lights switched on to ensure that it maintains a positive charge rate.

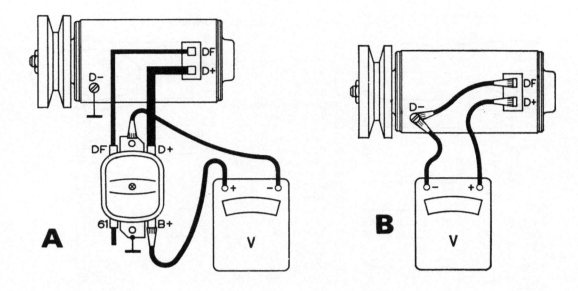

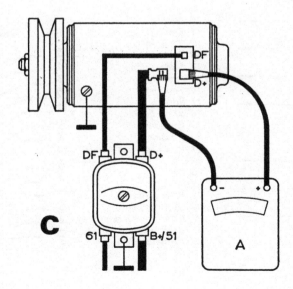

**Fig 10.1 DYNAMO AND REGULATOR TESTS**

A  *Voltmeter connection for dynamo no load regulated voltage check*

B  *Voltmeter connected for dynamo no-load unregulated voltage check*

C  *Ammeter connected for current output check and reverse current check*

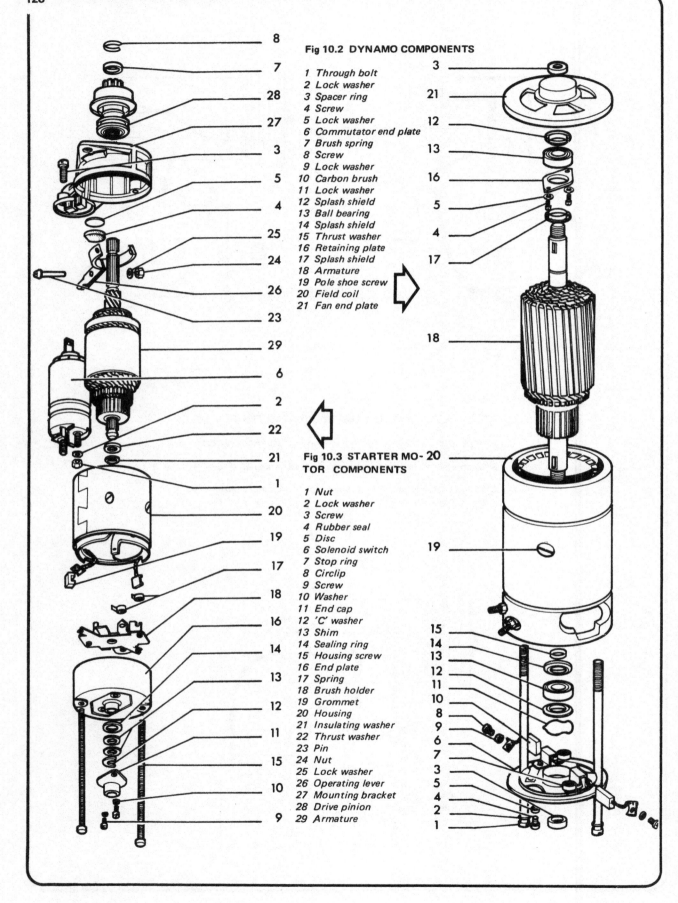

**Fig 10.2 DYNAMO COMPONENTS**

1 Through bolt
2 Lock washer
3 Spacer ring
4 Screw
5 Lock washer
6 Commutator end plate
7 Brush spring
8 Screw
9 Lock washer
10 Carbon brush
11 Lock washer
12 Splash shield
13 Ball bearing
14 Splash shield
15 Thrust washer
16 Retaining plate
17 Splash shield
18 Armature
19 Pole shoe screw
20 Field coil
21 Fan end plate

**Fig 10.3 STARTER MO-TOR COMPONENTS**

1 Nut
2 Lock washer
3 Screw
4 Rubber seal
5 Disc
6 Solenoid switch
7 Stop ring
8 Circlip
9 Screw
10 Washer
11 End cap
12 'C' washer
13 Shim
14 Sealing ring
15 Housing screw
16 End plate
17 Spring
18 Brush holder
19 Grommet
20 Housing
21 Insulating washer
22 Thrust washer
23 Pin
24 Nut
25 Lock washer
26 Operating lever
27 Mounting bracket
28 Drive pinion
29 Armature

Removing the aperture cover from the dynamo (Sec 12.2a)

Hooking up the spring to pull the brush from the holder (Sec 12.2b)

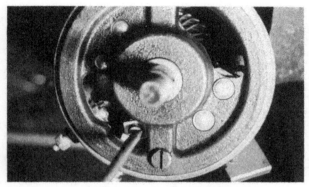

Undo the brush terminal tag screw (Sec 12.2c)

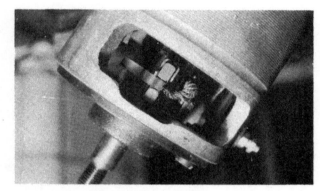

Brush and spring correctly fitted in position (Sec 12.4)

Removing the top starter motor bolt. Note the bolt head and the terminal (arrowed) for the main cable connection (Sec 13.2)

Undoing the connecting strap terminal nut (Sec 14.2a)

Removing the solenoid retaining screws (Sec 14.2b)

Unhook the solenoid from the operating lever (Sec 14.3)

**4** If the ammeter continues to show a discharge even at low idling speed it means that the cut-out is not functioning and current is flowing back from the battery to the generator.
**5** If the cut-out is not functioning the regulator unit must be changed.

## 11 Regulator - removal and replacement

**1** First disconnect the battery. The regulator is held by two screws to the body panel under the rear seat on the left. Disconnect the cables from the four terminals on the regulator.
**2** Replacement is a reversal of this procedure. Note that the thicker of the two wires from the generator is the one that connects to terminal + (D+). It is most important to get these connections correct. Otherwise the generator and regulator could be ruined in the first few seconds of operation.

## 12 Dynamo - removal, dismantling and replacement

**1** The generator is removed in the manner described for the fan in Chapter 2. Before deciding to take it out completely make sure that the renewal of the brushes and cleaning the commutator are not the sole things to be done because these can be dealt with without removing the dynamo.
**2** If the brushes need renewing remove the end cover. Hook up the ends of the springs which press them into the holders. Then pull the brushes out. Then undo the screw which connects the leads (photos).
**3** Whilst the brushes are removed the commutator can be cleaned with a piece of clean cloth soaked in petrol. If the commutator is very scored, changing the carbon brushes may improve things temporarily but the improvement in dynamo output is likely to be small and short lived.
**4** When fitting new brushes make sure that they are of the correct type and fit snugly in the holders and slide freely. Brushes which are too loose will clatter about and soon wear out. Those which are tight will probably stick and eventually lose contact with the commutator as they wear away (photo).
**5** If any of the brush retaining springs are broken or the commutator is scored the dynamo must be removed for the repairs to be made.
**6** To dismantle the dynamo is not a procedure we recommend, principally because there is very little the normal do-it-yourself man can do to repair it anyway. If the bearings have failed (a very rare occurrence) then the armature will need reconditioning. Skimming the commutator must be done in a lathe. Should the insulation of the armature or field coils have broken down then they will need renewal.
**7** Having removed the dynamo and taken off the fan, therefore, we recommend it be replaced with an exchange unit or overhauled by a specialist firm dealing with auto electrics. Make sure when taking it to the repair firm that the regulator goes with it as their tests after rebuild will cover the complete unit.
**8** Replacement of the dynamo is described in Chapter 2. Check that the spacer collars behind both the fan and pulley hubs are in position, otherwise when the nuts are tightened they will jam against the end frames.

## 13 Starter motor - testing, removal and replacement

**1** On the Volkswagen the starter is an inaccessible article and short of checking that the mounting bolts are tight and the electrical connections properly made to the solenoid, there is nothing else to be done except take it out if it malfunctions. If the starter fails to kick at all ascertain that current is being fed from the starter switch to the solenoid. This can be done by connecting a suitably long lead to test each of the terminals on the solenoid in turn. Connecting the other end via a voltmeter or bulb to earth. When connected to the smaller terminal (the lead from the ignition switch), there should be an indication on

the bulb or voltmeter when the starter switch is operated. If there is not then check the other end of the wire at the starter switch terminal in the same way. If there is no voltage then the fault is not with the starter. Then connect the lead to the larger terminal on the solenoid. If there is no voltage when the starter switch is operated the solenoid is defective. If there is voltage and the starter does not turn the starter is defective.
**2** The starter is held by a bolt at the top and a stud and nut at the bottom. The bolt head is not hexagonal (photo). It is circular with a flat which engages in a recess in the starter mounting flange. To remove it the nut on the other end must be undone and access to this is between the fan housing and the bulkhead in the engine compartment. The nut on the lower stud is accessible under the car.
**3** From underneath the car, pull off the small lead at the connection and then undo the nut securing the large cable. All this must be done mainly by feel. Do not confuse the two large terminal nuts on the solenoid. The lower one connects the strap between solenoid and starter.
**4** Remove the lower nut and the starter can be lifted out.
**5** Replacement is a reversal of the removal procedure. Before fitting, grease the end of the pinion shaft. It runs in a plain bush in the engine crankcase casting.

## 14 Starter motor - dismantling and reassembly

**1** The first stage of dismantling is to remove the end cover plate so as to get access to the brushes. If these do not protrude above the tops of their holders renewal is necessary, which calls for further dismantling.
**2** Undo the nut connecting the strap between the solenoid and the starter and then the two screws holding the solenoid to the end frame (photos).
**3** The solenoid can now be unhooked from the operating lever inside the end frame (photo).
**4** If the solenoid only is faulty this is as far as it is necessary to go. A new solenoid unit can be fitted now.
**5** Remove the two screws holding the end cover cap (photo).
**6** Slide out the 'U' clip and remove the shims from the end of the shaft. These shims control the endfloat (photos).
**7** Remove the two through bolts from the end cover and the end cover may then be taken off giving access to the commutator brushes (photos).
**8** Hook up the springs holding the carbon brushes in the holders and push them to one side so that the pressure is relieved. The yoke complete with the brush holder mounting plate may then be drawn off the armature. Watch out for the washers on the end of the shaft (photo).
**9** To renew the brushes, two may be detached by simply removing the screws whilst the other two need to be cut off and new ones soldered to the braided leads. Leave sufficient length to solder the new ones onto easily.
**10** To remove the end frame from the drive end of the shaft first push back the stop ring with a suitable tube so that the jump ring underneath can be released from its groove. The end cover assembly complete with pinion may then be drawn off.
**11** The pinion drive should turn one-way only inside the clutch easily. If it does not the whole unit needs renewing. The pinion teeth should not be badly worn or chipped. The yoke of the pinion operating lever should be a good fit in the groove of the pinion sleeve.
**11** Reassembly is a reversal of the dismantling procedure. Thoroughly grease the moving parts of the pinion operating lever first. When replacing the yoke engage the cut-out and tongue correctly (photo).
**12** The carbon brushes should all be held up in their holders and this can be achieved if the springs are jammed against the sides of the brushes. The armature has two washers on the end and these must be fitted so that the thrust washer goes on first and the insulating washer after that.
**13** When the pinion stop ring is refitted stake it into position over the jump ring after the latter has been fitted in its groove.

Removing the end cover cap screws (Sec 14.5)

Remove the U clip from the end of the shaft ... (Sec 14.6a)

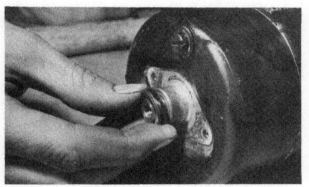

... and the shim washers (Sec 14.6b)

Remove the through bolts (Sec 14.7a)

Take off the end cover (Sec 14.7b)

Lifting the yoke and brush holder assembly off the armature (Sec 14.8)

Refitting the yoke so that the tongue and cut-out fit together (Sec 14.11)

Removing the direction indicator switch (Sec 16.3)

14 When refitting the solenoid ensure the plunger hooked end is securely placed over the operating lever.

15 The screw heads and joint faces of the commutator end cover, the solenoid and end frame should all be treated with sealing compound to keep water out. Use the Volkswagen product specially prepared for this if possible. It is important that it is not applied too thickly, otherwise clearance distances may be upset. If, after reassembly, the endfloat of the shaft exceeds 0.012 inch it should be reduced by adding shim washers under the U retaining clip on the end of the armature shaft under the small cover.

16 Because the pinion end bearing (bush) is located in the crankcase casting, it is not possible to rotate the starter under load or at speed when not fitted to the engine. The customary bench tests are therefore not applicable to this starter.

## 15 Fuses and relays

1 The fuses are located under the dash panel. The wire connections to the fuse block however, are to be found in the other side by removing the fibre cover panel inside the front luggage compartment. Their function is as detailed in the specifications. If any fuse should blow it is normally due to a short circuit in the circuit concerned. With the aid of the wiring diagram, therefore, first check visually at all the points in the circuit where such a fault is most likely to occur. The most likely places are where wires pass through individual holes into lamp units or through holes in the bodywork where grommets have been disturbed. In the ignition circuit check the connections at the coil and choke. Remove the fibre cover from behind the dash panel in the front luggage compartment and see if there are any broken or loose wires. Feel switches to see if they are hot, which they should not be.

2 If no obvious solutions occur disconnect all items on the particular circuit (e.g. the parking light bulbs if that is the circuit concerned). Fit another fuse of the proper rating. Then reconnect one item at a time, switching on each time until the fuse blows again. This will isolate the faulty part of the circuit and a closer examination can be made in that area. If you choose to fit a fuse of a much higher rating to try and overcome persistent blowing, the least that can happen is that the wiring will burn out somewhere. The worst result could be a fire.

3 Relays are in effect remote switches which avoid having to carry the full operating current of the apparatus through the actual operating switch (a starter solenoid is a relay). The fuse rack incorporates a relay console as well so that they may be simply plugged into it for renewal or additional wiring requirements. There are normally at least two relays fitted, one a combined relay for lights, flashers, horn etc, and another for the turn signal/emergency flasher circuit. Relays should be checked by substitution of a serviceable unit where malfunction of a circuit covered by them occurs.

## 16 Direction indicators - fault tracing and rectification

1 One of the most usual causes of failure is due simply to bad connections to earth. This can occur at the bulb holders (usual) or the terminal connections. If, therefore, the flashers can be heard but do not light - or only operate slowly - check all the bulbs, holders and screws for signs of whitish corrosion deposits (which may have been caused by seepage of water past the lamp housing seals). Check also the appropriate fuse.

2 First check that the flasher relay itself is not faulty. The simplest way to do this is by substitution with a new one. The

relay is located on the fuse rack behind the dash panel.

3 If the fault is in the switch itself the steering wheel must be removed (Chapter 11) so that the switch may be removed. This combined switch, if faulty, must be renewed as a unit (photo).

## 17 Windscreen wipers - fault finding

1 If the wipers do not work when they are switched on, first check the fuse. If this is sound then there is either an open circuit in the wiring or switch, the wiper motor is faulty, or the pivot spindles or linkages may be binding.

2 If the wipers work intermittently then suspect a short circuit in the motor or a poor contact to earth. The earth is connected at the main mounting screw. Alternatively, the armature shaft endfloat adjustment may be too tight or the wiper linkage may be binding.

3 Should the wipers not stop when they are turned off there must be a short circuit in the switch or wiring.

## 18 Windscreen wiper motor - removal and replacement

1 Disconnect the battery earth lead.

2 Slacken the clamping screw on the wiper arm brackets and pull the arms off the spindles.

3 Remove the hexagon nut, washers and seals from around the spindles.

4 Remove the glove box if necessary and the fresh air vent.

5 Disconnect the cables from the motor (photo).

6 Undo the screw which holds the motor and frame to the strip steel mounting bracket. The motor and the linkage can then be removed together.

7 To detach the motor from the linkage first remove the lock-washer and spring washer from the motor shaft and detach the connecting rod. Then undo the motor shaft clamp nut and the single screw holding the motor to the frame and take the motor away from the frame.

8 Replacement of the motor and wiper mechanism is a reversal of the removal procedure. Ensure the replacement of the spring washer between the motor shaft and frame and the coil spring between the connecting rod and frame. When refitting the unit to the car make sure the spindles are at right angles to the windscreen. The mounting hole in the frame is slotted to permit adjustment. The earthing strip contact at the mounting screw should be clean.

9 The sealing washers around the spindles must be correctly positioned and care taken not to overtighten the clamping screw - the correct torque being 2—3 lb/ft (30—40 cm kg).

## 19 Windscreen wiper motor - dismantling and reassembly

1 Other than for renewal of the carbon brushes, dismantling for further repair is not economical.

2 To renew the carbon brushes the wiper motor and frame assembly must be removed from the car as described in the previous sections and the motor separated from the frame.

3 Remove the armature end cover by undoing the clip.

4 The brush holders are held in tension against the commutator by a common spring. Unhook this and swing the holders outwards. The old brushes can be removed with a pair of fine nosed pliers. The new ones should be a tight fit in the holders and should seat squarely onto the commutator when the holder is moved back into position.

5 On motors fitted with a self-parking device check that the points gap is 0.8 mm (0.031 inch) and that the points are clean.

Disconnecting windscreen wiper leads (Sec 18.5)

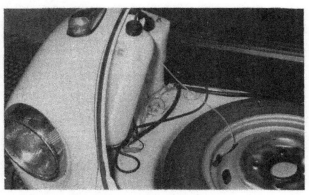
Windscreen washer reservoir. Note the pressurizing pipe running from the spare tyre valve (Sec 22.1)

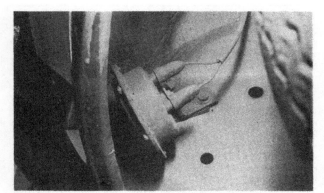
Position of the horn under the left front wing (Sec 24.1)

Checking the horn ring contact (Sec 24.2)

Removing the rear lamp lense (Sec 25.1a)

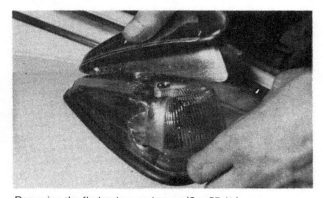
Removing the flasher lens and cover (Sec 25.1b)

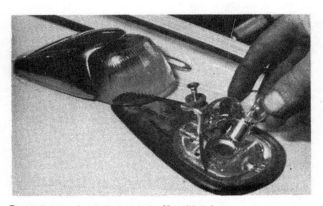
Removing the front flasher bulb (Sec 25.1c)

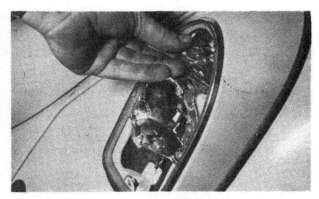
Removing the rear stop/tail bulbs (Sec 25.1d)

## 20 Windscreen wiper spindle bearings - renewal

1   One of the causes of jamming could be due to wear in the spindle bearings and these can be renewed after the assembly has been removed from the car.
2   Having disconnected the driving link and connecting rod by means of removing the spring clips and washer, take off the seal and washer and undo the locknut securing the bearings to the frame.
3   Replace any of the smaller nylon bushes that may be worn also.
4   When reassembling see that the hollow sides of the pressed steel links face towards the frame.

## 21 Windscreen wiper switch and washer pump - removal and replacement

1   The combined wiper switch and washer pump can be easily removed after first disconnecting the battery earth cable and unscrewing the knob from the switch.
2   Then, from behind the panel (in the front luggage compartment), pull off the wires and washer pipes. Unscrew the retaining ring and take off the switch.

## 22 Windscreen washer - fault finding

1   The washer is operated by a valve incorporated in the wiper switch. The water reservoir tank is pressurised from the spare wheel tyre so that water is automatically forced along the pipes when the valve is opened (photo).
2   If no water issues from the jets, first check that all pipes are connected and intact and that the reservoir is pressurised correctly.
3   Then check that the nozzles of the jets are clear. Use a piece of fine wire to poke them out if necessary.
4   If it becomes obvious that the pump/valve is not working, then it must be renewed.

## 23 Stop lamps - fault finding

1   The stop lamps are operated by either one or two hydraulic switches mounted on the brake master cylinder (see Chapter 9).
2   If, after checking that the bulbs, fuse and connections are in order, the brake lights still do not work (with the ignition switched on) pull off the leads from each hydraulic switch   and touch them together. If the stop lamps now light the switch is at fault and should be renewed. The brakes must be bled afterwards (see Chapter 9).
3   If the stop lights still do not work when bridging the terminals of the switch then the fault lies in the wiring circuit. First check that voltage is coming to the switch terminal and carry on from there, tracing back to the connections with the aid of the wiring diagram.

## 24 Horn

1   The single horn is mounted behind the left front wing (photo).
2   If the horn should fail to work after checking the fuse check that the horn ring is operating the contact in the centre of the steering wheel (photo). This can be seen after the steering wheel hub has been levered out. The three screws will release the ring. A contact spring is fitted in the turn signal switch to carry the horn earth wire. It must be remembered that when the ignition is switched on the current flows first to the horn and the circuit is made when the horn ring switch is earthed.
3   The terminals on the horn itself should be perfectly clean and the insulation in good condition.

4   If the horn has to be removed check it once again with an independent supply before condemning it. There is a central adjusting nut in the back of the horn which may possibly give advantageous results if rotated in one direction or the other. It is not normally adjustable and if wrongly set can damage an otherwise good horn. It is important to emphasise therefore that any 'fiddling' with this is a positively last resort, having checked the complete circuit first.
5   The horn is removed by undoing the mounting bolt which secures it to the bracket.
6   When refitting the horn it is important to make sure that it does not contact the surrounding bodywork in any way. If it does it will not function properly.

## 25 Headlamps, side lamps, rear lamps and interior lamp - bulbs and adjustment

1   Rear lamp bulbs are accessible after removing the lenses. These are held by two screws on the outside (photo). The same goes for the front direction indicator lamps mounted on the wings (photo). With the lenses removed the bulbs can be extracted by pressing them in firmly and turning them anticlockwise and releasing (photos). The twin filament stop/tail light bulb only fits one way and for this reason the bayonet pins are offset (photo). Check the offset when replacing them. A reversing light is incorporated in the same housing on some models.
2   Headlamp units also incorporate the front parking light which is a separate bulb set into the reflector casing (photo). On some models fitted with sealed beam units the parking light bulb holder is mounted in the lower part of the main casing instead.
3   To remove the headlamp unit from the car, unscrew the lowest screw which secures the rim. Do not confuse this with either of the two beam aiming screws (photo). Lift up the lower edge of the rim to unhook the top edge and then pull the whole lot out.
4   To remove the bulb undo the bulb holder from the back of the reflector by turning it anticlockwise and then pull the bulb and connection apart (photo).
5   When fitting the new bulb try to remember to avoid handling the glass with the fingers which will leave a deposit which can eventually cause discolouration. Fit the bulb and connector together and then fit the holder into the reflector so that the lugs and notches line up.
6   Should the headlamp lens need renewal proceed as described in paragraphs 3 and 4 and pull out the parking lamp bulb holder as well.
7   It will then be necessary to remove the adjusting screws; so if these are very rusty, clean them properly first.
8   The reflector is held into the rim with spring clips.
9   When fitting a new glass the same type must be used and the sealing ring should be in perfect condition. Make sure the glass is fitted the correct way up.
10  Replace the spring clips and put the adjusting screws back.
11  On sealed beam lamps the bulb and reflector are a single unit and can be identified by the absence of a bulb holder. The wire connection fits straight onto the three terminals at the back of the unit. This item is removed and replaced in the same way that would be used for releasing the reflector and glass on a conventional model.
12  Headlamp alignment is a task which can only be done properly with optical alignment equipment. However, a rough setting can be made until the time when the beams can be properly set. Regulations vary between countries and dimensions given here apply to right hand drive vehicles in the United Kingdom.
13  The car should be standing on level ground with the tyre pressures correct and the equivalent of a 70 kg (154 lbs) passenger in the back seat. For headlamps fitted with replaceable headlamp bulbs the car should face a vertical wall 5 metres (16½ feet) away. It is important that the centre line of the car be exactly

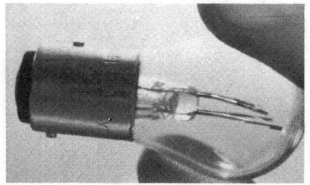

Double filament bulb. Note the offset bayonet pins (Sec 25.1e)

Parking light bulbs in the headlamp reflector (Sec 25.2)

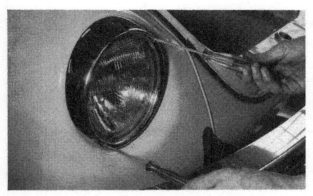

These are the beam aiming screws which should not be touched when removing the headlamp assembly (Sec 25.3)

Removing the bulb holder unit from the reflector (Sec 25.4a)

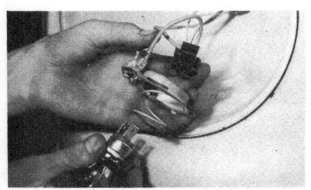

Detaching the bulb from the holder (Sec 25.4b)

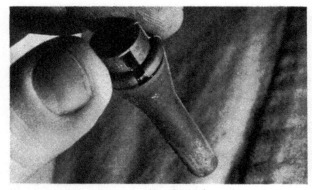

Headlamp housing drain plug (Sec 25.14a)

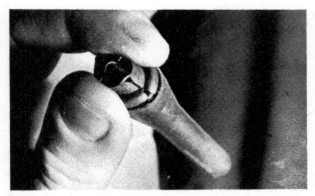

Drain plug with outlet slot squeezed shut if not properly fitted (Sec 25.14b)

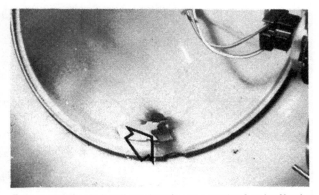

Rust developing in headlamp housing as a result of an ineffective drain plug (Sec 25.14c)

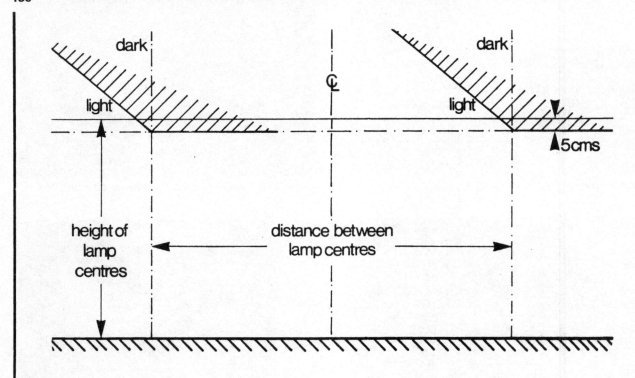

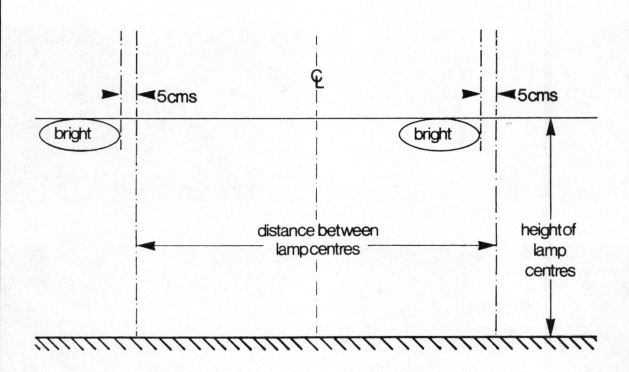

**Fig 10.4 DIAGRAM TO SHOW HEADLAMP BEAM ALIGNMENT**

*Top      Replaceable bulb units*
*Bottom   Sealed beam units*

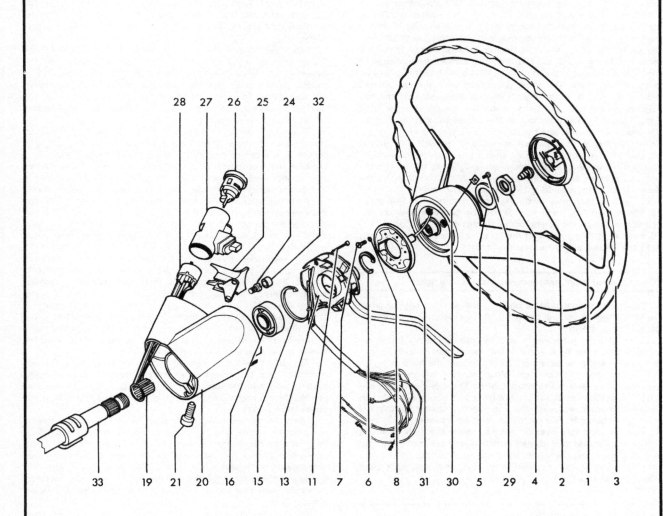

**Fig 10.5 STEERING COLUMN SWITCH AND TURN SIGNAL SWITCH — COMPONENTS**

1  Horn cap
2  Rubber plug
3  Steering wheel
4  Nut (27 mm spanner)
5  Spring washer
6  Circlip
7  Screw

8  Toothed washer
11  Turn signal switch screw
13  Turn signal switch
15  Circlip
16  Bearing
19  Contact ring and insulation
20  Column switch

21  Clamping screw
24  Scrəw
25  Retainer
26  Lock cylinder
27  Steering lock
28  Ignition/starter switch
29  Screw

30  Clip
31  Slip ring and cancelling cam
32  Insulating cap
33  Steering column

at right angles to the wall. Measure the height of the lamp centres above the ground and make a horizontal line on the wall at a height 5 cms (2 inches) less. Then mark the centre line of the car on the wall. This is best done by sighting. Measure the distance between the headlamps and mark two points on the horizontal line equal to this distance. The points should be equidistant from the car centre line. These are the reference points and with the headlamps dipped the angle point between the dark/light zones should coincide for each lamp. Cover the lamp not being adjusted. The adjusting screws are in the lamp rim and the upper one does the vertical adjustment. For sealed beam lamps follow the same procedure with the car 25 feet from the wall. Aim the light intensive areas so that the top edge coincides with the lamp centre line height and the right hand edge is 5 cms (2 inches) to the left of the vertical centres. The two sketches indicate the requirements (Fig 10.4).

14 Whilst the headlamps are removed it is well worthwhile checking the state of the rubber bung in the bottom of the housing in the wing. These bungs are designed to let water drain out and prevent any getting in. A slot in the top provides the drain. If this slot should get constricted and prevent the water from draining there may be the start of a rust problem (photos).

15 The registration plate light is held by two screws under the protective flap on the engine compartment cover (photo).

16 Access to the interior light bulb is effected after the lamp unit has been levered out of its location (photo).

## 26 Instrument panel, speedometer and warning lights

1 Access to all instruments on the panel is from behind, after the front luggage compartment lid has been raised, and the fibre backing panel taken off.

2 The ignition, main beam and oil warning lamp bulbs are contained in snap fit holders in the speedometer head and can be renewed and changed simply by pulling out the holders.

3 The speedometer cable can be detached from the head by unscrewing the knurled retaining collar. The other end is driven by the bearing dust cover on the front left wheel and this can be released after removing the hub cap and taking the clip off the end of the cable. The cable may then be drawn out.

4 The speedometer head is released once the two retaining screws are slackened. If turned anticlockwise the mounting lugs will disengage and the whole head can be lifted out. Make sure that the warning lamps, panel lamp and earth lead have been disconnected also.

## 27 Steering column switch

1 The steering column switch which also acts as a column lock may be removed if necessary once the steering column and direction indicator switch have been removed.

2 It is necessary to disconnect all wiring from both switches where they join their terminal connections behind the instrument panel. All these should be marked to prevent mix-ups later.

3 The column switch assembly is held to the column tube by a single screw requiring an Allan key to undo it. It may then be drawn off the top of the column.

4 It is important to set the switch/lock assembly in its correct position again on replacement. This is done when the flasher switch and steering wheel have been replaced. The gap above the switch casing should be 2–4 mm. If the gap is too large the horn will not work. If it is too small the headlamps will stay permanently on.

## 28 Computer diagnosis

Volkswagen has recently developed a maintenance check system linked into a recording and measuring apparatus.

The main purpose of the system is to reduce the human error, primarily one of omission, in the check list for their 6000 mile service.

A standard print-out sheet to cover all models lists 88 separate checks. 65 of these checks apply to all models.

It must be emphasised that the scheme is purely a diagnosis and that apart from ensuring that the tyre pressures are correct to start with (so that headlamp alignment may be measured correctly) the diagnosis service man does not do any rectification work.

All models from August 1971 onwards (1972 model year) are fitted with central multipin sockets which is wired to all the necessary points for the computer which is plugged into it. For models prior to that time back as far as about 1966 (depending on the model in question) the diagnosis equipment can be hooked up on a special cable fitted with crocodile clips attached to the strategic terminals.

The model of car is first determined together with any of the standard options fitted. Since the introduction of the plug-in socket every car carries a sticker in the engine compartment showing its computer diagnosis code number. This number corresponds with a plastic card measuring about 12 x 6 inches which is punched full of holes corresponding to the specifications for that particular car. This card is fed into the computer. From then on everything measured on the vehicle is compared with the norm on the punch card. The print-out indicates + (OK) or − (not OK) for those operations where the checking is done automatically.

The technician has a hand set connected to the computer and a window in this hand set shows each check requirement. At the time of writing only 24 of the 88 items are checked automatically. The rest are checked by the technician and where all is well he presses a button on the hand set marked '+'. If not applicable there is another button and if unsatisfactory a third button marked '−'. When any of these is pressed the mark is noted on the print-out sheet and the window in the hand set moves forward to the next item for checking.

The items which are measured by the equipment automatically are the steering geometry, ignition and charging systems and cylinder compression. Lights and battery condition are checked automatically only on those models fitted with the connection socket.

The steering geometry is checked by photo electric beams and mirrors as the steering wheel is turned through 180°, 90° each side of the straight ahead position. This is done within a 20 second period and measures toe and camber and prints out the answer in degrees and minutes. The ignition and charging systems are measured for the resistances of the various circuits. It is important that all connections are clean and that cable sizes are standard.

The cylinder compression is measured by calculating the load on the starter motor when the engine is turned over, the state of the battery and the temperature of the engine oil is measured and taken into account for this check.

There is no doubt that the system is quick, accurate and calculated to tell the unhappy customer all the awful things wrong with his vehicle in the shortest possible time. However, it is gratifying to be able to record that like all computer systems it is dependent on the information it is given and in this case the information is based on the experience and conscientiousness of the technician in control.

As far as the car owner is concerned there are a few words of warning to be given. The diagnosis can only be carried out accurately (as far as the automatic side of it is concerned) when the vehicle being processed conforms exactly to the types and options of the computer card which sets the standard. Addition and modifications in the electrical system can upset the measured resistances. Damage to the wiring system, or unusual resistances caused by faulty connections, corrosion or deteriorated insulation can also affect readings. It is perhaps for this reason that the automatic diagnosis is as yet not very extensive, depending as it does on electrical measurement within the vehicle circuitry.

To sum up therefore, it can be seen that the computer diagnosis system has the following positive advantages as part of any routine maintenance programme.

1   A complete check list which follows a logical sequence in the shortest possible time — thus saving time and money.

2   A great reduction in the possibility of human error by omission.

3   A printed record of the decision made on each and every check by the diagnosis technician.

4   Provided the record is kept regularly the car's value is maintained at a much higher level than otherwise.

But the system is still only as good as the personnel using it.

Removing the registration plate light (Sec 25.15)

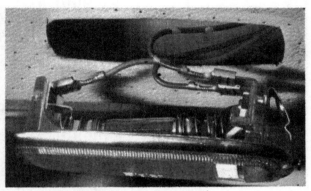

Access to the interior light bulb (Sec 25.16)

## WIRING DIAGRAM 1 FROM AUGUST 1970

| | |
|---|---|
| A | Battery |
| B | Starter |
| C | Generator |
| C1 | Regulator |
| D | Ignition/starter switch |
| E | Windshield wiper switch |
| E1 | Lighting switch |
| E2 | Turn signal switch (switch for dimmer and headlight flasher) |
| E3 | Emergency flasher switch |
| F | Brake light switch |
| F1 | Oil pressure switch |
| F2 | Door contact switch left |
| F3 | Door contact switch right |
| F4 | Back-up light switch |
| G | Fuel gauge sender unit |
| G1 | Fuel gauge |
| H | Horn half ring |
| H1 | Horn |
| J | Relay for headlight dimmer and flasher |
| J2 | Emergency flasher relay |
| J3 | Parking light relay (only for Austria) |
| J6 | Fuel guage vibrator |
| K1 | High beam warning lamp |
| K2 | Generator charging warning lamp |
| K3 | Oil pressure warning lamp |
| K5 | Turn signal warning lamp |
| K7 | Dual circuit brake warning lamp |
| L1 | Twin-filament bulb, left headlight |
| L2 | Twin-filament bulb, right headlight |
| L10 | Instrument panel light |
| M1 | Parking light, left |
| M2 | Tail/brake light, right |
| M3 | Parking light, right |
| M4 | Tail/brake light, left |
| M5 | Turn signal, front, left |
| M6 | Turn signal, rear left |
| M7 | Turn signal, front, right |
| M8 | Turn signal, rear, right |
| N | Ignition coil |
| N1 | Automatic choke |
| N3 | Electro-magnetic cut-off valve |
| O | Distributor |
| P1 | Spark plug connector, No. 1 cylinder |
| P2 | Spark plug connector, No. 2 cylinder |
| P3 | Spark plug connector, No. 3 cylinder |
| P4 | Spark plug connector, No. 4 cylinder |
| Q1 | Spark plug, No.1 cylinder |
| Q2 | Spark plug, No.2 cylinder |
| Q3 | Spark plug, No.3 cylinder |
| Q4 | Spark plug, No.4 cylinder |
| S | Fuse box |
| S1 | Single fuse for back-up light |

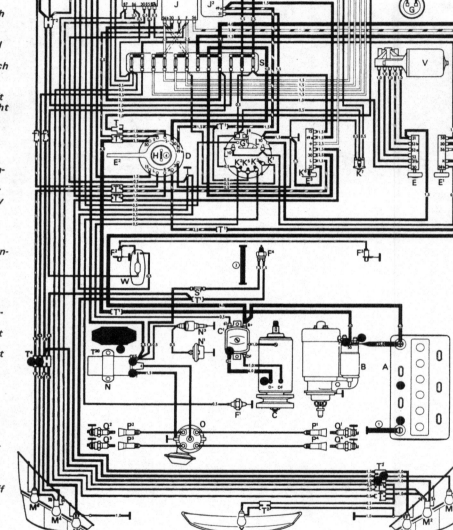

| | |
|---|---|
| T | Cable adaptor |
| T1 | Cable connector, single |
| T2 | Cable connector, 2 pin |
| T3 | Cable connector, 3 pin |
| T4 | Cable connector, 4 pin |
| V | Windshield wiper motor |
| W | Interior light |
| X | License plate light |
| X1 | Back-up light left |
| X2 | Back-up light right |
| 1 | Ground strap from battery to frame |
| 2 | Ground strap from transmission to frame |
| 4 | Horn is grounded through steering column |

The circular black spots are the connections in the test network which are wired to the central socket. The socket and test network were introduced during the 1971 model year.

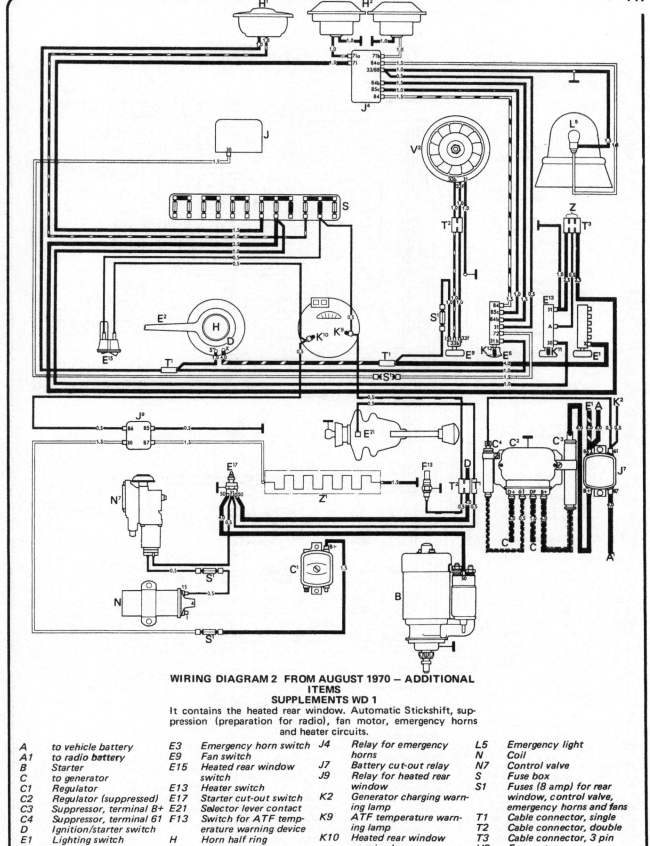

**WIRING DIAGRAM 2 FROM AUGUST 1970 – ADDITIONAL ITEMS**
**SUPPLEMENTS WD 1**

It contains the heated rear window. Automatic Stickshift, suppression (preparation for radio), fan motor, emergency horns and heater circuits.

| | | | | | | | |
|---|---|---|---|---|---|---|---|
| A | to vehicle battery | E3 | Emergency horn switch | J4 | Relay for emergency horns | L5 | Emergency light |
| A1 | to radio battery | E9 | Fan switch | | | N | Coil |
| B | Starter | E15 | Heated rear window switch | J7 | Battery cut-out relay | N7 | Control valve |
| C | to generator | | | J9 | Relay for heated rear window | S | Fuse box |
| C1 | Regulator | E13 | Heater switch | | | S1 | Fuses (8 amp) for rear window, control valve, emergency horns and fans |
| C2 | Regulator (suppressed) | E17 | Starter cut-out switch | K2 | Generator charging warning lamp | | |
| C3 | Suppressor, terminal B+ | E21 | Selector lever contact | | | | |
| C4 | Suppressor, terminal 61 | F13 | Switch for ATF temperature warning device | K9 | ATF temperature warning lamp | T1 | Cable connector, single |
| D | Ignition/starter switch | | | | | T2 | Cable connector, double |
| E1 | Lighting switch | H | Horn half ring | K10 | Heated rear window warning lamp | T3 | Cable connector, 3 pin |
| E2 | Turn signal switch (switch for headlight dimmer and flasher) | H1 | Horn | K11 | Heater warning lamp | V2 | Fan motor |
| | | H2 | Dual horns | K12 | Emergency horn warning lamp | Z | to heater |
| | | J | Relay for headlight dimmer and flasher | | | Z1 | Heated rear window |

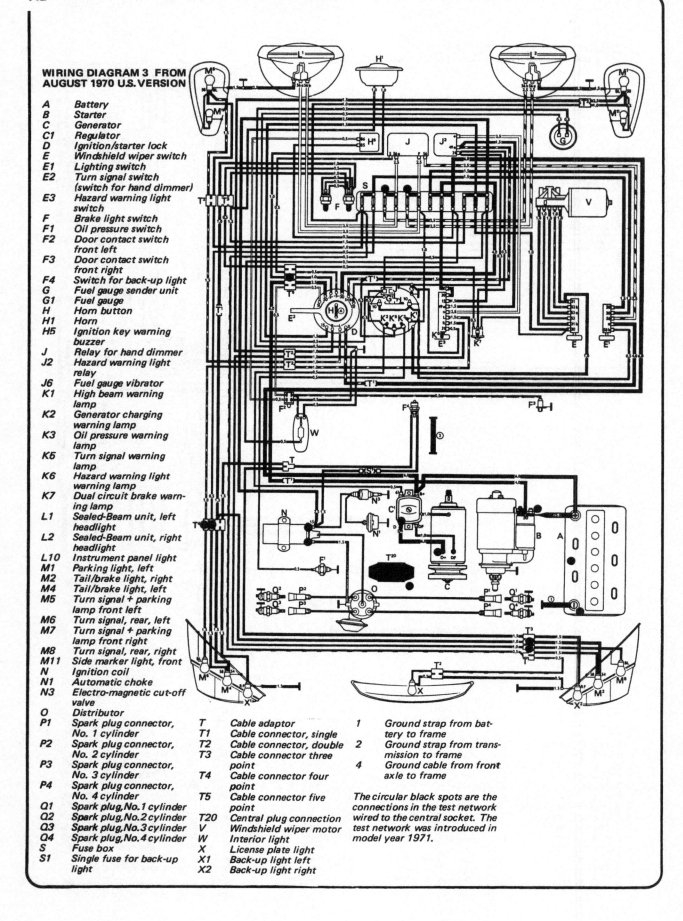

**WIRING DIAGRAM 3 FROM AUGUST 1970 U.S. VERSION**

A Battery
B Starter
C Generator
C1 Regulator
D Ignition/starter lock
E Windshield wiper switch
E1 Lighting switch
E2 Turn signal switch (switch for hand dimmer)
E3 Hazard warning light switch
F Brake light switch
F1 Oil pressure switch
F2 Door contact switch front left
F3 Door contact switch front right
F4 Switch for back-up light
G Fuel gauge sender unit
G1 Fuel gauge
H Horn button
H1 Horn
H5 Ignition key warning buzzer
J Relay for hand dimmer
J2 Hazard warning light relay
J6 Fuel gauge vibrator
K1 High beam warning lamp
K2 Generator charging warning lamp
K3 Oil pressure warning lamp
K5 Turn signal warning lamp
K6 Hazard warning light warning lamp
K7 Dual circuit brake warning lamp
L1 Sealed-Beam unit, left headlight
L2 Sealed-Beam unit, right headlight
L10 Instrument panel light
M1 Parking light, left
M2 Tail/brake light, right
M4 Tail/brake light, left
M5 Turn signal + parking lamp front left
M6 Turn signal, rear, left
M7 Turn signal + parking lamp front right
M8 Turn signal, rear, right
M11 Side marker light, front
N Ignition coil
N1 Automatic choke
N3 Electro-magnetic cut-off valve
O Distributor
P1 Spark plug connector, No. 1 cylinder
P2 Spark plug connector, No. 2 cylinder
P3 Spark plug connector, No. 3 cylinder
P4 Spark plug connector, No. 4 cylinder
Q1 Spark plug, No.1 cylinder
Q2 Spark plug, No.2 cylinder
Q3 Spark plug, No.3 cylinder
Q4 Spark plug, No.4 cylinder
S Fuse box
S1 Single fuse for back-up light

T Cable adaptor
T1 Cable connector, single
T2 Cable connector, double
T3 Cable connector three point
T4 Cable connector four point
T5 Cable connector five point
T20 Central plug connection
V Windshield wiper motor
W Interior light
X License plate light
X1 Back-up light left
X2 Back-up light right

1 Ground strap from battery to frame
2 Ground strap from transmission to frame
4 Ground cable from front axle to frame

The circular black spots are the connections in the test network wired to the central socket. The test network was introduced in model year 1971.

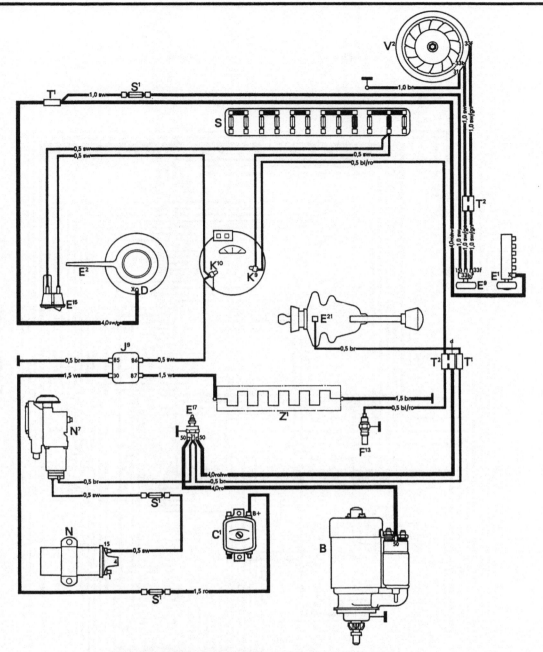

**WIRING DIAGRAM 4 FROM AUGUST 1970 – ADDITIONAL ITEMS. U.S. VERSION**
**SUPPLEMENTS WD 3**

| | | | |
|---|---|---|---|
| B | Starter | J9 | Relay for heated rear window |
| C1 | Regulator | | |
| D | Starter/ignition switch | K9 | Warning light for ATF temperature |
| d | to starter/ignition switch terminal 50 | | |
| | | K10 | Warning light for rear window |
| E1 | Light switch | N | Ignition coil |
| E2 | Turn signal switch (hand dimmer switch) | N7 | Control valve |
| | | S | Fuse box |
| E9 | Switch for fan motor | S1 | Fuses for rear window control valve and fan motor |
| E15 | Switch for heated rear window | | |
| E17 | Starter cut out switch | | |
| E21 | Selector lever contact | T1 | Cable connector, single |
| F13 | Switch for ATF temperature warning device | T2 | Cable connector, double |
| | | V2 | Fan motor |
| | | Z1 | Heated rear window |

**Cable colours:-** *SW – black. ro – red. ws – white. br – brown.*
*bl – blue. gn – green. ge – yellow.*

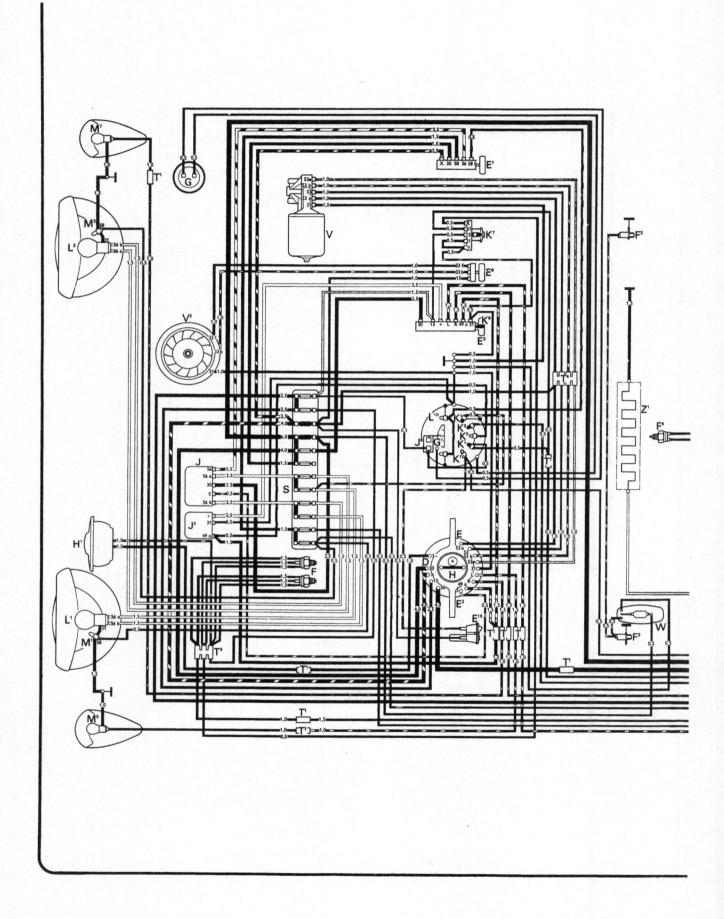

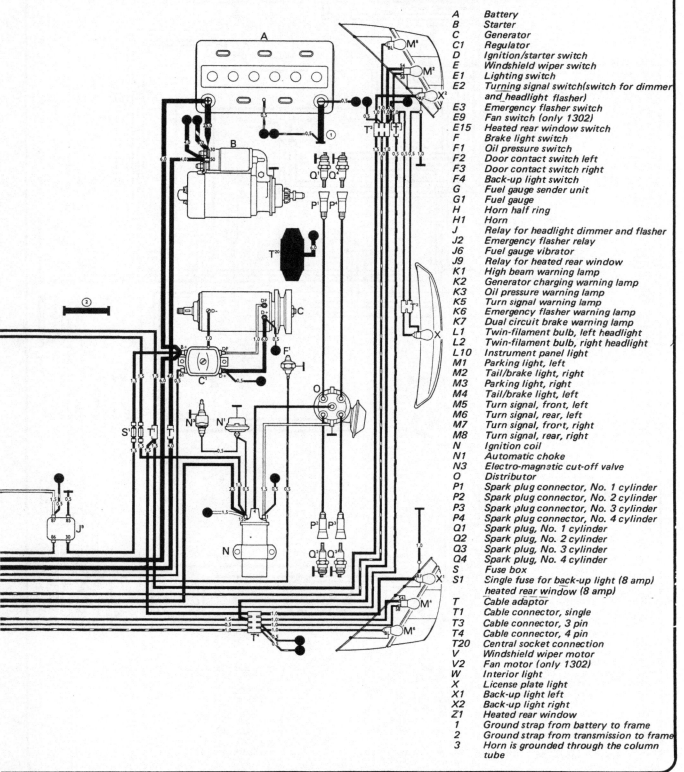

*The circular black spots are the connections in the test
network wired to the central socket.*

| | |
|---|---|
| A | Battery |
| B | Starter |
| C | Generator |
| C1 | Regulator |
| D | Ignition/starter switch |
| E | Windshield wiper switch |
| E1 | Lighting switch |
| E2 | Turning signal switch(switch for dimmer and headlight flasher) |
| E3 | Emergency flasher switch |
| E9 | Fan switch (only 1302) |
| E15 | Heated rear window switch |
| F | Brake light switch |
| F1 | Oil pressure switch |
| F2 | Door contact switch left |
| F3 | Door contact switch right |
| F4 | Back-up light switch |
| G | Fuel gauge sender unit |
| G1 | Fuel gauge |
| H | Horn half ring |
| H1 | Horn |
| J | Relay for headlight dimmer and flasher |
| J2 | Emergency flasher relay |
| J6 | Fuel gauge vibrator |
| J9 | Relay for heated rear window |
| K1 | High beam warning lamp |
| K2 | Generator charging warning lamp |
| K3 | Oil pressure warning lamp |
| K5 | Turn signal warning lamp |
| K6 | Emergency flasher warning lamp |
| K7 | Dual circuit brake warning lamp |
| L1 | Twin-filament bulb, left headlight |
| L2 | Twin-filament bulb, right headlight |
| L10 | Instrument panel light |
| M1 | Parking light, left |
| M2 | Tail/brake light, right |
| M3 | Parking light, right |
| M4 | Tail/brake light, left |
| M5 | Turn signal, front, left |
| M6 | Turn signal, rear, left |
| M7 | Turn signal, front, right |
| M8 | Turn signal, rear, right |
| N | Ignition coil |
| N1 | Automatic choke |
| N3 | Electro-magnetic cut-off valve |
| O | Distributor |
| P1 | Spark plug connector, No. 1 cylinder |
| P2 | Spark plug connector, No. 2 cylinder |
| P3 | Spark plug connector, No. 3 cylinder |
| P4 | Spark plug connector, No. 4 cylinder |
| Q1 | Spark plug, No. 1 cylinder |
| Q2 | Spark plug, No. 2 cylinder |
| Q3 | Spark plug, No. 3 cylinder |
| Q4 | Spark plug, No. 4 cylinder |
| S | Fuse box |
| S1 | Single fuse for back-up light (8 amp) heated rear window (8 amp) |
| T | Cable adaptor |
| T1 | Cable connector, single |
| T3 | Cable connector, 3 pin |
| T4 | Cable connector, 4 pin |
| T20 | Central socket connection |
| V | Windshield wiper motor |
| V2 | Fan motor (only 1302) |
| W | Interior light |
| X | License plate light |
| X1 | Back-up light left |
| X2 | Back-up light right |
| Z1 | Heated rear window |
| 1 | Ground strap from battery to frame |
| 2 | Ground strap from transmission to frame |
| 3 | Horn is grounded through the column tube |

**WIRING DIAGRAM 6 FROM AUGUST 1971 — ADDITION-AL ITEMS SUPPLEMENTS WD6**

Containing:- Emergency flasher system for trailer towing, auto-matic stick shift, suppression, (preparation for radio), dual tone horn system, connection for fuel/electric heater, fog-lights and rear foglight, interval switch for windshield wiper system.

| | |
|---|---|
| A | to vehicle battery |
| A1 | to second battery |
| B | Starter |
| C | to generator |
| C2 | Regulator, suppressed |
| C3 | Suppressor terminal B + |
| C4 | Suppressor terminal 61 |
| D | Ignition/starter switch |
| D1 | to ignition/starter ter-minal 50 |
| E | Windshield wiper switch |
| E5 | Dual tone horn switch |
| E13 | Fuel/electric heater switch |
| E17 | Starter cut-out switch |
| E21 | Selector lever contact |
| E23 | Foglights front and rear, switch |
| F13 | ATF temperature warn-ing switch |
| H | Horn half ring |
| H1 | Horn |
| H2 | Dual tone horns |
| J2 | Emergency flasher relay for trailer towing |
| J4 | Dual tone horn relay |
| J5 | Foglights front and rear, relay |
| J7 | Battery — separating re-lay |
| J11 | Interval switch relay |
| K2 | to generator warning lamp |
| K9 | ATF temperature warn-ing lamp |
| K11 | Fuel/electric heater warning lamp |
| K12 | Dual tone horn warning lamp |
| K17 | Front and rear fog lights, warning lamp |
| K18 | Trailer towing warning lamp |
| L5 | Rotating emergency light |
| L9 | Fog light bulb |
| M2 | R/H tail and brake light bulb |
| M4 | L/H tail and brake light bulb |
| M6 | L/rear turn signal bulb |
| M8 | R/rear turn signal bulb |
| N7 | Control valve (stick shift) |

| | | | |
|---|---|---|---|
| S | Fuse box | T5 | Cable connector five point |
| S1 | Single fuse for heater | | |
| S2 | To fuse box terminal 30 | U | Trailer towing socket |
| T | Cable adaptor | V | to windshield wiper motor |
| T1 | Cable connector single | | |
| T2 | Cable connector double | X1 | L/H back-up light |
| T3 | Cable connector three point | X2 | R/H back-up light |
| | | X3 | Rear fog light |
| T4 | Cable connector four point | Z | to fuel/electric heater |

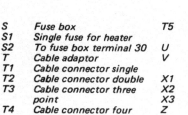

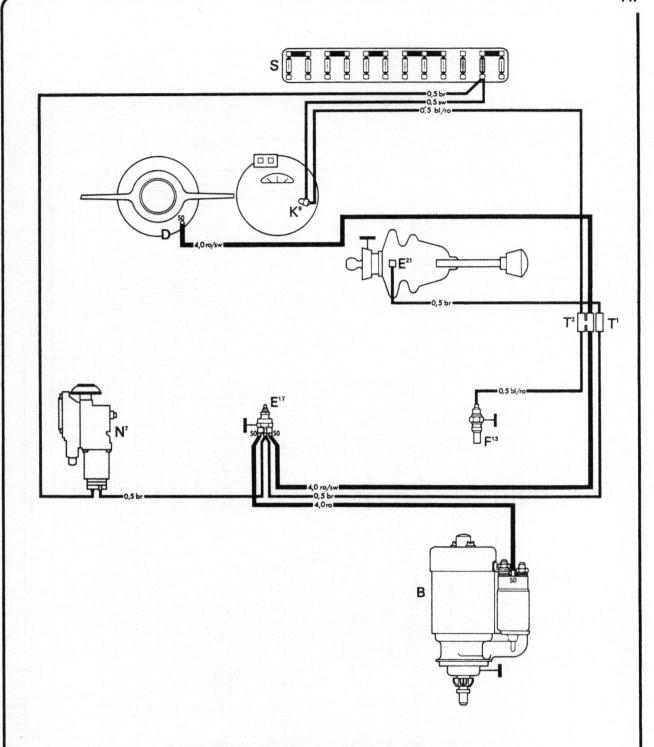

**WIRING DIAGRAM 8 FROM AUGUST 1971 — ADDITIONAL ITEMS. U.S. VERSION**
**SUPPLEMENTS WD 7**

| | | | |
|---|---|---|---|
| B | Starter | K9 | ATF temperature warning lamp |
| D | Ignition/starter switch | | |
| E17 | Starter cut-out switch | N7 | Control valve (stick shift) |
| E21 | Selector lever contact | S | Fuse box |
| F13 | ATF temperature warning switch | T1 | Cable connector, single |
| | | T2 | Cable connector, double |

**WIRING DIAGRAM 7 FROM AUGUST 1971 – U.S. VERSION**

| | | | | | |
|---|---|---|---|---|---|
| A | Battery | E | Windshield wiper switch | E9 | Switch for fresh air motor (only 1302) |
| B | Starter | E1 | Lighting switch | E15 | Switch for heated rear window |
| C | Generator | E2 | Turn signal switch (switch for hand dimmer) | F | Brake light switch |
| C¹ | Regulator | | | F1 | Oil pressure switch |
| D | Ignition/starter lock | E3 | Hazard warning light switch | | |

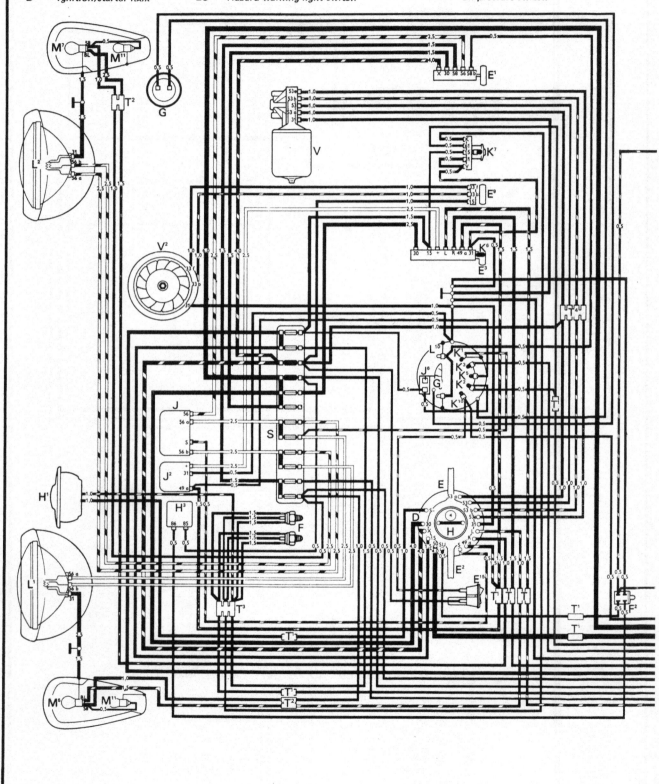

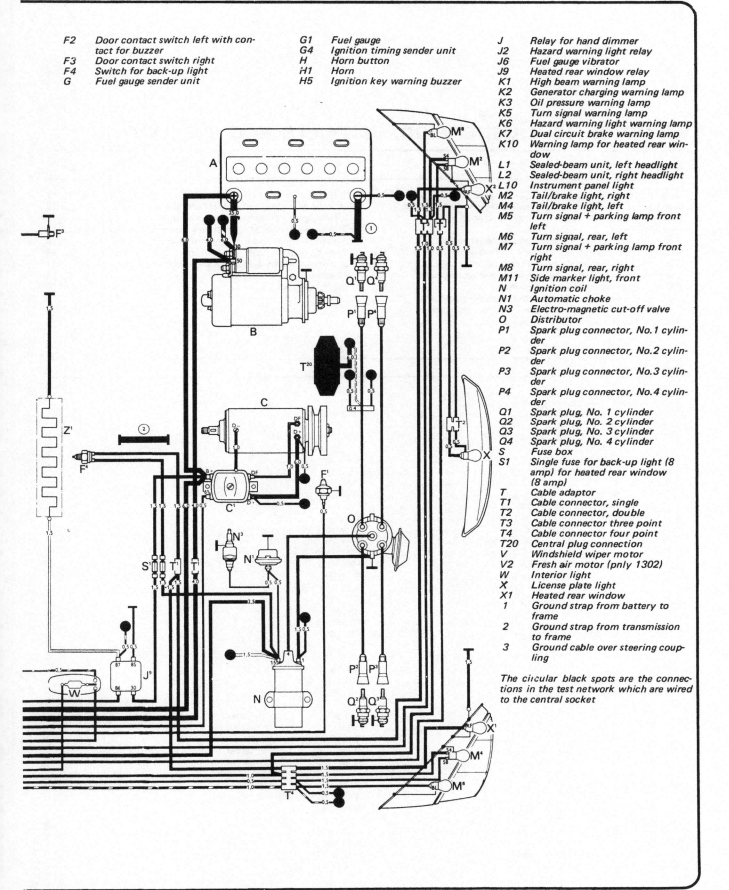

| | |
|---|---|
| F2 | Door contact switch left with contact for buzzer |
| F3 | Door contact switch right |
| F4 | Switch for back-up light |
| G | Fuel gauge sender unit |
| G1 | Fuel gauge |
| G4 | Ignition timing sender unit |
| H | Horn button |
| H1 | Horn |
| H5 | Ignition key warning buzzer |
| J | Relay for hand dimmer |
| J2 | Hazard warning light relay |
| J6 | Fuel gauge vibrator |
| J9 | Heated rear window relay |
| K1 | High beam warning lamp |
| K2 | Generator charging warning lamp |
| K3 | Oil pressure warning lamp |
| K5 | Turn signal warning lamp |
| K6 | Hazard warning light warning lamp |
| K7 | Dual circuit brake warning lamp |
| K10 | Warning lamp for heated rear window |
| L1 | Sealed-beam unit, left headlight |
| L2 | Sealed-beam unit, right headlight |
| L10 | Instrument panel light |
| M2 | Tail/brake light, right |
| M4 | Tail/brake light, left |
| M5 | Turn signal + parking lamp front left |
| M6 | Turn signal, rear, left |
| M7 | Turn signal + parking lamp front right |
| M8 | Turn signal, rear, right |
| M11 | Side marker light, front |
| N | Ignition coil |
| N1 | Automatic choke |
| N3 | Electro-magnetic cut-off valve |
| O | Distributor |
| P1 | Spark plug connector, No. 1 cylinder |
| P2 | Spark plug connector, No. 2 cylinder |
| P3 | Spark plug connector, No. 3 cylinder |
| P4 | Spark plug connector, No. 4 cylinder |
| Q1 | Spark plug, No. 1 cylinder |
| Q2 | Spark plug, No. 2 cylinder |
| Q3 | Spark plug, No. 3 cylinder |
| Q4 | Spark plug, No. 4 cylinder |
| S | Fuse box |
| S1 | Single fuse for back-up light (8 amp) for heated rear window (8 amp) |
| T | Cable adaptor |
| T1 | Cable connector, single |
| T2 | Cable connector, double |
| T3 | Cable connector three point |
| T4 | Cable connector four point |
| T20 | Central plug connection |
| V | Windshield wiper motor |
| V2 | Fresh air motor (only 1302) |
| W | Interior light |
| X | License plate light |
| X1 | Heated rear window |
| 1 | Ground strap from battery to frame |
| 2 | Ground strap from transmission to frame |
| 3 | Ground cable over steering coupling |

The circular black spots are the connections in the test network which are wired to the central socket

# Chapter 11 Suspension, dampers and steering

## Contents

## Specifications

| | |
|---|---|
| Wheel base ... ... ... ... ... ... ... ... ... ... ... ... | 2420 mm |
| Track (front) disc brakes ... ... ... ... ... ... ... ... ... | 1379 mm |
|             drum brakes ... ... ... ... ... ... ... | 1375 mm |
| Turning circle (kerb) ... ... ... ... ... ... ... ... ... | 9.0 m |
| Coil springs - no of coils ... ... ... ... ... ... ... ... | 10.5 |
|             effective coils ... ... ... ... ... ... | 9 |
|             wire diameter ... ... ... ... ... ... | 10.45 mm |
|             mean coil diameter ... ... ... ... | 110 mm |
| Steering gear ratio ... ... ... ... ... ... ... ... ... | 17.8 |
| Overall steering ratio ... ... ... ... ... ... ... ... | 16.5 |
| Steering wheel turns lock to lock ... ... ... ... ... | 2¾ |
| Steering geometry - toe in ... ... ... ... ... ... ... | 30' |
|          - toe in (pressed) ... ... ... ... ... | 10' (under 10 kg wheel load) |
|          - front wheel camber ... ... ... | 1º (+ 20' or − 40') |
|          - toe angle difference ... ... ... | − 30' Lhd |
|            at 20º lock ... ... ... ... ... ... | + 30' Rhd |
|          - caster angle ... ... ... ... ... | 2º ± 35' |
|          - rear wheel camber ... ... ... | negative 1º 20' ± 40' |
|          - rear wheel toe ... ... ... ... | 0º ± 15' |
| Suspension strut ball joint clearance - new ... ... ... | 1.00 mm |
|                       - maximum ... ... ... ... | 2.5 mm |
| Rear suspension spring plate angle ... ... ... ... ... ... | 20º 30' |

### Wheels and tyres

| | |
|---|---|
| Rims ... ... ... ... ... ... ... ... ... ... ... ... | 4J x 15  4 bolt fixing |
| Standard crossply tyres... ... ... ... ... ... ... ... ... | 5.60 x 15  4PR |
| Radial tyres ... ... ... ... ... ... ... ... ... ... | 155 SR 15 |

| Pressures | Normal | Laden |
|---|---|---|
| Front (crossply) ... ... ... ... ... ... ... ... ... | 16 psi | 18 psi |
| Rear (crossply) ... ... ... ... ... ... ... ... ... | 27 psi | 27 psi |
| Front (radial) ... ... ... ... ... ... ... ... ... | 18 psi | 18 psi |
| Rear (radial) ... ... ... ... ... ... ... ... ... | 27 psi | 27 psi |

### Torque wrench settings

| | |
|---|---|
| Strut upper bearing nut ... ... ... ... ... ... ... ... | 51 - 61 lb ft/7 - 8.5 mkg |
| Steering knuckle and ball joint to strut bolts ... ... ... | 29 lb ft/4.0 mkg |
| Front wheel bearing clamp nut screw (max) ... ... ... | 7 - 10 lb ft/1.0 - 1.3 mkg |
| Strut to body nuts ... ... ... ... ... ... ... ... ... | 14 lb ft/ 2 mkg |
| Frame head to body bolts ... ... ... ... ... ... ... | 25 lb ft/3.5 mkg |
| Track control arm to frame head nut ... ... ... ... ... | 29 lb ft/4.0 mkg |
| Track control arm to ball joint nut ... ... ... ... ... | 29 lb ft/4.0 mkg |

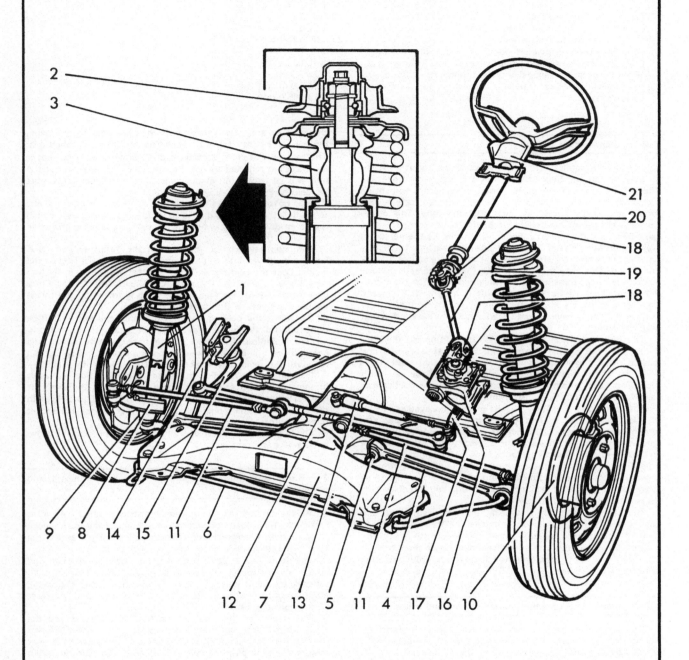

Fig 11.1 FRONT SUSPENSION — GENERAL LAYOUT

1 Suspension strut
2 Detail of strut upper bearing
3 Rubber buffer
4 Track control arm
5 Track control arm eccentric pin for camber adjustment
6 Stabilizer bar
7 Frame head
8 Steering knuckle
9 Suspension ball joint
10 Brake disc
11 Tie rod
12 Centre tie rod
13 Steering damper
14 Idler arm mounting bracket
15 Idler arm
16 Steering gear
17 Drop arm
18 Universal joint
19 Steering column shaft lower section
20 Steering column tube
21 Steering column switch

| | |
|---|---|
| Stabilizer to track control arm nut ... ... ... ... ... ... ... ... | 22 lb ft/3.0 mkg |
| Stabilizer clip to frame head bolt... ... ... ... ... ... ... ... | 14 lb ft/2.0 mkg |
| Steering gear to body bolts ... ... ... ... ... ... ... ... | 29 lb ft/4.0 mkg |
| Drop arm to steering gear nut ... ... ... ... ... ... ... | 72 lb ft/10.0 mkg |
| Steering tie rod joint nuts ... ... ... ... ... ... ... ... | 22 lb ft/3.0 mkg |
| Steering damper to frame head bolt ... ... ... ... ... ... | 43 lb ft/6.0 mkg |
| Steering damper to drop arm bolt ... ... ... ... ... ... | 29 - 32 lb ft/4.0 p 4.5 mkg |
| Rear suspension spring plate bolts ... ... ... ... ... ... | 80 lb ft/11.0 mkg |
| Diagonal arm socket head pivot screw ... ... ... ... ... | 87 lb ft/12.0 mkg |
| Shock absorber to diagonal arm and frame nuts ... ... ... ... | 50 lb ft/7.0 mkg |
| Rear wheel bearing cover bolts ... ... ... ... ... ... | 43 lb ft/6.0 mkg |
| Wheel bolts ... ... ... ... ... ... ... ... ... ... ... ... | 108 lb ft/15.0 mkg |

## 1 General description

One of the significant changes which came about with the introduction of the Super Beetle was a redesigned suspension. The well-tried, tough torsion bars used for the front suspension ever since the vehicle came into being were replaced by coil springs and struts known as the McPherson type. This design will be well known by owners of British built Fords from the early 50's until the late 60's. Some advantages are the increase in available space in the front luggage compartment, slightly superior road-holding and obviation of the need for regular lubrication. One disadvantage seems to be an increase in noise due to the direct transference of wheel vibrations to the top of the wheel arch where the strut unit is anchored. Time and experience will show how robust it is by comparison, especially in those countries where rugged road conditions have in the past been no problem.

The rear suspension is still torsion bar sprung but the drive shafts are now double jointed and the wheel is carried and located on a diagonal suspension arm and spring plates. The wheel no longer moves in an arc on the end of the axle shaft tube. This form of suspension was fitted to earlier Beetles that had stick shift automatic transmission.

The road holding of the vehicle is greatly improved as a result of this change, the 'tuck-in' propensities of the swinging arm having been eliminated. Drive shaft constant velocity universal joints are now an additional point of wear in the drive train but on the other hand the servicing procedures have been considerably simplified. Removal of the drive shafts, which is quite straightforward, enables the transmission unit and wheel bearings to be removed and repaired much more readily and without disturbing the suspension settings.

The steering gear itself remains the well-tried worm and roller design with provision for adjustment. The steering movement is transmitted to the wheels via a central track rod supported by the drop arm and idler arm and two short tie-rods from the track rod to each steering knuckle. A hydraulic steering damper is also installed.

## 2 Front wheel bearings - removal, replacement and adjustment

1   The front wheel hubs each run on two taper roller bearings. Adjustment is effected by a clamp nut which is locked into position by a socket head cap screw incorporated into it.
2   The left hand front hub has a left hand thread. The axle is hollow to permit the speedometer drive cable to go through it. This cable is driven by a square hole in the bearing dust cover. Jack up the wheel and remove the securing bolts and wheel.
3   To remove the bearing dust cover, first take out the split pin or circlip securing the speedometer cable and tap the dust cover from side to side until it comes free.
4   Undo the socket head cap screw and undo the wheel bearing clamp nut.
5   If the thrust washer is now taken off, the complete drum may be removed. There will be the outer races of each bearing left in the hub and the inner race of the inner bearing left on the axle. These should be drifted out of the hub from the inside if

the bearings are to be renewed. If the same bearings are being replaced, they may be left in position and merely flushed out. The race on the shaft should be drifted off also. Note that if the races are renewed then the oil seal on the inner part of the hub will be driven out at the same time as the race. This must be renewed as well.
6   It is possible that the bearing race is a loose fit on the shaft. If this is so, which would tend to let it turn, a few centre punch marks around the axle where it fits will give it some grip once again when fitted.
7   Refitting new bearings means that the outer races will first have to be driven into the hub and the new oil seal fitted on the inside. Coat the bearings and the space between them in the hub with liberal quantities of Castrol LM Grease and place the hub back on the shaft. Fit the outer bearing followed by the thrust washer and screw on the clamp nut (photos).
8   To adjust the bearing endfloat correctly the nut should be tightened up firmly to make sure the bearings are properly located, spinning the wheel at the same time to ensure the bearings are not overtightened. Then the nut should be backed off until the axial play is between 0.03 — 0.12 mm (0.001 — 0.005 inch) at the spindle. This seems quite a lot and can result in some quite noticeable rock at the outer rim of the wheel. It is nevertheless correct although the axial play should be kept to the lower limit where possible. When correct tighten the socket screw (photo).
9   Replace the hub cover and re-secure the speedometer drive cable where appropriate.

## 3   Front suspension ball joint - inspection, removal and replacement

1   At the bottom of the suspension strut a single ball joint carries the main load and steering movement of the front wheel. It is secured to the track control arm on a taper pin and to the base of the strut and steering knuckle by three screws.
2   The joint has a spring loaded nylon shell for the ball and when new the spring can be compressed 1 mm before the shell touches the joint casing inside. As the shell wears the spring holds it onto the ball. The gap between the shell increases accordingly and must not exceed 2.5 mm.
3   To check the clearance the bottom of the strut and the track control arm must be forced apart. If the wheel is raised they must be forced together. Theoretically this latter movement may be achieved by putting a jack under the ball pin nut when the wheel is off the ground. In practise the wheel lifts also. The solution is to make up a lever which will rest on the top flange of the steering knuckle at the base of the strut and can hook under the track control arm (see Fig 11.2). The play can then be ascertained.
4   To renew a joint jack the car up and remove the wheel. Undo the nut on the joint pin. Drive the pin out of its seat in the end of the track control arm. The arm can be forced down to release it. Undo the three bolts that secure the joint to the strut and take the joint off.
5   Replacement is a straightforward reversal of this procedure. Fit new lock plates and tighten the screws and nut to the correct torque.

Pack the bearing with grease (Sec 2.7a)

Replace the thrust washer (Sec 2.7b)

Tightening the clamp screw (Sec 2.8)

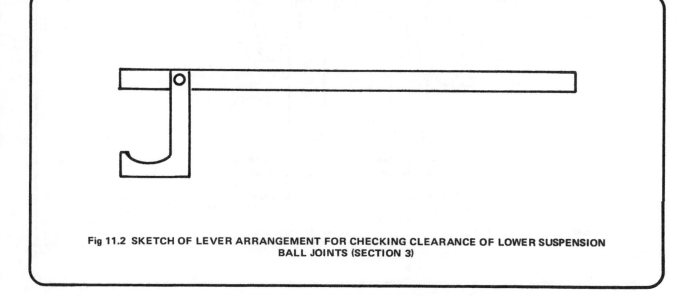

Fig 11.2 SKETCH OF LEVER ARRANGEMENT FOR CHECKING CLEARANCE OF LOWER SUSPENSION
BALL JOINTS (SECTION 3)

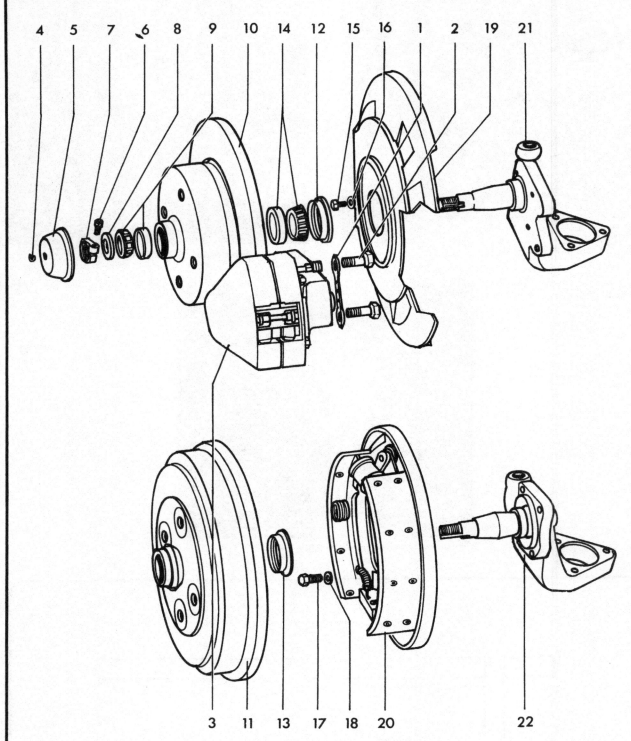

**Fig 11.3 FRONT WHEEL HUB BEARING DETAILS
DRUM OR DISC BRAKES (SEE SEC 11.2)**

| | | | |
|---|---|---|---|
| 1 Lock plate | 7 Bearing adjusting nut | 13 Seal for drum | 18 Washer |
| 2 Caliper mounting bolts | 8 Thrust washer | 14 Taper roller bearing 50 mm | 19 Backplate |
| 3 Caliper | 9 Taper roller bearing 40 mm | 15 Backplate bolt | 20 Brake shoe |
| 4 Circlip for speedo cable | 10 Brake disc | 16 Spring washer | 21 Stub axle assembly |
| 5 Hub cap | 11 Brake drum | 17 Bolt | 22 Stub axle assembly |
| 6 Clamp screw | 12 Seal for disc | | |

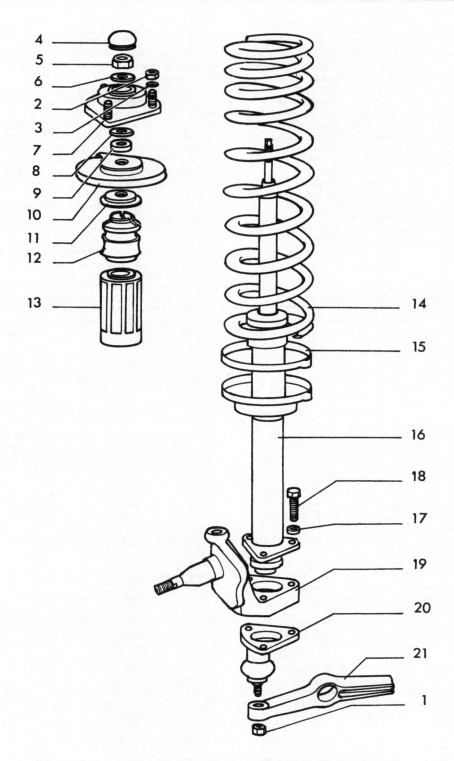

**Fig 11.4 FRONT SUSPENSION STRUT DETAILS (SEC 5)**

1  Self-locking nut
2  Self-locking nut
3  Spring washer
4  Cap
5  Self-locking nut
6  Washer

7  Strut bearing
8  Small washer
9  Spacer
10 Spring cap
11 Large washer
12 Rubber buffer

13 Protective sleeve
14 Coil spring
15 Damping ring
16 Damper
17 Lockwasher
18 Bolt

19 Steering knuckle
20 Ball joint
21 Track control arm

## 4 Front suspension strut - removal and replacement

1   A defective spring or damper means that the whole front suspension must be removed from the car. As this point review the spare situation and the facilities available and decide whether renewal or repair is the most economic process to adopt.
2   To remove the unit first take off the brake assembly. It is not necessary to disconnect the hydraulic line. With drum brakes, the backplate and shoes can all be taken off as an assembly once the drum/hub has been removed. With discs remove the caliper and hang it up with wire nearby. Then remove the disc/hub unit.
3   Remove the three bolts securing the lower end of the strut to the steering knuckle and track control arm (photo).
4   Remove the three nuts holding the top of the strut assembly to the wing valance in the luggage compartment (photo).
5   The steering knuckle can be separated from the bottom of the strut and swung away on the end of the steering tie-rod.
6   The strut assembly is then drawn down to disengage it from the wing valance and lifted away from the car (photos).

## 5 Front suspension strut - dismantling and reassembly

1   If either the spring or damper needs renewal check first whether it would be best to renew the whole assembly. The damper cannot be repaired.
2   To separate the spring and damper it is essential to obtain a proper and suitable spring compressor to hold the spring in compression whilst the securing nut on the top stud of the damper is released. It is dangerous to attempt to release the spring without proper retainers.
3   Once the spring seat is released the damper can be checked, held in its installed position. The damping action should be felt throughout its stroke in both directions. Any very slight leaks which are visible on the outer casing need not give cause for concern provided that the damping action continues to be satisfactory.
4   Coil springs come in three versions each with a colour code. Make sure a new spring fitted has the same colour code as the one removed. The close coils of the spring go at the top.
5   When reassembling make sure that the upper strut bearing is in good condition. Tighten the upper strut retaining nut to the correct torque holding the damper rod end with a suitable spanner.

## 6 Front stabilizer bar - removal and replacement

1   The stabilizer bar is clamped to the front of the frame head and the ends are fixed into the track control arm at each side. All mounting points are in renewable rubber bushes.
2   The stabilizer bar has two functions. It acts as an anti-roll bar but more importantly it provides fore and aft location of the front suspension struts taking the loading of the braking torque.
3   To remove the bar first remove the clips holding the rubber mountings to the frame head. Then remove the split pins from the retaining nuts on the track control arms and take off the nuts and large washers. The stabilizer bar is then taken out.
4   If the stabilizer bar bush in the track control arm is worn it is possible to renew it in place provided a suitable draw bolt and tube can be made up to pull the old one out and draw the new one in. If the inner track control arm bush is in need of renewal as well it would be simpler to do it after removing the track control arm as described in the next section. In any case check the details mentioned in the next section.
5   When replacing the stabilizer bar it is particularly important that the nuts holding the ends into the track control arms are tightened to the specified torque. They should then be tightened further as necessary in order to be able to replace the split pins.

## 7 Track control arms and bushes - removal and replacement

1   The track control arm and bushes control the main aspects of the steering geometry so if they are damaged or worn they must be attended to.
2   The inner pivot pin of the track control arm is eccentric and fitted with eccentric washers to provide adjustment in the setting of the wheel camber angle (photo). Any disturbance therefore, will require checking and re-aligning of the steering geometry after reassembly. It is helpful to mark the position of the eccentric pin before removal so that it will be as near as possible accurate until such time as the geometry can be checked properly.
3   To remove the control arm jack up the car and remove the wheel. Remove the stabilizer bar and disconnect the strut ball joint pin from the end of the control arm.
4   Mark the position of the eccentric washers at the inner end. Undo the self-locking nut and washer and drive out the pin. The arm may then be taken off.
5   Bushes should be pressed or drawn in and out. A tool may be made up from a bolt, washers and a piece of pipe of suitable diameter to draw them in and out. However, as you will most likely be obtaining the new parts at a VW agency it would be easier to ask them to fit them into the arm for you.
6   Two points must be noted when fitting the bushes. The inner pivot bush has a recess which must be on the arm centre line and facing the wheel end. The stabilizer bar bush has two lugs which must be horizontal and face the rear of the car (see Fig 11.7)
7   The track control arm is refitted to the car in the reverse order. The inner pivot pin nut should be tightened to the correct torque when the car is standing on the wheels. This will normally be done when the camber angle is being set.

## 8 Rear dampers - removal and replacement

1   The rear dampers are fixed top and bottom by bolts securing them to the suspension support frame and the diagonal arms.
2   The upper and lower securing nuts are easily accessible but very tight. Make sure the car is stable when undoing and tightening them (photos).
3   Dampers can be tested by operating them, after removal, throughout the full length of their stroke. The damping action should be felt in both directions. Any leaks, provided they are not excessive, may be ignored provided the damping action is in order. If otherwise the damper must be renewed.

## 9 Rear suspension diagonal arm - removal and replacement

1   Fig 8.1. in Chapter 8 is relevant to this section. To remove the diagonal arm first jack up the car and disconnect the outer end of the drive shaft from the wheel shaft (see Chapter 8). The rear brakes may be removed with the arm and wheel shaft if wished in which case the hydraulic pipe connection should be undone. Otherwise the wheel shaft nut should be slackened whilst the car is still on its wheels. The brake drum and backplate complete with shoes may then be taken off and hung to one side.
2   Before undoing the bolts securing the spring plates to the diagonal arm it is important to mark both the arm and plates with a chisel before moving their relative positions. The rear wheel geometry can be upset if this setting is lost (photo).
3   Unclip the brake pipes from the arm.
4   The inner end of the diagonal arm pivots on a socket head bolt (photo). Once this is undone the arm may be taken out. Note the position of the spacer washers which are both located on the outside of the pivot bush.
5   The bushes may be renewed as required. When replacing the pivot bolt it must be tightened to the correct torque of 87 lb/ft and peened into the arm in order to lock it in position.
6   When clamping the spring plates back to the diagonal arm the line up marks made on dismantling must correspond.
7   If extensive repairs are being made (due to damage) which

Undoing the lower strut securing bolts (Sec 4.3)

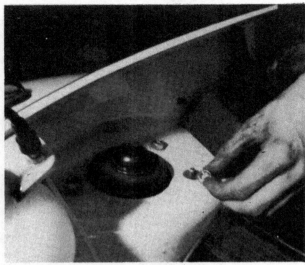
Undoing the upper strut securing nuts (Sec 4.4)

Taking away the strut assembly (Sec 4.6a)

Showing the lower ball joint and steering knuckle which are also secured by the lower strut bolts (Sec 4.6b)

Inner end of track control arm showing eccentric pin and washer (Sec 7.2)

Rear damper upper mounting bolt (Sec 8.2a)

Rear damper lower mounting bolt (Sec 8.2b)

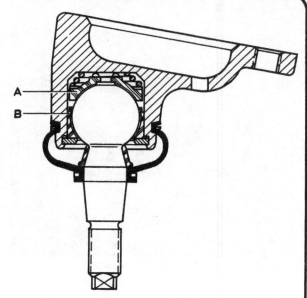

**Fig 11.5 SUSPENSION STRUT BALL JOINT — CROSS SECTION (SECTION 5)**

A  Upper plastic shell - spring loaded
B  Lower plastic shell

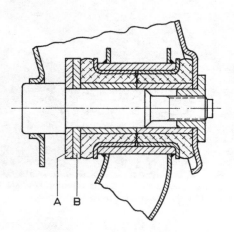

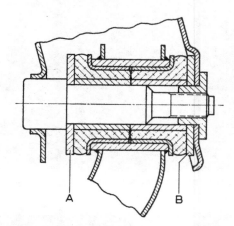

**Fig 11.6  REAR SUSPENSION DIAGONAL ARM — CROSS SECTION OF PIVOT MOUNTING AND BUSH (SECTION 9)**

A and B  Spacer washers

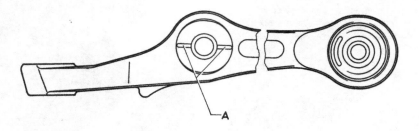

**Fig 11.7  TRACK CONTROL ARM — DETAIL OF BUSHES (SEC 7)**

A. Rubber lugs on stabilizer bar bush facing rearwards. Note position of slot in pivot bush.

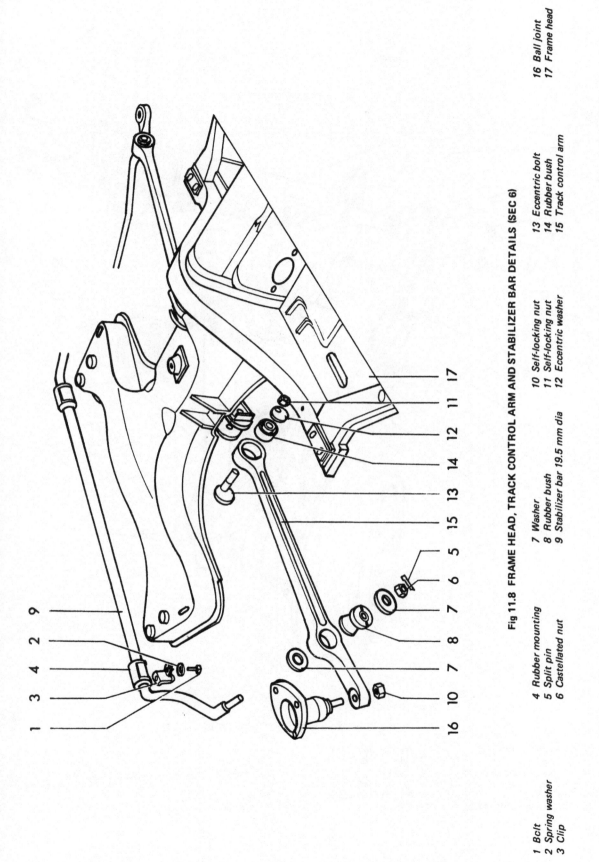

Fig 11.8 FRAME HEAD, TRACK CONTROL ARM AND STABILIZER BAR DETAILS (SEC 6)

1 Bolt
2 Spring washer
3 Clip

4 Rubber mounting
5 Split pin
6 Castellated nut

7 Washer
8 Rubber bush
9 Stabilizer bar 19.5 mm dia

10 Self-locking nut
11 Self-locking nut
12 Eccentric washer

13 Eccentric bolt
14 Rubber bush
15 Track control arm

16 Ball joint
17 Frame head

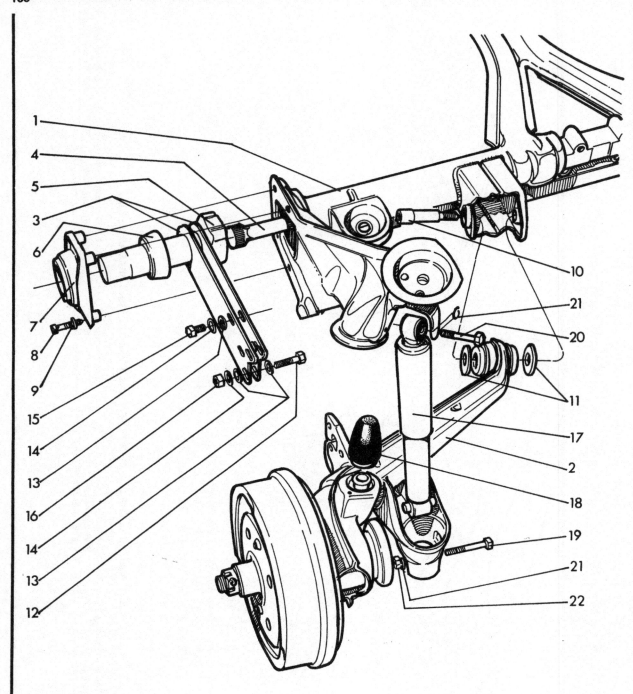

**Fig 11.9 REAR SUSPENSION DETAILS (SEC 9)**

1 Frame cross tube
2 Diagonal arm
3 Spring plate (double leaf version
4 Torsion bar
5 Rubber bush (left inner)

6 Rubber bush (outer)
7 Cover plate
8 Screw
9 Spring washer
10 Socket head screw
11 Spacer

12 Screw
13 Washer
14 Spring washer
15 Screw
16 Nut
17 Damper

18 Bump stop
19 Screw
20 Screw
21 Spring washer
22 Nut

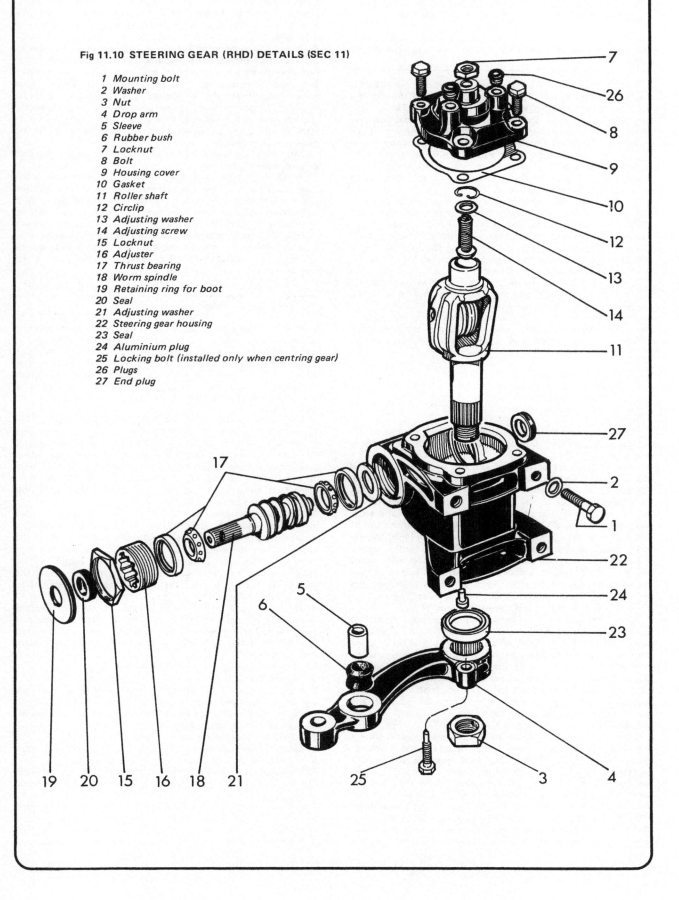

**Fig 11.10 STEERING GEAR (RHD) DETAILS (SEC 11)**

1 Mounting bolt
2 Washer
3 Nut
4 Drop arm
5 Sleeve
6 Rubber bush
7 Locknut
8 Bolt
9 Housing cover
10 Gasket
11 Roller shaft
12 Circlip
13 Adjusting washer
14 Adjusting screw
15 Locknut
16 Adjuster
17 Thrust bearing
18 Worm spindle
19 Retaining ring for boot
20 Seal
21 Adjusting washer
22 Steering gear housing
23 Seal
24 Aluminium plug
25 Locking bolt (installed only when centring gear)
26 Plugs
27 End plug

call for renewal of the arm it is important to have the whole assembly checked on a VW alignment jig after assembly.

## 10  Rear torsion bars and spring plates - removal, replacement and setting

1   Before the nuts and bolts attaching the spring plates to the diagonal arm are loosened the relative positions of the arm and the plates must be marked with a chisel (see Section 9).
2   Early models have a double leaf spring plate but they are joined at the torsion bar end and cannot move up or down independently. It will therefore be referred to throughout in the singular. The spring plate rests on a lug in the frame casting along its lower edge and to relieve residual tension in the torsion bar it must be sprung out so that it rides over the lug. This can be done quite easily with a tyre lever.
3   At this stage the setting of the suspension can be checked. The angle of the plate in this unstressed position should be 20° 30' from the horizontal line of the car. For this measurement therefore a spirit level and protractor are needed. The horizontal line of the car is taken from the bottom of the door opening in the body shell. Using a level and protractor work out how far this deviates from the true horizontal.
4   Measure the angle of the spring plate from the true horizontal in the same way, eliminating any play there may be by lifting the plate while the measurement is taken.
5   Depending on which way the body deviates, the angle is added or subtracted to the plate angle to give the differences between the two. Reference to Fig 11.11 will illustrate the examples given below.

| | |
|---|---|
| Body deviation angle | 4° |
| Plate deviation angle | 20° |
| Plate/body angle (AA) | 16° |
| Plate/body angle (BB) | 24° |

If the correct plate/body angle is 20° 3' then in situation AA the plate angle needs increasing by 4° 30'. In BB it needs decreasing by 3° 30'.
6   The torsion bars are splined at each end. The inner end anchors to a splined bracket fixed in the centre of the cross tube. The outer end is splined to the spring plate. The inner end has forty splines (9° per spline) and the outer has forty-four splines (8° 10' per spline) affording an alteration possibility in graduations of 50' (9° − 8° 10'). In example AA, if the inner end of the torsion bar is rotated anticlockwise five splines (45°) and the spring plate rotated clockwise on the outer end by five splines (4° 50') the net increase in the angle will be 45° minus 40° 50' = 4° 10' which is as near as one can get. In example BB the inner end is rotated clockwise four splines (36°) and the plate on the outer end rotated anticlockwise four splines (32° 40'). The net decrease in the angle is thus 3° 20'.
7   To withdraw the torsion bar sufficiently to rotate the splines for adjustment first remove the four screws which secure the cover clamping the rubber cushion mounting. The spring plate can now be pulled off the torsion bar and at the same time the inner end of the bar may be drawn out of the centre splined location. (Note that if one wishes to take the torsion bar right out then about five or six of the screws which hold the forward edge of the rear mudguard to the body must be removed. The mudguard can then be pulled out of the way. Torsion bars are not interchangeable side for side.)
8   Having reset the torsion bar so that the plate angle is correct make sure that the rubber mounting bushes are in good condition. Renew if in doubt. Cover with flake graphite (to prevent squeaking) and make sure the inner one is installed the proper way up. (The top edge is marked 'Oben'.) Before the cover is reinstalled over the rubber bush it will be necessary to raise the plate above the stop lug on the frame casting. If this is not done now the pre-loading of the rubber bushing will be all wrong when the cover is put back. It will also be very nearly impossible to move the plate. To lift the plate put a jack under the end. If it

looks as though the car is going to lift before the plate is up in position get some people to sit in the back seat for a minute or two. With the plate held in position replace the cover plate and setscrews.
9   It may be difficult to get the four plate securing screws to pick up their threads on replacement - particularly with a new bush. In such instances two longer screws will have to be obtained and used diagonally so that the plate may be drawn down enough to refit the shorter screws. (The short screws must be used finally otherwise the cover plate will not pull down far enough to stress the rubber bush properly.)
10  With the cover tightened down the diagonal arm may be reassembled to the spring plate.
11  The angle adjustment of the spring plates must be the same on both sides of the car.
12  If the spring plates have been renewed or any other work has been carried out on the rear suspension which could affect the alignment then it is important that the camber and toe settings be checked with alignment equipment. It would also be timely to mention here that if the rear suspension spring plate settings are purposely altered to give an increased or reduced ground clearance then the effects on handling under certain circumstances are, to say the least, unusual. Tyre wear is also greatly increased if the rear wheel alignment is incorrect.

## 11  Steering gear - adjustments

1   If play in the steering can be positively traced to the steering gear rather than wear in the track rod ends or suspension linkage it is possible to make certain adjustments (with the steering gear fitted in the car) to improve the situation. Play occurs at two main points - in the worm shaft bearings and between the worm and roller. A third point - axial play of the roller can also cause sloppiness but rectification of this requires dismantling of the steering gear.
2   To check the worm axial play (i.e. in the bearings) first set the wheels straight ahead and move the steering wheel from side to side until resistance is felt. The circumferential movement of the wheel should not exceed 25 mm total across this central position. If it does, begin the adjustment check by getting hold of the steering column at the coupling (with the wheels now lifted from the ground) and turning it from side to side. Any endfloat in the shaft will be visible.
3   To adjust the play turn the steering to either side on full lock. Then loosen the large locknut on the adjuster plug. The adjuster plug on RHD models is round the worm pinion on the upper side of the gear. On LHD models it is on the opposite lower side. With a suitable box spanner turn the adjuster until no more end play can be discerned in the worm shaft. Hold the adjuster and tighten the locknut. Turn the steering from lock to lock. There should be no tight spots whatsoever.
4   If the original overall steering play (as measured at the steering wheel) is still not eliminated, go the next step which is adjustment of the play between the worm and roller. With the front wheels still off the ground set the steering to the straight ahead position.
5   Turn the steering wheel 90° only to left or right.
6   Loosen the roller shaft adjuster locknut which can be reached through the hole in the luggage compartment floor. Turn the adjuster anticlockwise about one turn. Then turn it clockwise until the roller can be felt just to make contact with the worm. Do not overtighten (photo).
7   Hold the screw and tighten the locknut.
8   Lower the vehicle to the ground and with the steering wheel set in turn at the 90° position both left and right, check that the circumference backlash does not exceed 25 mm at each position. If it does repeat the adjustment on the affected side only.
9   Before a conclusive road test can be made the toe-in adjustment must be checked. Then go on the road and check that the steering still has its self centring action. If it does not then the roller shaft adjustment must be slackened off, otherwise damage

Marking the rear suspension diagonal arm and spring plate for realignment Sec 9.2.

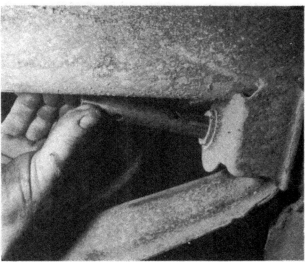

A tubular spanner inserted in the diagonal arm socket head pivot bolt (Sec 9.4)

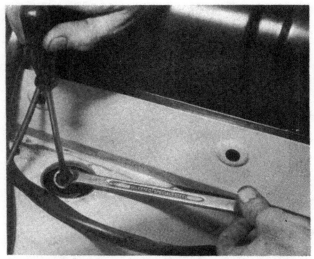

Steering gear. Adjustment of the roller to worm clearance through access hole in luggage compartment floor (Sec 11.6)

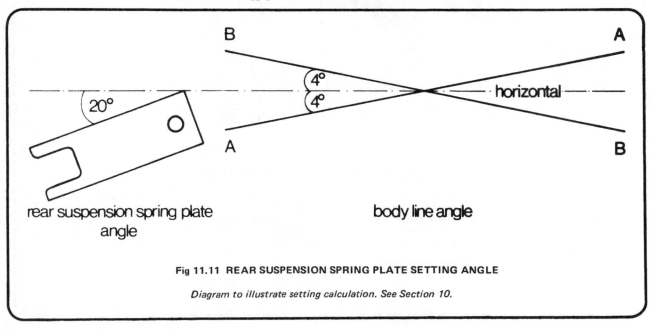

rear suspension spring plate angle

body line angle

**Fig 11.11 REAR SUSPENSION SPRING PLATE SETTING ANGLE**

*Diagram to illustrate setting calculation. See Section 10.*

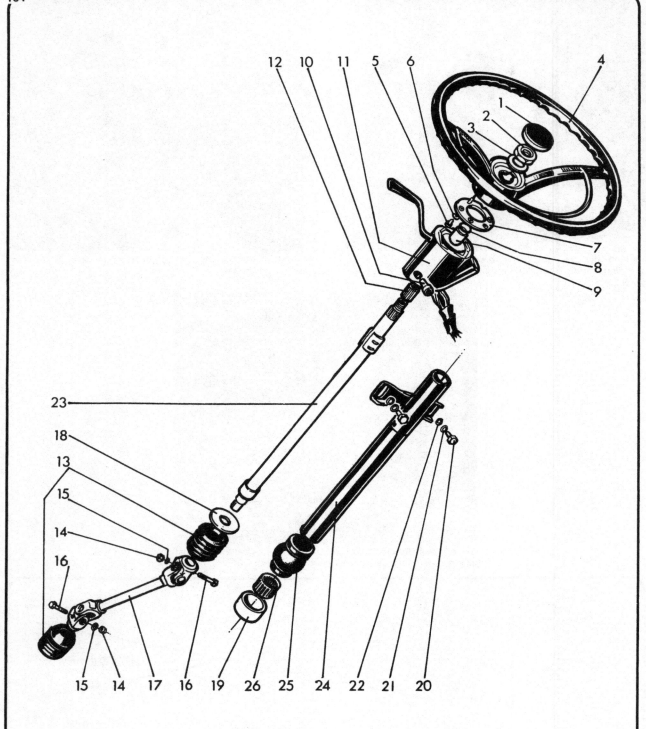

**Fig 11.12 STEERING COLUMN DETAILS (SEC 14)**

| 1 Cap | 8 Circlip | 15 Spring washer | 21 Washer |
|---|---|---|---|
| 2 Nut | 9 Spacer | 16 Bolt | 22 Washer |
| 3 Lockwasher | 10 Socket head screw | 17 Universal joint shaft | 23 Column shaft |
| 4 Steering wheel | 11 Column switch | 18 Washer | 24 Column tube |
| 5 Screw | 12 Contact ring | 19 Bush | 25 Boot |
| 6 Lockwasher | 13 Boot | 20 Bolt | 26 Needle bearing |
| 7 Cancelling ring | 14 Self-locking nut | | |

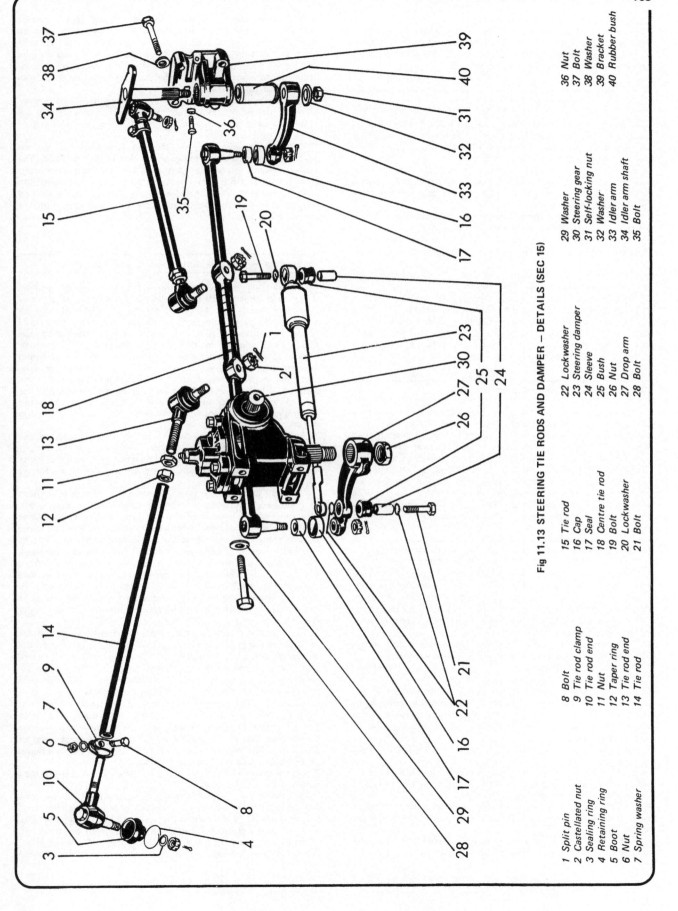

Fig 11.13 STEERING TIE RODS AND DAMPER – DETAILS (SEC 15)

1 Split pin
2 Castellated nut
3 Sealing ring
4 Retaining ring
5 Boot
6 Nut
7 Spring washer

8 Bolt
9 Tie rod clamp
10 Tie rod end
11 Nut
12 Taper ring
13 Tie rod end
14 Tie rod

15 Tie rod
16 Cap
17 Seal
18 Centre tie rod
19 Bolt
20 Lockwasher
21 Bolt

22 Lockwasher
23 Steering damper
24 Sleeve
25 Bush
26 Nut
27 Drop arm
28 Bolt

29 Washer
30 Steering gear
31 Self-locking nut
32 Washer
33 Idler arm
34 Idler arm shaft
35 Bolt

36 Nut
37 Bolt
38 Washer
39 Bracket
40 Rubber bush

can occur to either the worm or roller.

10 If neither of the foregoing adjustments rectifies the play in the steering gear then the third involves dismantling the assembly to check the axial play on the roller itself. If this is excessive the whole unit needs renewal or reconditioning.

## 12 Steering gear - removal and replacement

1   The steering gear is mounted on the sidemember of the body frame and may be removed from underneath the car. It is connected to the lower section of the steering column by a splined coupling at the universal joint.

2   First of all the steering damper and tie-rod ends must be detached from the drop arm. For the tie-rod this will require a suitable claw extractor. There are lugs on the drop arm to enable the extractor claws to grip.

3   Undo the bolt and nut on the universal joint attachment to the splined worm shaft and take the bolt right out.

4   Remove the three bolts holding the gear to the sidemember. They are accessible under the wheel arch alongside the suspension strut.

5   The steering gear may now be pulled off the universal joint and taken down and out from underneath.

6   Replacement is a reversal of the removal procedure. When fitting the splined worm spindle into the universal joint see that the recess in the splined section matches up with the bolt hole in the joint. If it does not the clamp bolt will not go through. Install a new self-locking nut onto the clamp bolt and tighten it to the correct torque of 18 lb ft/2.5 mkg.

## 13 Steering gear - dismantling and overhaul

1   The decision to dismantle and rebuild a steering gear assembly will depend to a large extent on the availability of parts. It is inevitable that if adjustments fail to rectify play adequately then most of the interior components will need renewal. The steering gear with its hour glass worm and roller is subject to some very critical settings and requires shims and setting jigs which only a Volkswagen agency is likely to have. We do not therefore, recommend that the do-it-yourself owner attempts this job. The time and cost expended to do the job properly cannot justify any saving over the purchase of a replacement unit.

## 14 Steering wheel and column shafts - removal and replacement

1   The steering shaft is in two parts linked by two universal joints. The lower section which joins on to the steering gear runs at an angle to the main column so that in case of end thrust (as in a collision) the assembly will collapse rather than be pushed up inside the passenger compartment. The column tube surrounds the upper section of shaft.

2   To remove the steering wheel prise the centre cap out of the wheel. Undo the screw holding the horn switch earth wire.

3   Put the wheel in position with the spokes horizontal and then undo the centre clamping nut and washer (photos).

4   Pull the wheel off the splined end of the shaft (photo).

5   If the column and shaft are being removed next remove the fuel tank from the front luggage compartment as described in Chapter 3. Underneath the lower section of steering shaft is accessible (photo).

6   Undo the clamp bolt on the upper universal joint.   Take the bolt out.

7   Disconnect all wires from the steering column switch where they join behind the instrument panel and then pull them all through into the passenger compartment.

8   Remove the bolts securing the column tube to the instrument panel and lift the assembly out from inside the passenger compartment.

9   The column shaft and tube may be separated after the column switch has been removed from the column.

10 The lower shaft together with the universal joints may be removed after the lower universal joint bolt has been removed from the steering gear end. If it is intended to remove the lower shaft and universal joints only the upper column need only be unfixed on the mounting bracket bolts. This will enable it to be lifted just far enough to disengage the upper steering shaft from the universal joint.

11 Replacement of all components is a straightforward reversal of these procedures. Make sure the splined connections to the universal joints are made so that the locking bolt will engage in the cut-out.

12 It is important that the steering wheel spokes are set horizontal when the steering gear is in the central position. The steering gear is central when the hole in the drop arm lug is directly in line with the countersunk depression in the aluminium plug in the bottom of the steering gear casing. Use a drill of suitable diameter to put through the hole and engage in the depression to line them up.

## 15 Steering tie-rods and joints - removal and replacement

1   The steering gear transmits the motion of the steering wheel to the road wheels via three tie-rods. The end of the drop arm is connected to one end of a central tie-rod the other end of which is supported by an idler arm on the opposite side. From this tie-rod two other tie rods run to the steering knuckle of each wheel. Each end of the tie-rods has a swivel ball joint which allows the variety of angles to be adopted by the wheels during movement of steering and suspension. If the track rods are bent, or of the incorrect length, or if the swivel joints are worn, the wheels will take up an incorrect position of alignment, or, in the case of worn joints, be able to move independently of the steering gear. Both these conditions result in inaccurate steering and control.

2   Each ball joint is attached to the steering knuckle at the outer end, or centre tie-rod at the inner end by a tapered pin through a tapered hole and secured by a hexagon nut. The joints are screwed on to the tie-rods with a left and right hand thread on each rod.

3   The ball joints on the outer tie-rod ends are held in position to the tie-rods by a clamp round the split end of the tie-rods. The joints on the inner ends of these rods are clamped by sleeves with a hexagonal nut and a tapered inner sleeve. The two joints at each end of the central tie-rod are in fact rubber bushed pins and if either of these becomes worn the whole tie-rod is renewed.

4   The main problem normally is removing the joint pin from the steering knuckle or from the centre tie-rod. First remove the split pin and castellated nut. The joint pin may be a very tight fit. If you have no proper extractor hold a hammer to one side of the eye and strike opposite with another. This usually succeeds.

5   Once the joint pin has been extracted from its location the position of the joint should be carefully noted in relation to the tie-rod before it is unclamped and screwed off. This will ensure that the replacement is positioned as accurately as possible. However it must be emphasised that the front wheel alignment must be checked after any renewal of tie-rod joints.

6   When obtaining new joints be careful to note whether or not there is a left or right hand thread. Also note that the joints at the outer ends of the tie-rods are not interchangeable with those from other Beetles. This 1302 model requires a large range of movement. The proper type can be identified by either a bump or depression on the ball retaining plug.

7   Screw the new track rod end on to the rod but do not lock it tight yet.

8   If a track rod is bent it must be replaced with a new one. Attempts to straighten track rods can only weaken the metal and may result in fracture with disastrous restuls on the road.

9   It is most important that the rubber seals on the track rod joints are intact and capable of retaining grease. On sealed joints any grease which escapes or which is contaminated needs special

Undoing the steering wheel nut (Sec 14.3a)

Steering wheel nut and washer (Sec 14.3b)

Pulling off the steering wheel (Sec 14.4)

Steering column lower shaft section (fuel tank removed) (Sec 14.5)

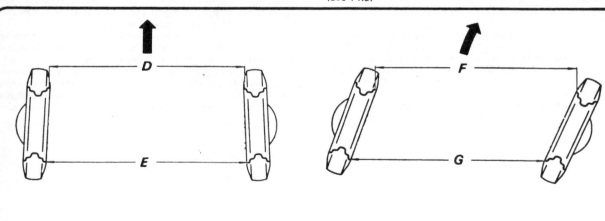

**Fig 11.14 STEERING GEOMETRY — WHEEL ALIGNMENT TOE (SEC 17)**

*Toe in D is less than E*
*Toe out F is greater than G*

attention. It is possible to fit new seals and have them repacked but more often than not it is too late by the time the fault is seen in which case the joint must be renewed.

10 When the track rods are fitted with the ends replace the taper pins into their respective eyes and refit and tighten the hexagon nuts to the correct torque. Replace the split pins after lining up the holes.

11 It is important to see that both ball joints are correctly aligned on the rod so push both of them either fully forward or backwards. Then tighten the nut or pinch bolt and bend over the lock tabs.

12 It is important to have the wheel alignment checked properly at the earliest opportunity.

## 16 Steering damper - removal, checking and replacement

1 The steering damper is a double acting piston which serves to smooth out vibration and shocks through the steering. One end is fixed to the centre of the frame head and the other to the drop arm. Each fixing bolt is rubber bushed.

2 If the bushes are worn allowing play the damper should be removed and new bushes fitted. New bushes comprise a rubber buffer with a steel central sleeve. Old ones can be cut or driven out and new ones pressed in between the jaws of a vice.

3 The bolts securing the ends of the damper are accessible from underneath for the tie-rod connection and from the luggage compartment for the frame head attachment. For the latter lift out the spare wheel and prise out the small circular cover plate in the floor of the compartment.

4 If the damper is leaking fluid badly and there is inadequate damping action in either direction it should be renewed. To test the action of the damper push and pull the piston throughout its full travel. There should be no roughness or variations in resistance anywhere along the travel of the piston. Note that the dampers fitted to right hand drive vehicles are different from those fitted to left hand drive.

5 Replace the damper (with the cylinder end mounted on the frame head) by fitting the securing bolts and nuts and tightening them to the specified torques.

## 17 Steering geometry and wheel alignment

1 The correct alignment of the front wheels does not normally alter and the need for checking and realigning occurs only after certain conditions, namely:

a) Renewal of track rod joints
b) Damage to front suspension or steering linkage

Theoretically, if worn ball joints, wheel bearings and so on, are all renewed the steering geometry will automatically be correct. This, of course, presumes that no adjustment has been made in a misguided attempt to compensate for wear. If adjustments have been made then, of course, when the various parts are renewed the steering will have to be realigned.

2 The only adjustments which can be made to the geometry (except of course outside the standard specifications) are on the track rods for toe-in and on the eccentric washers of the track control arm inner pivot bushes for the camber angle and king pin inclination. Alteration of the king pin inclination automatically alters the camber angle because the relationship between these two is fixed in the design of the king pin carrier/steering knuckle assembly. The term 'king pin inclination' is the same as 'steering pivot angle'. The former expression dates from the time when front wheels pivoted on spindles rather than joints.

3 Adjustments of steering geometry should never be made in a haphazard manner. In order to check all the angles correctly proper equipment is needed. Furthermore it is quite pointless trying to realign the steering if one or more of the components is worn. A reputable garage would not normally undertake to re-adjust steering which had significant wear - although they may be prepared to inform you of the state of the alignment.

## 18 Wheels and tyres

1 To provide equal, and obtain maximum wear from all the tyres, they should be rotated on the car at intervals of 6,000 miles to the following pattern:

> Spare to offside rear
> Offside rear to nearside front
> Nearside front to nearside rear
> Nearside rear to offside front
> Offside front to spare

Wheels should be re-balanced when this is done. However, some owners baulk at the prospect of having to buy five new tyres all at once and tend to let two run on and replace a pair only. The new pair should always be fitted to the front wheels, as these are the most important from the safety aspect of steering and braking.

2 Never mix tyres of a radial and crossply construction on the same car, as the basic design differences can cause unusual and, in certain conditions, very dangerous handling and braking characteristics. If an emergency should force the use of two different types, make sure the radials are on the rear wheels and drive particularly carefully. If three of the five wheels are fitted with radial tyres then make sure that no more than two radials are in use on the car (and those at the rear). Rationalise the tyres at the earliest possible opportunity.

3 Wheels are normally not subject to servicing problems, but when tyres are renewed or changed the wheels should be balanced to reduce vibration and wear. If a wheel is suspected of damage - caused by hitting a kerb or pot hole which could distort it out of true, change it and have it checked for balance and true running at the earliest opportunity.

4 The tightening of the wheel bolts is to be done carefully. The torque requirement is quite high — 108 lbs/ft — which is just about all you can give it using the spanner and handle provided for changing the wheel in the event of a puncture. Bolts should be tightened evenly and if they have to be undone in an emergency get them checked properly as soon as possible. The tightness of wheel bolts is included in the service check.

**19 Fault diagnosis**

Before diagnosing faults in the mechanics of the suspension and steering itself, check that any irregularities are not caused by:

1 Binding brakes
2 Incorrect 'mix' of radial and cross-ply tyres
3 Incorrect tyre pressures
4 Misalignment of the bodyframe and suspension due to accident damage

| Symptom | Reason/s | Remedy |
|---|---|---|
| Steering wheel can be moved considerably before any sign of movement of the wheels is apparent | Wear in the steering linkage, gear and column coupling | Check movement in all joints, and steering gear and adjust, overhaul and renew as required. |
| Vehicle difficult to steer in a consistent straight line - wandering | As above | As above. |
| | Wheel alignment incorrect (indicated by excessive or uneven tyre wear) | Check wheel alignment. |
| | Front wheel hub bearings loose or worn | Adjust or renew as necessary. |
| | Worn suspension ball joints | Renew as necessary. |
| Steering stiff and heavy | incorrect wheel alignment (indicated by excessive or uneven tyre wear) | Check wheel alignment. |
| | Excessive wear or seizure in one or more of the joints in the steering linkage or suspension | Repair as necessary. |
| | Excessive wear in the steering gear unit | Adjust if possible, or renew. |
| Wheel wobble and vibration | Road wheels out of balance | Balance wheels. |
| | Road wheels buckled | Check for damage. |
| | Wheel alignment incorrect | Check wheel alignment. |
| | Wear in the steering linkage or suspension | Check and renew as necessary. |
| | Ineffective steering damper | Check and renew as necessary. |
| Excessive pitching and rolling on corners during braking | Defective dampers and/or broken springs | Check and renew as necessary. |

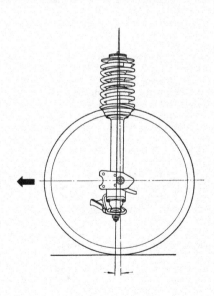

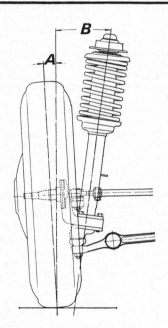

FIG.11.15 STEERING GEOMETRY — ILLUSTRATION TO SHOW CASTER ANGLE (SECTION 17) ARROW INDICATES FORWARD DIRECTION

FIG.11.16 STEERING GEOMETRY — ILLUSTRATION TO SHOW CAMBER ANGLE (A) AND STEERING PIVOT ANGLE (B) (SECTION 17)

# Chapter 12 Bodywork and underframe

## Contents

## 1 General description

The bodywork of the Volkswagen is noted for its simplicity, rigidity and corrosion free properties.

It consists basically of a flat floor pan stiffened down the centre with a fabricated sheet steel tube. At the front is a 'frame head' to which the front suspension track control arms and stabilizer bar are attached. (See Chapter 11, Fig 11.8). At the rear of the floor pan is a 'frame fork' into which the engine/ transmission assembly is bolted. Just forward of the frame fork is a lateral tube to which the rear suspension spring plate supports are fitted at the outer ends. The frame tunnel is closed in underneath and carries inside it the necessary guide tubes for brake cables, heater cables, clutch cable, accelerator cable and gearchange connecting rods.

The bodywork is a unit fabricated from steel panels welded together with the exception of sill panels, wings, doors and engine and luggage compartment lids. The unit is bolted to the floor frame. The doors, wings, lids and sill panels are bolted to the body and are readily detachable.

The whole frame body assembly is remarkable for its lack of 'nooks and crannies' where water/dirt can collect and is notable for being almost airtight (it is virtually impossible to slam the doors shut with the windows closed due to the air pressure build up inside).

## 2 Maintenance - bodywork and underframe

1  The Volkswagen is a particularly easy car to keep clean due to its aerodynamic shape. The general condition of a car's bodywork is the one thing that significantly affects its value. Maintenance is easy but needs to be regular and particular. Neglect, particularly after minor damage, can lead quickly to further deterioration and costly repair bills. It is important also to keep watch on those parts of the car not immediately visible, for instance, the underside, inside all the wheel arches and the engine compartment.

2  The basic maintenance routine for the bodywork is washing - preferably with a lot of water, from a hose. This will remove all the solids which may have stuck to the car. It is important to flush these off in such a way as to prevent grit from scratching the finish. The wheel arches and underbody need washing in the same way to remove any accumulated mud which will retain moisture and tend to encourage rust. Paradoxically enough, the best time to clean the underbody and wheel arches is in wet weather when the mud is thoroughly wet and soft. In very wet weather the underbody is usually cleaned of large accumulations automatically and this is a good time for inspection.

3  Periodically it is a good idea to have the whole of the underside of the car steam cleaned engine compartment included, so that a thorough inspection can be carried out to see what minor repairs and renovations are necessary. Steam cleaning is available at many garages and is necessary for removal of accumulations of oily grime which sometimes cakes thick in certain areas near the engine and transmission. The facilities are usually available at commercial vehicle garages but if not there are one or two excellent grease solvents available which can be brush applied. The dirt can then be hosed off.

4  After washing paintwork, wipe it with a chamois leather to give an unspotted clear finish. A coat of clear protective wax polish will give added protection against chemical pollutants in the air. If the paintwork sheen has dulled or oxidised, use a cleaner/polisher combination to restore the brilliance of the shine. This requires a little more effort, but is usually caused because regular washing has been neglected. Always check that drain holes and pipes are completely clear so that water can drain out (photo). Brightwork should be treated the same way as paintwork. Windscreens and windows can be kept clear of the smeary film which often appears if a little ammonia is added to the water. If they are scratched, a good rub with a proprietary metal polish will often clear them. Never use any form of wax or chromium polish on glass (photo 2.4, page 175).

## 3 Maintenance - upholstery and floor coverings

1  Mats and carpets should be brushed or vacuum cleaned regularly to keep them free of grit. If they are badly stained remove them from the car for scrubbing or sponging and make quite sure they are dry before replacement. Seats and interior trim panels can be kept clean by a wipe over with a damp cloth. If they do become stained (which can be more apparent on light coloured upholstery) use a little liquid detergent and a soft nailbrush to scour the grime out of the grain of the material. Do not forget to keep the head lining clean in the same way as the upholstery. When using liquid cleaners inside the car do not over-wet the surfaces being cleaned. Excessive damp could get

into the seams and padded interior causing stains, offensive odours or even rot. If the inside of the car gets wet accidentally, it is worthwhile taking some trouble to dry it out properly, particularly where carpets are involved. Do NOT leave oil or electric heaters inside the car for this purpose.

## 4 Minor body repairs

1 A car which does not suffer some minor damage to the bodywork from time to time is the exception rather than the rule. Even presuming the gatepost is never scraped or the door opened against a wall or high kerb, there is always the likelihood of gravel and grit being thrown up and chipping the surface, particularly at the lower edges of the doors and sills.

2 If the damage is merely a paint scrape which has not reached the metal base, delay is not critical, but where bare metal is exposed action must be taken immediately before rust sets in.

3 The average owner will normally keep the following 'first aid' materials available which can give a professional finish for minor jobs:

a) Matching paint in liquid form - often complete with brush attached to the lid inside. (Aerosols should only be bought for painting areas larger than 6 inches square - they are extravagant and expensive for anything less and give no better results. In fact spraying from aerosols is generally less perfect than the makers would have one expect.)
b) Thinners for the paint (for brush application).
c) Cellulose stopper (a filling compound for small paint chips).
d) Cellulose primer (a thickish grey coloured base which can be applied and rubbed down in several coats to give a perfect paint base).
e) Proprietary resin filler paste (for larger areas of in-filling).
f) Rust-inhibiting primer.

4 Where the damage is superficial (i.e. not down to the bare metal and not dented) fill the scratch or chip with sufficient filler/stopper to smooth the area, rub down with paper and apply the matching paint.

5 Where the bodywork is scratched down to the metal, but not dented, clean the metal surface thoroughly and apply the primer (it does not need to be a rust-inhibitor if the metal is clean and dry), and then build up the scratched part to the level of the surrounding paintwork with the stopper. When the primer/stopper is hard it can be rubbed down with wet and dry paper. Keep applying primer and rubbing it down until no surface blemish can be felt. Then apply the colour, thinned if necessary. Apply as many coats and rub down as necessary.

6 If more than one coat of colour is required rub down each coat before applying the next.

7 If the bodywork is dented, first beat out the dent as near as possible to conform with the original contour. Avoid using steel hammers - use hardwood mallets or similar and always support the back of the panel being beaten with a hardwood or metal 'dolly'. In areas where severe creasing and buckling has occurred it will be virtually impossible to reform the metal to the original shape. In such instances a decision should be made whether or not to cut out the damaged piece or attempt to re-contour over it with filler paste. In large areas where the metal panel is seriously damaged or rusted, the repair is to be considered major and it is often better to replace a panel or sill section with the appropriate part supplied as a spare. When using filler paste in largish quantities, make sure the directions are carefully followed. It is false economy to try and rush the job as the correct hardening time must be allowed between stages or before finishing. With thick application the filler usually has to be applied in layers - allowing time for each layer to harden.

8 Sometimes the original paint colour will have faded and it will be difficult to obtain an exact colour match. In such instances it is a good scheme to select a complete panel - such as a door, or boot lid, and spray the whole panel. Differences will be less apparent where there are obvious divisions between the original and re-sprayed areas.

9 Finally, a general word of advice. Do not expect to be able to prepare, fill, rub down and paint a section of damaged bodywork in one day and expect good results. It cannot be done. Give plenty of time for each successive application of filler and primers to harden before rubbing it down and applying the next coat.

## 5 Major body repairs

1 Volkswagen owners are fortunate in that what would be relatively severe damage in some cars is not so for them. This is where wings or sills are badly damaged beyond economical repair. Being bolted on they can be removed and a new unit fitted by the owner (see subsequent sections).

2 Where serious damage has occurred or large areas need renewal due to neglect it means certainly that completely new sections or panels will need welding in and this is best left to professionals. If the damage is due to impact it will also be necessary to check the alignment of the body structure. In such instances the services of a Volkswagen agent with specialist checking jigs are essential. If a body is left misaligned it is first of all dangerous as the car will not handle properly - and secondly, uneven stresses will be imposed on the steering, engine and transmission, causing abnormal wear or complete failure. Tyre wear will also be excessive.

## 6 Front wings - removal and replacement

1 Jack up the car and remove the headlamp and direction indicator lamp housing.
2 Pull the wires and grommets out of the holes where they pass through the wing.
3 Remove the nut and bolt holding the wing to the sill panel and subsequently the nine bolts holding the wing to the bodywork. It is more than likely that these bolts are difficult to move. If this is so clean the heads and surrounds thoroughly and use plenty of penetrating fluid to ease the threads. If resort to cutting is necessary - with either saw or chisel - take care not to damage or bend the bodywork. One of the safest ways if you have a power drill and stone is to grind the heads off stubborn bolts (see Fig 12.3, page 174).
4 When clear, lift off the wing and beading strip.
5 It is a good idea to fit a new beading strip when putting the wing back. If the wing is a new one do any necessary paint spraying before fitting.
6 Use new bolts and treat them with grease or some anti-seize compound before fitting. There should be a new rubber washer on the bolt between the wing and sill panel.
7 The headlamp must be realigned after repalcement. Make sure all the wires and grommets are properly replaced to avoid chafing or strain which could lead to failure.

## 7 Rear wings - removal and replacement

1 The principle of removing and replacing the rear wing is exactly the same as that for the front wing as described in the previous section except that the rear bumper and bumper brackets should be removed first. Do not forget to remove the bolt securing the wing to the sill panel.
2 On replacement fit new beading and rubber washer between wing and sill as required. See Fig 12.4, page 174.

## 8 Sill panels - removal and replacement

1 The sill panel is bolted to the body and to the wings at the front and rear. Once all the bolts have been removed - bearing in mind that precautions for stubborn bolts as mentioned in the

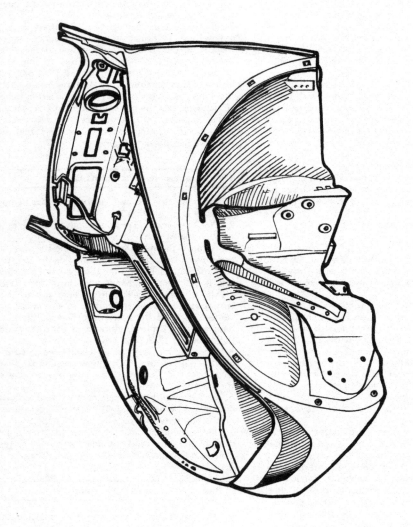

Fig 12.1. FRONT BODY SHELL

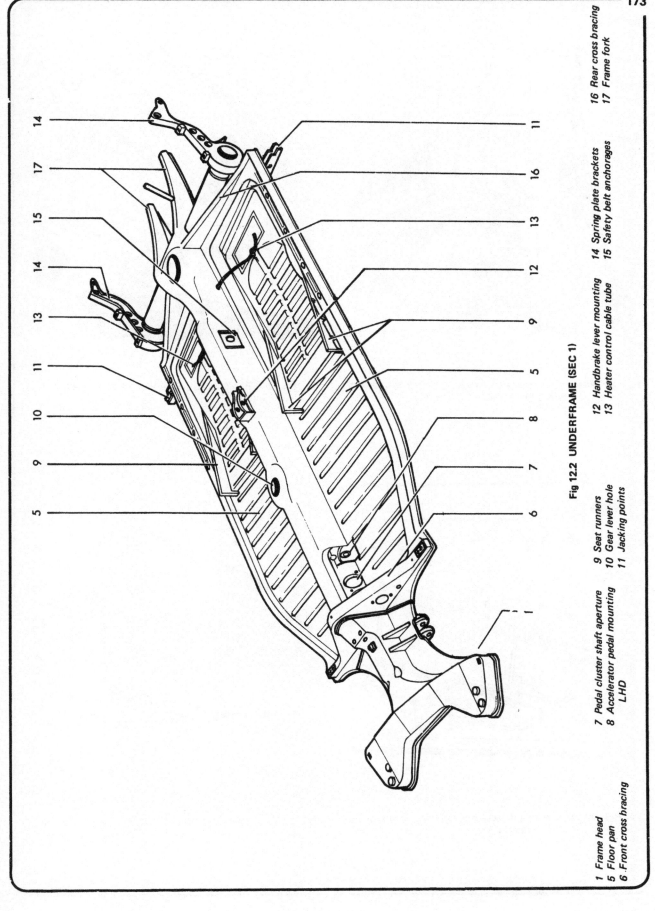

**Fig 12.2 UNDERFRAME (SEC 1)**

1 Frame head
5 Floor pan
6 Front cross bracing

7 Pedal cluster shaft aperture
8 Accelerator pedal mounting
   LHD

9 Seat runners
10 Gear lever hole
11 Jacking points

12 Handbrake lever mounting
13 Heater control cable tube

14 Spring plate brackets
15 Safety belt anchorages

16 Rear cross bracing
17 Frame fork

174

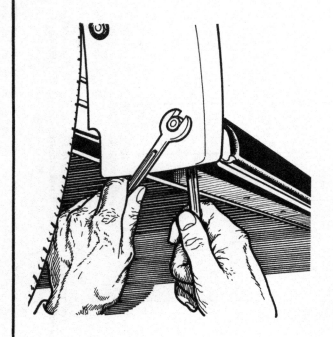

**Fig 12.3 REMOVING THE BOLT CONNECTING THE FRONT WING TO DOOR SILL (SEC 6)**

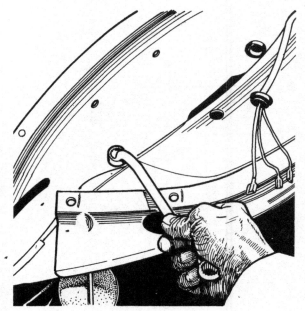

**Fig 12.4 REMOVING REAR WING BOLTS (SEC 7)**

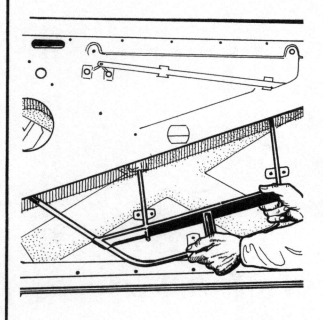

**Fig 12.5 TAKING OUT THE WINDOW LIFTER MECHANISM (SEC 15)**

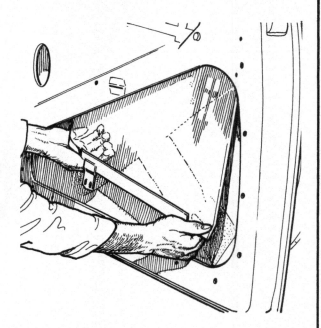

**Fig 12.6 REMOVING THE WINDOW GLASS (SEC 16)**

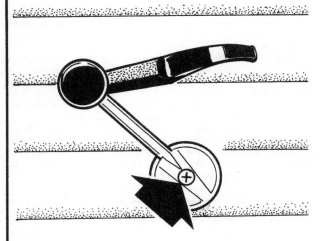

Fig 12.7  THE WINDOW REGULATOR HANDLE RETAINING
SCREW (ARROWED) IS BEHIND THE ESCUTCHEON (SEC 14)

Fig 12.8  THE LATCH LEVER SCREW (ARROWED) IS UNDER
THE FINGER PLATE BEHIND THE LEVER (SECTION 14)

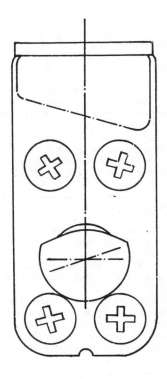

Fig 12.9  DOOR LATCH STRIKER PLATE (SEC 19)

Tunnel drain plug near frame fork (Sec 2.4)

section on front wing removal - the sill can be lifted off.
2  When fitting a new sill panel make sure the washers fit correctly over the slots and when tightening the bolts tighten up the ones to the bodywork before the ones to the wings.

## 9  Front bumper - removal and replacement

1  The bumper can be removed together with the brackets or otherwise as wished. The bumper can be detached from the brackets by undoing the two screws holding it to each bracket. To remove the brackets unship the spare wheel from its well and undo the two screws holding the brackets in place.
2  When replacing a bumper assemble the bumper to the brackets (loosely at first) and then bolt the brackets in position. If the bumper is not level or the gaps at each end between the bumper and wing are uneven then the brackets must be bent (if the bumper is new).
3  Make sure the bracket rubber seals are in good condition if you wish to prevent water getting into the space behind the panel.

## 10  Rear bumper - removal and replacement

The rear bumper is mounted in exactly the same way as the front one and should be removed and refitted in the same manner.

## 11  Windscreen and fixed glass - removal and replacement

1  Make sure you know what kind of glass if fitted. Toughened safety glass will stand a certain amount of impact without breaking but any other kind will crack at least and only carefully applied sustained pressure may be used with safety.
2  After taking off the windscreen wiper arms, loosen the rubber sealing strip on the inside of the car where it fits over the edge of the window frame. Use a piece of wood for this. Anything sharp may rip the rubber weatherstrip. The screen can be pushed out, weatherstrip attached, if pressure is applied at the top corners. Two people are needed on this to prevent the glass falling out. Push evenly and protect your hands to avoid accidents. Remove the finisher strip from the weatherstrip.
3  When fitting a screen first make sure that the window frame edges are even and smooth. Examine the edges of the screen to see that it is ground smooth and no chips or cracks are visible. Any such cracks could be the start of a much bigger one. The rubber weatherstrip should be perfectly clean. No traces of sealing compound should remain on rubber, glass or metal. If the sealing strip is old, brittle or hard, it is advisable to fit a new one even though they are not cheap.
4  Fit the weatherstrip to the screen first so that the joint comes midway along the top edge.
5  Next fit the decorative moulding into the weatherstrip. This is done by first feeding fine cord into the slot (use a piece of thin tubing as a guide and time saver) and leave the ends overlapping long enough to be able to grip later. The two halves of the moulding are then put in place and the cord drawn out so that the edge of the strip locks them into place.
6  Apply suitable sealing compound to the weatherstrip where it will seat onto the metal window frame and also onto the outside faces of the frame at the lower corners.
7  Fit a piece of really strong thin cord into the frame channel of the weatherstrip as already described and then offer up the screen to the aperture. A second person is essential for this.
8  When you are sure that the screen is centrally positioned, pull the cord out so that the lip of the weatherstrip is drawn over the inner edge of the frame flange. One of the most frequent difficulties in this job is that the cord breaks. This is often because of sharp or uneven edges on the frame flange so a little extra time in preparation will pay off.

## 12  Doors - removal and replacement

1  The door hinges are welded to the door and fixed to the car by four countersunk crosshead screws. One screw is concealed under a plastic plug (photo). The check strap rivet must also be drilled out (photo).
2  If the same door is being put back the simplest way to take it off is to drive out the hinge pins with a punch but you will have to remove the sill panel to get at the bottom one. If this is done no re-alignment problems will occur.
3  To slacken the hinge screws an impact screwdriver is essential. Similarly for tightening them properly on replacement.
4  When hanging a new door (or re-aligning one which is out of position) insert all hinge screws loosely and then tighten just one in each hinge sufficiently to hold the door whilst it is set centrally and flush in the opening. It makes things easier if you remove the latch striker plate whilst this is being done.

## 13  Door rattles - tracing and rectification

Door rattles are due either to loose hinges, worn or maladjusted catches, or loose components inside the door. Loose hinges can be detected by opening the door and trying to lift it. Any play will be felt. Worn or badly adjusted catches can be found by pushing and pulling on the outside handle when the door is closed. Once again any play will be felt. To check the window mechanism open the door and shake it with the window first open and then closed. Rattles will normally be heard.

## 14  Door trim panels - removal and replacement

1  First remove the window winder and door latch lever. The winder handle has a plastic cover which should be prized off at the spindle end. A crosshead screw is then accessible and should be removed (photo). The recessed finger plate behind the inner door handle lever can be prized out also with a screwdriver (photo). The crosshead screw behind it can then be removed to release the assembly (photo). Then use a piece of flat metal strip to put round the edge of the panel and pull out the retaining clips. Take care not to tear the clips off the trim panel itself. It will be necessary to lift the panel a little to disengage the arm rest inner support from the door panel (photo).
2  Replacement is a reversal of the removal procedure. Make sure the tension spring is fitted in position behind the trim panel over the window regulator spindle (photo).
3  Remember the rubbing washer behind the window handle (photo). (See also Figs 12.7 and 12.8, page 175.)

## 15  Window regulator mechanism - removal and replacement

1  Remove the door trim panel and plastic sheet covering.
2  With the window in the lowered position undo the bolts holding the glass to the lifter channel.
3  Push the window to the raised position and wedge it there.
4  Remove the guide channel bolts and take out the channel (photo). (See Fig 12.5, page 174.)
5  Undo the bolts holding the lifter mechanism in to the door and lower the mechanism out from the bottom (photo).
6  Replacement is a reversal of this procedure. Take care to re-align the glass position correctly and also the guide strip. Check the operation fully throughout the window positions.

## 16  Door window glass - removal and replacement

1  Remove the door trim and lifter mechanism.
2  Take out the wedges used to jam the glass in position when the lifter was taken out and then lower and tilt the glass so that it comes out of the bottom of the door. Replacement is a

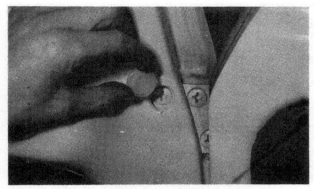

Nylon plug covering door hinge screw (Sec 12.1a)

Door check strap rivet (Sec 12.1b)

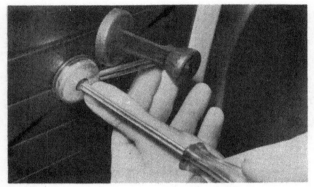

Removing the window winder handle (Sec 14.1a)

Prising out the door latch lever finger plate (Sec 14.1b)

Removing the escutcheon retaining screw (Sec 14.1c)

The door handle strap clips over the inner door panel (Sec 14.1d)

Refit the pressure spring between door and trim panel (Sec 14.2)

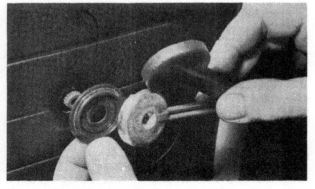

Do not forget the rubbing washer behind the window winder handle (Sec 14.3)

reversal of the procedure. See Fig 12.6, page 174.

3   If new glass is being fitted into the existing channel the rear end of the channel must be positioned 90 mm from the rear corner of the glass.

### 17 Quarterlight - removal and replacement

1   If only the glass is being renewed the top pivot pin must be drilled out (photo). The glass may then be lifted up and out.

2   When fitting a new glass the upper pin should be properly rivetted and hard material used, otherwise the car security is jeopardised.

3   If the lower pivot is giving trouble it will be necessary to remove the main window and lifter and take out the whole main frame channel to get to it. This involves removing all the weatherstrips and undoing the securing bolts at the rear edge of the door frame. The channel strip is then taken out complete with the window dividing strip.

### 18 Door latch mechanism - removal and replacement

1   Remove the door trim.

2   Take out the bolts holding the remote control handle shaft to the door frame and disconnect the link arm.

3   Remove the crosshead screws holding the latch to the door and then push it inside the door and down - manoeuvring the link arm sufficiently to enable it to come clear so that it can be disconnected.

4   Replacement is a reversal of the removal procedure.

### 19 Door latch striker plates - adjustment and renewal

1   Rattles in doors are usually due to an incorrect striker plate position.

2   First check that the door fits the aperture properly by seeing that the gaps are more of less equal all round and that it fits flush with the side panel of the bodywork. There should be no rubbing and all the weatherstrip should show signs of equal compression.

3   Then make sure that the latch on the door is working properly.

4   If the door will shut and latch only when slammed it means that the rubber wedge at the top of the striker plate is too far out thus preventing the corresponding wedge on the door from moving right in. If the door can be rattled in and out when latched the wedge on the striker plate is too far in. To remedy either of these conditions slacken the striker plate fixing screws and move the upper end in or out as required (Fig 12.9).

5   If adjustment still fails to prevent any looseness when the door is shut then it is in order to put some packing between the wedge and the bracket, to which it is held by two screws.

### 20 Engine compartment cover - removal and replacement

1   The lid is held by two conventional hinges and is kept open by a strong spring.

2   Mark the position of the hinge and brackets as clearly as possible and slacken off all the hinge and bracket bolts. Remove the spring by squeezing the two 'L' shaped ends out of their holes. If you have doubts about the spring flying off and causing an accident leave it where it is and undo the bolts, using the cover to hold and eventually ease the spring tension.

3   If the cover is being removed in order to remove the engine fan housing the hinge brackets will need taking off as well.

4   When replacing the cover the spring can be fitted after the lid has been attached provided you are able to get sufficient leverage on to it. If not, replace the brackets and then hook the spring into position and use the cover once again to take up the tension whilst the hinge bolts are replaced.

5   Do not first attach the hinge brackets to the cover. It is much easier to fit the brackets to the body and then fit the cover to the brackets.

6   It is important to position the lid so that when closed it is central in the aperture. For this reason the bracket holes are slotted to allow adjustment.

### 21 Luggage compartment cover - removal and replacement

1   Mark the position of the hinge plates on the cover and then slacken mounting bolts and remove one from each side.

2   Remove the other hinge bolts with assistance from another person and lift the cover off (photo).

3   Replacement is a reversal of the removal procedure. Fit the hinge bolts loosely to start with so that the cover can be positioned correctly in the slotted holes.

### 22 Engine compartment cover latch - adjustment

1   Before adjusting the latch the cover must be correctly set on its hinges so that it fits centrally in the aperture. If the cover is distorted or out of position no adjustment of the latch can rectify it.

2   The adjustment is confined to the striker plate fitted to the body. The hook on the latch should centralise in the notch and the plate should be raised or lowered to ensure adequate engagement. Slacken the two striker plate mounting screws and move the plate as required.

### 23   Luggage compartment cover latch and release cable - adjustment

1   Before any adjustment is made see that the cover fits centrally over the aperture. If it has been buckled the latch can be adjusted only a limited amount to compensate for it.

2   To centralise the lock bolt (on the cover) to the aperture in the latch, the latch must be removed after first slackening the latch securing screws. To adjust the engagement of the lock bolt into the latch plate the lock bolt can be lengthened or shortened in its mounting. The bolt should engage when firm pressure is applied to the bottom of the cover. If the cover needs slamming the bolt should be screwed out a little. If the cover rattles, move the bolt in.

3   The latch has a fail safe arrangement in the design so that if the cable breaks the latch will release rather than lock the cover.

4   To gain access to the cable end the latch mounting screws should be removed and the cover plate eased down from the lower half. The clamping screw it undone and the cable drawn out of the bracket. It can then be drawn out from inside the car.

5   When fitting a new cable into the bracket push the bracket back against the spring tension before tightening the screw.

### 24 Fresh air ventilation

1   In addition to the two heater controls on the floor, one each side of the handbrake lever (see Chapter 2) there are two rotary knobs on the facia panel (photo). These control flaps which permit outside air to enter through the slots on the top edge of the facia panel. The air enters through the grille just forward of the windscreen (photo). On some models exported to hot' countries the air stream is boosted by an electric blower fan. Otherwise if the air enters under the pressure caused by the car's movement.

2   Each control knob adjusts the air inlet independently on the driver's and passenger's side.

3   The fresh air inlet is quite independent of the heating

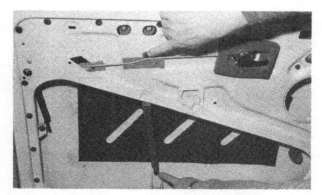

Securing screws for the window guide rail (Sec 15.4)

Securing screws for the window winder (Sec 15.5)

Quarterlight upper pivot (Sec 17.1)

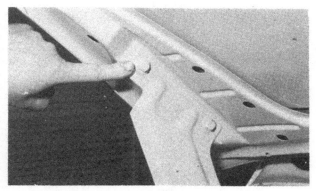

Luggage compartment mounting screws (Sec 21.2)

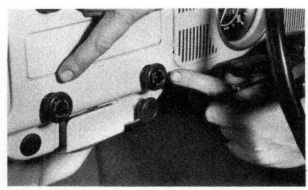

Fresh air inlet dashboard control knobs (Sec 24.1a)

Fresh air intake grille (Sec 24.1b)

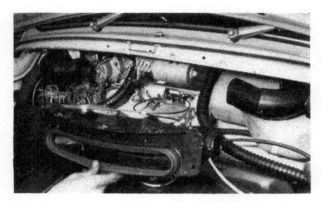

Fresh air inlet scoop withdrawn. Note the inlet pipes at each side (Sec 24.5)

Fresh air inlet flap controls behind the fascia panel (Sec 24.6)

system.
4   So that the car may be properly ventilated even when all the windows are shut and the heater/fresh air inlets are in operation special outlet slots are incorporated in the bodywork behind the rear side window glasses. This ensures that stale air is exhausted and keeps interior condensation to a minimum under certain conditions of humidity.

5   Access to the cables is from inside the luggage compartment. When the compartment lining is removed the air intake duct is removed by undoing the self-tapping screws (photo).

6   The air control flaps are controlled by nylon racks fitted to the cables which move the pinions on the valve spindles (photo).

# Metric conversion tables

| Inches | Millimetres | Inches | Millimetres | Inches | Decimals | Millimetres |
|---|---|---|---|---|---|---|
| 0.001 | 0.0254 | 0.1 | 2.54 | 1/64 | 0.0156 | 0.3969 |
| 0.002 | 0.0508 | 0.2 | 5.08 | 1/32 | 0.0313 | 0.7937 |
| 0.003 | 0.0762 | 0.3 | 7.62 | 1/16 | 0.0625 | 1.5875 |
| 0.004 | 0.1016 | 0.4 | 10.16 | 1/8 | 0.125 | 3.1750 |
| 0.005 | 0.1270 | 0.5 | 12.70 | 3/16 | 0.1875 | 4.7625 |
| 0.006 | 0.1524 | 0.6 | 15.24 | 1/4 | 0.25 | 6.3500 |
| 0.007 | 0.1778 | 0.7 | 17.78 | 5/16 | 0.3125 | 7.9375 |
| 0.008 | 0.2032 | 0.8 | 20.32 | 3/8 | 0.375 | 9.5250 |
| 0.009 | 0.2286 | 0.9 | 22.96 | 7/16 | 0.4375 | 11.1125 |
| 0.01 | 0.254 | 1.0 | 25.4 | 1/2 | 0.5 | 12.7000 |
| 0.02 | 0.508 | 2.0 | 50.8 | 9/16 | 0.5625 | 14.2875 |
| 0.03 | 0.762 | 3.0 | 76.2 | 5/8 | 0.625 | 15.8750 |
| 0.04 | 1.016 | 4.0 | 101.6 | 11/16 | 0.6875 | 17.4625 |
| 0.05 | 1.270 | 5.0 | 127.0 | 3/4 | 0.75 | 19.0500 |
| 0.06 | 1.524 | 6.0 | 152.4 | 13/16 | 0.8125 | 20.6375 |
| 0.07 | 1.778 | 7.0 | 177.8 | 7/8 | 0.875 | 22.2250 |
| 0.08 | 2.032 | 8.0 | 203.2 | 15/16 | 0.9375 | 23.8125 |
| 0.09 | 2.286 | 9.0 | 228.6 | | | |
| | | 10.0 | 254.0 | | | |

| Miles | Kilometres | Kilometres | Miles | lb ft | kg m | lb/sq in | kg/sq cm |
|---|---|---|---|---|---|---|---|
| 1 | 1.61 | 1 | 0.62 | 1 | 0.128 | 1 | 0.07 |
| 2 | 3.22 | 2 | 1.24 | 2 | 0.276 | 2 | 0.14 |
| 3 | 4.83 | 3 | 1.86 | 3 | 0.414 | 3 | 0.21 |
| 4 | 6.44 | 4 | 2.49 | 4 | 0.553 | 4 | 0.28 |
| 5 | 8.05 | 5 | 3.11 | 5 | 0.691 | 5 | 0.35 |
| 6 | 9.66 | 6 | 3.73 | 6 | 0.829 | 6 | 0.42 |
| 7 | 11.27 | 7 | 4.35 | 7 | 0.967 | 7 | 0.49 |
| 8 | 12.88 | 8 | 4.97 | 8 | 1.106 | 8 | 0.56 |
| 9 | 14.48 | 9 | 5.59 | 9 | 1.244 | 9 | 0.63 |
| 10 | 16.09 | 10 | 6.21 | 10 | 1.382 | 10 | 0.70 |
| 20 | 32.19 | 20 | 12.43 | 20 | 2.765 | 20 | 1.41 |
| 30 | 48.28 | 30 | 18.64 | 30 | 4.147 | 30 | 2.11 |
| 40 | 64.37 | 40 | 24.85 | | | | |
| 50 | 80.47 | 50 | 31.07 | | | | |
| 60 | 96.56 | 60 | 37.28 | | | | |
| 70 | 112.65 | 70 | 43.50 | | | | |
| 80 | 128.75 | 80 | 49.71 | | | | |
| 90 | 144.84 | 90 | 55.92 | | | | |
| 100 | 160.93 | 100 | 62.14 | | | | |

| Pints | Litres | Litres | Pints | Gallons | Litres | Litres | Gallons |
|---|---|---|---|---|---|---|---|
| 1 | 0.57 | 1 | 1.76 | 1 | 4.55 | 1 | 0.22 |
| 2 | 1.14 | 2 | 3.52 | 2 | 0.09 | 2 | 0.44 |
| 3 | 1.70 | 3 | 5.28 | 3 | 13.64 | 3 | 0.66 |
| 4 | 2.27 | 4 | 7.04 | 4 | 18.18 | 4 | 0.88 |
| 5 | 2.84 | 5 | 8.80 | 5 | 22.73 | 5 | 1.10 |
| 6 | 3.41 | 6 | 10.56 | 6 | 27.28 | 6 | 1.32 |
| 7 | 3.98 | 7 | 12.32 | 7 | 31.82 | 7 | 1.54 |
| 8 | 4.55 | 8 | 14.08 | 8 | 36.37 | 8 | 1.76 |
| 9 | 5.11 | 9 | 15.841 | 9 | 40.91 | 9 | 1.98 |
| 10 | 5.58 | 10 | 17.60 | 10 | 45.46 | 10 | 2.20 |
| 11 | 6.25 | 11 | 19.36 | 11 | 50.01 | 20 | 4.40 |
| 12 | 6.82 | 12 | 21.12 | 12 | 54.56 | 30 | 6.60 |

# Safety first!

Professional motor mechanics are trained in safe working procedures. However enthusiastic you may be about getting on with the job in hand, do take the time to ensure that your safety is not put at risk. A moment's lack of attention can result in an accident, as can failure to observe certain elementary precautions.

There will always be new ways of having accidents, and the following points do not pretend to be a comprehensive list of all dangers; they are intended rather to make you aware of the risks and to encourage a safety-conscious approach to all work you carry out on your vehicle.

## Essential DOs and DON'Ts

**DON'T** rely on a single jack when working underneath the vehicle. Always use reliable additional means of support, such as axle stands, securely placed under a part of the vehicle that you know will not give way.

**DON'T** attempt to loosen or tighten high-torque nuts (e.g. wheel hub nuts) while the vehicle is on a jack; it may be pulled off.

**DON'T** start the engine without first ascertaining that the transmission is in neutral (or 'Park' where applicable) and the parking brake applied.

**DON'T** suddenly remove the filler cap from a hot cooling system – cover it with a cloth and release the pressure gradually first, or you may get scalded by escaping coolant.

**DON'T** attempt to drain oil until you are sure it has cooled sufficiently to avoid scalding you.

**DON'T** grasp any part of the engine, exhaust or catalytic converter without first ascertaining that it is sufficiently cool to avoid burning you.

**DON'T** allow brake fluid or antifreeze to contact vehicle paintwork.

**DON'T** syphon toxic liquids such as fuel, brake fluid or antifreeze by mouth, or allow them to remain on your skin.

**DON'T** inhale dust – it may be injurious to health (see *Asbestos* below).

**DON'T** allow any spilt oil or grease to remain on the floor – wipe it up straight away, before someone slips on it.

**DON'T** use ill-fitting spanners or other tools which may slip and cause injury.

**DON'T** attempt to lift a heavy component which may be beyond your capability – get assistance.

**DON'T** rush to finish a job, or take unverified short cuts.

**DON'T** allow children or animals in or around an unattended vehicle.

**DO** wear eye protection when using power tools such as drill, sander, bench grinder etc, and when working under the vehicle.

**DO** use a barrier cream on your hands prior to undertaking dirty jobs – it will protect your skin from infection as well as making the dirt easier to remove afterwards; but make sure your hands aren't left slippery. Note that long-term contact with used engine oil can be a health hazard.

**DO** keep loose clothing (cuffs, tie etc) and long hair well out of the way of moving mechanical parts.

**DO** remove rings, wristwatch etc, before working on the vehicle – especially the electrical system.

**DO** ensure that any lifting tackle used has a safe working load rating adequate for the job.

**DO** keep your work area tidy – it is only too easy to fall over articles left lying around.

**DO** get someone to check periodically that all is well, when working alone on the vehicle.

**DO** carry out work in a logical sequence and check that everything is correctly assembled and tightened afterwards.

**DO** remember that your vehicle's safety affects that of yourself and others. If in doubt on any point, get specialist advice.

**IF,** in spite of following these precautions, you are unfortunate enough to injure yourself, seek medical attention as soon as possible.

## Asbestos

Certain friction, insulating, sealing, and other products – such as brake linings, brake bands, clutch linings, torque converters, gaskets, etc – contain asbestos. *Extreme care must be taken to avoid inhalation of dust from such products since it is hazardous to health.* If in doubt, assume that they *do* contain asbestos.

## Fire

Remember at all times that petrol (gasoline) is highly flammable. Never smoke, or have any kind of naked flame around, when working on the vehicle. But the risk does not end there – a spark caused by an electrical short-circuit, by two metal surfaces contacting each other, by careless use of tools, or even by static electricity built up in your body under certain conditions, can ignite petrol vapour, which in a confined space is highly explosive.

Always disconnect the battery earth (ground) terminal before working on any part of the fuel or electrical system, and never risk spilling fuel on to a hot engine or exhaust.

It is recommended that a fire extinguisher of a type suitable for fuel and electrical fires is kept handy in the garage or workplace at all times. Never try to extinguish a fuel or electrical fire with water.

**Note:** *Any reference to a 'torch' appearing in this manual should always be taken to mean a hand-held battery-operated electric lamp or flashlight. It does NOT mean a welding/gas torch or blowlamp.*

## Fumes

Certain fumes are highly toxic and can quickly cause unconsciousness and even death if inhaled to any extent. Petrol (gasoline) vapour comes into this category, as do the vapours from certain solvents such as trichloroethylene. Any draining or pouring of such volatile fluids should be done in a well ventilated area.

When using cleaning fluids and solvents, read the instructions carefully. Never use materials from unmarked containers – they may give off poisonous vapours.

Never run the engine of a motor vehicle in an enclosed space such as a garage. Exhaust fumes contain carbon monoxide which is extremely poisonous; if you need to run the engine, always do so in the open air or at least have the rear of the vehicle outside the workplace.

If you are fortunate enough to have the use of an inspection pit, never drain or pour petrol, and never run the engine, while the vehicle is standing over it; the fumes, being heavier than air, will concentrate in the pit with possibly lethal results.

## The battery

Never cause a spark, or allow a naked light, near the vehicle's battery. It will normally be giving off a certain amount of hydrogen gas, which is highly explosive.

Always disconnect the battery earth (ground) terminal before working on the fuel or electrical systems.

If possible, loosen the filler plugs or cover when charging the battery from an external source. Do not charge at an excessive rate or the battery may burst.

Take care when topping up and when carrying the battery. The acid electrolyte, even when diluted, is very corrosive and should not be allowed to contact the eyes or skin.

If you ever need to prepare electrolyte yourself, always add the acid slowly to the water, and never the other way round. Protect against splashes by wearing rubber gloves and goggles.

When jump starting a car using a booster battery, for negative earth (ground) vehicles, connect the jump leads in the following sequence: First connect one jump lead between the positive ( + ) terminals of the two batteries. Then connect the other jump lead first to the negative (–) terminal of the booster battery, and then to a good earthing (ground) point on the vehicle to be started, at least 18 in (45 cm) from the battery if possible. Ensure that hands and jump leads are clear of any moving parts, and that the two vehicles do not touch. Disconnect the leads in the reverse order.

## Mains electricity and electrical equipment

When using an electric power tool, inspection light etc, always ensure that the appliance is correctly connected to its plug and that, where necessary, it is properly earthed (grounded). Do not use such appliances in damp conditions and, again, beware of creating a spark or applying excessive heat in the vicinity of fuel or fuel vapour. Also ensure that the appliances meet the relevant national safety standards.

## Ignition HT voltage

A severe electric shock can result from touching certain parts of the ignition system, such as the HT leads, when the engine is running or being cranked, particularly if components are damp or the insulation is defective. Where an electronic ignition system is fitted, the HT voltage is much higher and could prove fatal.

# Index